VAT on Property:
Law and Practice

VAT on Property: Law and Practice

Dermot O'Brien

THE INSTITUTE OF
Chartered Accountants
IN IRELAND

Institute of Chartered Accountants in Ireland
Burlington House, Burlington Road
Dublin 4

Published in 2009

© VAT on Property: Law and Practice, Institute of Chartered
Accountants in Ireland, 2009

ISBN: 978-0-903854-67-2

Printed by Colour Books, Ireland
Typeset by: Amnet International, Ireland

Contents

Chapter 4 The Supply of Non-Transitional Property .. 125

Chapter 5 The Supply of Transitional Property 147

Chapter 6 Lettings of Immovable Goods 169

Introduction

A look back to the old regime – why the need for change?

Value Added Tax, or VAT, was introduced in Ireland on 1 November 1972 as a prerequisite for Ireland's accession to the European Economic Community on 1 January 1973. Prior to the introduction of VAT, Ireland's exchequer received income from two other indirect taxes – Turnover Tax and Wholesale Tax. Both of those taxes were abolished with the introduction of VAT. European rules in relation to VAT provide that no Member State is allowed to have any tax on supplies other than VAT.

Specifically, Member States shall not be prevented from "maintaining or introducing taxes on insurance contracts, taxes on betting and gambling, excise duties, stamp duties and, more generally, any taxes, duties or charges which cannot be categorised as turnover taxes" (Article 401, Council Directive 2006/112/EC). Council Directive 2006/112/EC recast the 6th EC VAT Directive (77/388/EEC).

The 6th Directive was the governing European Directive on VAT from its implementation on 1 January 1978 until the recast Directive was effected on 28 November 2006. The recast Directive has now assumed that role and it will be referred to in this publication as the recast Directive.

For now, it is useful to reproduce the provisions of Articles 4(3) and 13B(b) and 13C of the Sixth Directive and note the changes in presentation and wording as those provisions have been transposed into the recast Directive, and it is useful to remind the reader that, where different language is used in the recast Directive to that of the Sixth Directive, there may be different nuances to those of the earlier work and – ultimately – this could lead to the courts arriving at a different interpretation to one which might have emerged under the similar, but different, Sixth Directive wording.

Taxable persons

Article 4(3) of the Sixth Directive:

"Member States may also treat as a taxable person anyone who carries out, on an occasional basis, a transaction relating to the activities referred to in paragraph 2 (Economic Activities) and in particular one of the following:

(a) *the supply before first occupation of buildings or parts of buildings and the land on which they stand; Member States may determine the conditions of application of this criterion to transformations of buildings and the land on which they stand.*

Member States may apply criteria other than that of first occupation such as the period elapsing between the date of completion of the building and the date of first supply or the period elapsing between first occupation and the date of subsequent supply, provided that these periods do not exceed five years and two years respectively.

"A building" shall be taken to mean any structure fixed to or in the ground.

(b) *the supply of building land.*

"Building land" shall mean any unimproved or improved land defined as such by the Member States.

Article 12 of the recast Directive states:

"1. *Member States may regard as a taxable person anyone who carries out, on an occasional basis, a transaction relating to the activities referred to in the second subparagraph of Article 9(1) (Economic Activities) and in particular one of the following transactions:*

(a) *the supply, before first occupation, of a building or parts of a building and of the land on which the building stands;*

(b) *the supply of building land.*

2. *For the purposes of paragraph 1(a), "building" shall mean any structure fixed to or in the ground.*

Member States may lay down the detailed rules for applying the criterion referred to in paragraph 1(a) to conversions of buildings and may determine what is meant by "the land on which a building stands".

Member States may apply criteria other than that of first occupation, such as the period elapsing between the date of completion of the building and the date of first supply, or the period elapsing between the date of first occupation and the date of subsequent supply, provided that those periods do not exceed five years and two years respectively.

3. *For the purposes of paragraph 1(b), "building land" shall mean any improved or unimproved land defined as such by the Member States."*

Exemptions

Article 13B 6th Directive:

"Without prejudice to other Community provisions, Member States shall exempt the following under conditions which they shall lay down for the

purpose of ensuring the correct and straightforward application of the exemptions and of preventing any possible evasion, avoidance or abuse:

...

(b) *the leasing or letting of immovable property excluding:*

1. *the provision of accommodation, as defined in the laws of the Member States, in the hotel sector or in sectors with a similar function, including the provision of accommodation in holiday camps or on sites developed for use as camping sites;*

2. *the letting of premises and sites for parking vehicles;*

3. *lettings of permanently installed equipment and machinery;*

4. *hire of safes.*

Member States may apply further exclusions to the scope of this exemption;

...

(g) *the supply of buildings or parts thereof, and of the land on which they stand, other than as described in Article 4(3)(a);*

(h) *the supply of land which has not been built on other than building land as described in Article 4(3)(b)."*

Article 13C 6th Directive:

"Member States may allow taxpayers a right of option for taxation in cases of:

(a) *letting and leasing of immovable property;*

.

.

Member States may restrict the scope of this right of option and shall fix the details of its use."

A derogation for Ireland

Under the rules which existed prior to the introduction of the new VAT on Property system on 1 July 2008, Irish VAT law recognised as a supply of goods a sale of a freehold interest in property or the disposal of a leasehold interest of 10 years or longer.

This structure was not compatible with the 6th EU Directive as it sought to treat the letting of immovable goods – a service – as a supply of goods for VAT purposes. Ireland sought, and was granted, a derogation from the Directive allowing it to treat the disposal of a leasehold interest of 10 years or more in a property as a supply of goods.

This was a critical development in Irish VAT legislation because almost every difficulty and complication in Irish VAT and Property law which emerged over subsequent years has its roots in such leases being treated as supplies of goods.

Why was this so?

When a supply of goods is made, VAT becomes due at the time of the supply unless there has been an earlier advance payment when the VAT point is brought forward to the time of payment. Since the disposal of a leasehold interest of 10 years or more was treated as a supply of goods, VAT became due when the lease was executed or the property was occupied by the tenant, whichever event happened first.

This meant that the supply had to be capable of being valued when it was created. The consideration which passes under a lease – the rent (perhaps with an additional premium) – is usually paid over the life of the lease. However, for VAT purposes, the supply is a one-off made at the outset of the lease and it was necessary to ascribe consideration to that lease and calculate a VAT liability based on a notional figure. Legislation provided that a lease of 10 years or longer – where a taxable interest was passing – would be liable to VAT on the capitalised value of the rents passing under that lease. The methods provided under the legislation for capitalising the rent did not necessarily give a value which bore any resemblance to the market value passing.

For many years, this did not present practical difficulties. When VAT was introduced in 1972, the rate of VAT on the disposal of a taxable interest in property was 3%. This remained the case until 1983. Even then, when the rate was increased by the Minister for Finance, it only went up to 5%. It was increased to 10% in 1985.

Whilst the VAT rates through the 1970s and into the mid-1980s were low, it was also a period when the Irish economy was reasonably depressed and price inflation in the property sector was relatively unheard of. The method of calculating the VAT charge on an occasional lease of 10 years or more was regarded widely as being unimportant.

In addition, specialist VAT planning in the private sector was scarce. It was not until the very late 1980s that the larger accounting firms saw VAT services as an area of expertise for which clients were willing to pay. Ernst & Whinney, as it was, was probably the first firm to engage tax specialists whose tax expertise was largely confined to VAT. The other large accountancy firms gradually followed suit.

As the rates of VAT on property transactions continued their inexorable rise (the rate increased to 12.5% in 1993 and to 13.5% in 2003) and as

VAT practitioners became more numerous and had to justify their existence, it became clear that the VAT legislation as it applied to property transactions was riddled with inconsistencies and opportunities were there to achieve VAT savings by clever use of the legislation.

VAT on property in Ireland prior to Finance Act 1997

Finance Act 1997 marked a watershed in VAT legislation in Ireland. It was the first time that the legislators made a serious attempt to introduce anti-avoidance legislation in the VAT and property area. Although it was characterised by some astonishingly cumbersome legislation, it served its purpose – to a degree.

It put an end to certain VAT planning ideas which had become widely used during the previous decade but, in doing so, as is often the case with anti-avoidance legislation, it spawned a host of new ideas.

So, what did Finance Act 1997 achieve?

It effectively brought about an end to situations whereby institutions which normally had little or no VAT recovery – such as banks, insurance companies, hospitals, universities and even State bodies – could acquire a long-term leasehold interest in a brand new building and pay out almost no VAT. This could be engineered by judicious use of assignments or surrenders of leases as the legislation which might have been expected to tax an assignment or surrender of a lease was hopelessly inadequate at the time.

As a result of the weak legislation, it was possible (for example) for Oncea Bank plc to set up a subsidiary company to acquire a long lease in a new headquarters property and recover the large amount of VAT charged to it by the landlord because this subsidiary carried out some taxable activities. The subsidiary could assign, shortly afterwards, its leasehold interest to the bank for a nominal consideration – say ten pounds – and the bank then had a brand, spanking new head office for a VAT cost of less than £1.50p.

Many people can see the sense in introducing legislation that brings opportunistic schemes of this kind to an end, but it is rare for such a door to be closed without another opening.

VAT avoidance post-Finance Act 1997

In the late 1990s, Ireland's economy began to grow and the demand for property, both residential and commercial, grew also. Prices began to rise more sharply than previously and the rate of VAT attaching to new property was significant at 12.5%.

Finance Act 1997, as we have seen, put an end to certain VAT saving schemes involving the (occasionally) imaginative use of lease assignments or surrenders, but other opportunities remained, and there was a great appetite to exploit those opportunities, fuelled by the desire of non-vatable organisations to acquire commercial property with as little a VAT cost as possible, and by the desire of developers and builders of residential accommodation to be able to sell houses and apartments with as little of the sale price as possible being subject to VAT.

It was as though certain sectors of the economy saw value added tax as an optional extra in a property transaction.

In commercial property transactions, it was legitimate to dispose of a long term leasehold interest in a property at market value. Usually, that amount was determined by whatever valuation a professional valuer said the interest was worth on the open market.

Consider, for example, what a library on a university campus might be worth on the open market. In short, not very much because of its location and restricted usefulness. Nonetheless, it might be very expensive to build.

So, a university which recovers no input on its expenditure is looking at building a new library for IR £10 million. This will carry a VAT cost of roughly IR £1.5 million.

If that university granted a lease of the land, pre-development, to another company which may, or may not, be connected to it, and that company were to build the library and then grant a taxable lease back to the university for, say, 25 years then the development company could recover the IR £1.5 million. The lease to the university might be valued at no more than IR £2 million which would carry an irrecoverable VAT cost for the university of IR £250,000.

So, using a very uncomplicated arrangement, the university reduced its VAT cost from IR £1.5 million to IR £250,000. This type of arrangement proved to be quite attractive in certain quarters. Unsurprisingly, it found little favour with the Revenue Commissioners who countered it in Finance Act 2002 with the introduction of a piece of legislation which came to be known as the Economic Value Test (EVT).

Briefly, the EVT provided that the capital value of a lease of more than 10 years, for VAT purposes, must be at least as high as the cost of developing or acquiring the interest out of which the lease was being created.

The EVT was a clumsy, but effective, piece of legislation. It achieved what it set out to achieve by closing down the "university-type" structure shown above but it also impacted adversely on hundreds of ordinary, arm's length transactions. In meetings with practitioners, Revenue gave assurances that the EVT was an anti-avoidance measure and would not be used in arm's length transactions where no VAT avoidance planning was involved. Unfortunately, this message often failed to reach the Revenue Auditor "in the field" who delighted in using the EVT as a way of generating VAT assessments and penalties even where the most innocent of transactions were at issue. The EVT became a serious obstacle to commerce because of its poorly conceived drafting and wide-ranging impact. It, probably more than any other single factor, led to the eventual breakdown of the "old" VAT on property system.

The various arrangements described above were designed to save VAT for businesses which had little or no VAT recovery potential and which were building or acquiring expensive new properties. But these were not the only VAT saving arrangements on the go.

Sellers of new residential property were also keen to find an angle whereby they could reduce the amount of VAT liability on sales. This could have the effect of enabling property developers to keep prices down or, more often, inflate their own profits.

Certain structures became widely known under which the site value included in a property sale could potentially escape VAT, thereby removing a large element of the sale price of any house or apartment from the VAT charge. These structures, as a whole, came into the limelight when John Perry TD raised the question publicly as to how developers could be avoiding VAT on the sale of new properties. Speculation mounted in the media as to how much tax was being lost to the Exchequer under such arrangements and, while some figures quoted bordered on the ridiculous, it seemed that the figure was likely to amount to many tens of millions of euro.

The big difference between the schemes designed to save VAT on the sales of residential property and those designed for commercial property transactions was that the latter were far more straightforward. Schemes designed to reduce the VAT amount included in a house or apartment sale were far more contrived and difficult to execute. In general, they lacked commercial substance or reality.

Along with the EVT referred to above, these residential property schemes were a major contributor in persuading Revenue that the system of VAT on property needed a fundamental re-think.

Since 1997, almost every Finance Act carried an amendment to the VAT on property rules, most of them being anti-avoidance in nature. By the early 2000s, VAT on property law resembled a legislative patchwork quilt. It had become extremely cumbersome and it is not unreasonable to say that it was comprehensively understood by few people. There was widespread demand for the system to be simplified and, in the interests of taxpayers and Revenue alike, the time had come to start again.

A clean white sheet of paper

In May 2005, Revenue Commissioner, Josephine Feehily, convened a Forum in Dublin Castle of the various stakeholders in the area of VAT and property. She announced that she had set up a Review Group comprising officials from Revenue and the Department of Finance to look at the area of VAT and property with a view to – hopefully – introducing a more simplified piece of legislation that would be less cumbersome to work with, that would be secure from Revenue's perspective and would not diminish the Exchequer yield from VAT on property. Of course, since then, the Exchequer yield from VAT on property has all but collapsed but the revised VAT legislation is hardly to blame for that.

The Review Group worked at its task and received significant assistance from VAT practitioners. The overwhelming view was that a new system was required. The existing system was already creaking and groaning and any further tinkering with it would only make a bad system worse. Proposals for draft legislation were put forward by the Review Group and debated in a wider forum.

Ultimately, the new VAT on property legislation was enacted in Finance Act 2008 and became law on 1 July 2008. Finance (No. 2) Act 2008 brought in further changes – mostly minor amendments to tidy up some of the initial drafting but also, astonishingly, one anti-avoidance clause.

The new system certainly seems to be simpler for the majority of transactions but is extremely complex for others. Property transactions, by their nature, can be complex things – so the VAT legislation which taxes them sometimes has to be complex too.

Ironically, once the new legislation became law the property market in Ireland (for all sorts of non-VAT related reasons) collapsed and, at the time of writing, the robustness of the new legislation remains largely untested. But that will change in time and the chapters which follow attempt to take the reader through the detail of the new legislation with examples to help clarify the trickier issues.

It has been said that the new, simplified, rules will reduce the demand for the services of specialist VAT practitioners and make life easier for the administrators. Time will tell.

About this book

This book is an analysis of the VAT on property laws as they apply in Ireland since 1 July 2008. For this reason and to avoid confusing even the most avid reader, very little reference is made to the "old rules". The book is aimed at the accountant, solicitor or practising tax professional who already has some knowledge of the law of VAT on property.

The material is presented in a concise and relevant format and the temptation to pad out the work with largely irrelevant material has been avoided, it is hoped.

However, there may be occasions when practitioners must still have recourse to the "old" rules, particularly if retrospective issues arise, e.g. in the course of Revenue audits.

The book is primarily an analysis of the legislation of VAT on property and is intended to guide the reader through whatever property transaction or conundrum presents itself.

VAT on property always was and still is a complex area. This book aims to make understanding it a little easier for the practitioner through the use of straightforward terminology and numerous illustrative examples. The book does not attempt to offer a substitute for professional advice.

Acknowledgements

The author wishes to express his deep appreciation to his colleague, Geraldine Crowley, for her Trojan work in assisting in the work on this book. Her dedication, patience and contribution were truly immense. In addition, Tom James in Revenue was extremely helpful and prompt in offering Revenue's interpretation of some of the trickier aspects of the new rules and his input is much appreciated.

Chapter 1

Outline of the New Provisions

Introduction

This book considers the new VAT and property legislation as introduced [1–01] under the 2008 and 2009 Finance Acts. The 2008 Finance Acts were enacted on 1 July 2008 and the second on 24 December 2008. The Finance Act 2009 was enacted on 3 June 2009.

The stated objective of the new VAT and property provisions is to rationalise and simplify the VAT treatment of property transactions.

Josephine Feehily, Chairman of the Revenue Commissioners, states in [1–02] the Foreword to the *VAT on Property Guide* from April 2008 (see Appendix 1) that "the new system is a fundamental change in the way VAT is applied to property transactions and represents one of the most significant changes in the Irish VAT system since its introduction in 1972". She confirms her belief that it is "a significant improvement in the application of VAT to property transactions", representing "a major long-term simplification in what had become a very complex part of the law".

Some of the "old" property provisions still have application in certain [1–03] cases, e.g. Section 7 and parts of Section 4. The "old" property-related definitions in Section 1 continue to apply and new definitions are included. The general principles of VAT still apply, notwithstanding the changes in the property provisions. Measures derived from other sections of the VAT Act continue to have relevance, e.g. that in relation to the amount of taxable consideration.

The new legislation

The new legislation changes completely many aspects of the VAT and [1–04] property provisions with which practitioners have had to become familiar over almost four decades. The changes in some cases are sweeping.

While many parts of the legislation would appear to be quite clear, it is still largely untested.

This book sets out the new provisions and, using various examples, attempts to clarify how they would apply in practical terms.

Chapter 2 contains an analysis of the new legislation and is cross-referenced to the detailed chapters dealing with specific sections of the VAT Act.

The Capital Goods Scheme

[1-05] Chapter 3 considers the capital goods scheme (CGS) introduced in the new Section 12E of the VAT Act. Under the CGS, a VAT life (referred to in the legislation as an adjustment period) is attributed to land and buildings which have been developed as defined in the VAT Act. Section 12E contains a series of definitions and procedures whereby the capital goods owner "tracks" changes in the taxable use of immovable goods. The CGS provides for the adjustment of VAT deductibility over the adjustment period, depending on the extent to which the property is put to a taxable use. No periodic adjustments will apply unless there is a change in the taxable use of a property. Consequently when the taxable use remains unchanged, then the CGS has very little impact on the capital goods owner. However, s/he is nonetheless required to keep a capital goods record and this must contain *"sufficient information to determine any adjustments in respect of that capital good"*.

[1-06] The CGS also sets out certain procedures for calculating adjustments relating to the disposal of capital goods or the exercise/cancellation of the option to tax. The CGS does *not* determine whether a supply of the property is subject to VAT. This matter is dealt with by other provisions of the VAT Act, notably Sections 4B and 4C.

Freehold interests and freehold equivalent interests

[1-07] Chapter 4 examines Section 4B of the VAT Act, which sets out the new general rules in relation to supplies of freehold interests and "freehold equivalent interests" in immovable goods. Some exceptions/variations for transitional properties are set out in Section 4C (see chapter 5). Transitional properties are capital goods acquired or developed prior to 1 July 2008.

[1-08] Before the changes introduced in the first Finance Act 2008, the general rules for supplies of property were contained to a large extent in Section 4 of the VAT Act. However, with effect from 1 July 2008, the new Section 4(11) confines the application of Section 4 to a small number of specified situations relating to disposals of transitional property (see below).

Section 4B applies not only to supplies of freehold interests but also to *"freehold equivalent interests"*. The concept of the freehold equivalent interest (FEI) was introduced under the Finance Act 2008 via a new Section 3(1C) of the VAT Act. The definition was simplified in the Finance (No. 2) Act 2008. In brief, the FEI includes very long ownership-type leasehold interests, which would still be treated as immovable goods under the new rules. **[1–09]**

Section 4B sets out provisions which exempt the vendor of a capital good from charging VAT in relation to its disposal. The exemptions are based on the period of time the property has been held or occupied since the date of its "completion" as defined. These exemptions are commonly referred to as the two- and five-year rules. The extent to which the property has been developed is also taken into account and the concept of "minor" development is introduced. This is the new *de minimis* provision and it replaces the old 10% rule, which was in any event not a legislative provision. **[1–10]**

If a vendor makes an exempt disposal of a capital good during its adjustment period, then the capital good is still in the VAT "net" and the vendor could suffer a clawback of input VAT based on the proportion of the adjustment period which has elapsed in relation to the full adjustment period. The clawback can be avoided if vendor and purchaser opt to tax the disposal, as provided for in Section 4B(5). Under Section 4B(6), the purchaser in an opted sale becomes the accountable person in relation to the VAT. **[1–11]**

Section 4B also contains certain anti-avoidance provisions. Section 4B(3) provides that the supply of property which would otherwise be exempt will be taxable if it is made in connection with an agreement to develop the property. Section 4B(3) replaces Section 4(5) of the VAT Act but it is in essence the same anti-avoidance provision. **[1–12]**

In addition, Section 4B(7) provides that the first sale of developed residential property by a property developer within the adjustment period will always be subject to VAT, regardless of the two- and five-year rules. This section also provides that, if a property developer puts residential property into exempt lettings prior to the first sale, then the CGS clawback would be an interval-based adjustment and not a lump sum clawback. **[1–13]**

"Transitional" properties and "legacy" leases

Chapter 5 examines Section 4C, which deals with certain exceptions/ variations to the general rules in Section 4B. Specific provisions are set **[1–14]** out in relation to interests in capital goods which were acquired or developed prior to 1 July 2008 and are not disposed of until after that date. These are commonly referred to as "transitional" properties and they include "legacy leases", i.e. long leases granted by a taxable person under the **old** regime and still in existence under the **new** regime. The transitional measures for what were **short** leases under the old rules are contained in Section 7B.

[1–15]   When considering the provisions contained in Section 4C, it is important to be aware that the **general** rules in relation to the supply of immovable goods are contained in Section 4B. Unless Section 4C deals with a specific provision in relation to transitional property, then Section 4B would generally apply.

[1–16]   To the extent that long leases granted pre-1 July 2008 simply continue in place after that date and the relevant property is not further developed, then the leases are not affected by the new rules. This is because any VAT on legacy leases would have been dealt with under the old regime, i.e. when the leases were granted initially. However, specific measures were needed to deal in particular with the assignment and surrender of legacy leases from 1 July 2008 onwards.

[1–17]   Section 4C confirms that developed transitional property is a capital good and it sets out the adjustment period applicable in various circumstances.

Lettings

[1–18]   Chapter 6 examines lettings of immovable goods. Under the old VAT and property rules, short lettings (i.e. lettings of less than 10 years in duration) were *prima facie* VAT exempt. However, under Section 7 of the VAT Act, lessors seeking an entitlement to recover input VAT were entitled to waive their short-term letting exemption, thereby making the otherwise exempt short letting taxable. Once the waiver was in place, it extended to all short-term lettings by the same taxable person, with some exceptions in relation to short lettings of residential property following changes introduced in the Finance Act 2007.

[1–19]   The changes introduced under the first Finance Act 2008 provided that no new waivers of exemption would commence on or after 1 July 2008 and that in general waivers existing at that date would not extend to lettings of property acquired or developed on or after 1 July 2008.

[1–20]   Under the new system, all new lettings of property (i.e. all lettings commencing on or after 1 July 2008) are *prima facie* exempt, **regardless**

of **duration**. There is no longer a requirement to calculate capitalised values or to pass the economic value test.

This general exemption would not apply to the following: **[1–21]**

- New lettings which are still covered by pre-existing waivers of exemption.
- Long leases which were put in place prior to 1 July 2008 – these are dealt under the new Section 4C.
- Leases of a duration such that they would be regarded as FEIs.

In certain circumstances, waivers of exemption already in place **[1–22]** at 1 July 2008 were allowed to remain in place. The provisions dealing with the continuation of pre-existing waivers are set out in Section 7B.

The option to tax lettings

In relation to new lettings of property **not** covered by pre-existing **[1–23]** waivers, an alternative to the waiver of exemption, the option to tax, is set out in the new Section 7A. If a letting is subject to VAT by virtue of a pre-existing waiver of exemption, then it is not an "opted" letting.

Section 7A sets out the circumstances in which the option to tax is **[1–24]** available. Taxing a letting makes the rents subject to VAT at the standard rate. The lessor is required to issue VAT invoices to the tenant and to account for output VAT in the normal manner.

Once the option to tax is exercised, a letting is no longer exempt but con- **[1–25]** stitutes a VAT-able supply of services. Putting the property to a VAT-able use gives the lessor an entitlement in principle to recover input VAT in relation to costs associated with acquisition/development of the relevant property. Revenue has confirmed in e-brief 37/2008 (reproduced in Appendix 2) that, in its view, a refund of purchase VAT (a CGS positive adjustment) does **not** arise when a lessor had a short-term letting pre-1 July 2008 without a waiver and opts to tax it on or after 1 July 2008.

A significant difference between the old "waiver" system and the new **[1–26]** "option" system is that the option to tax is exercised on a "per letting" basis. The previous broad application associated with the waiver does not apply under the new system.

In addition, the option to tax a letting is unilateral, i.e. under the **[1–27]** legislation, a lessor does not need the tenant's acquiescence in order to tax a letting. This is different from opting to tax a sale, which has to be done jointly. However, the legislation does require the lessor to notify the tenant in writing that a letting will be opted.

The option to tax clause can be included in a letting contract or notified by separate letter. It is important to be aware that the standard VAT clause recommended by the Law Society of Ireland still applies and would be a separate matter from an "option to tax" clause.

[1-28] Chapter 7 provides a straightforward reference guide for readers seeking direction as to the main points they should consider in relation to a VAT and property issue.

[1-29] The Appendices to the book contain copies of:

- Revenue's *VAT on Property Guide* from April 2008 (Appendix 1);

- e-brief 37/2008: FAQs 2008 VAT on Property (Appendix 2); and

- from Tax Briefing, Issue 69, September 2008, measures explaining Revenue's approach to the VAT aspects of lettings of property pending sale of same (Appendix 3).

Chapter 2

The New Legislation

The amendments to the VAT Act introduced under the Finance Act 2008 took effect from 1 July 2008. Certain amendments and clarifications were introduced in Finance (No. 2) Act 2008, which was enacted on 24 December 2008. Some further changes were also introduced in the Finance Act 2009, enacted on 3 June 2009. **[2–01]**

Section 1

Section 83 of the Finance Act made a number of changes to Section 1 of the VAT Act, i.e. the definitions section. However, many additional new definitions are introduced directly in the relevant sections rather than being contained in Section 1. **[2–02]**

Accounting year

The definition of the term "accounting year" is relevant in the context of the CGS. It is defined as: **[2–03]**

> *"a period of 12 months ending on 31 December, but if a taxable person customarily makes up accounts for periods of 12 months ending on **another** fixed date, then for such a person, a period of 12 months ending on **that** fixed date."*

In other words, the term "accounting year" means a period of 12 months ending on 31 December, but can be a period of 12 months ending on another fixed date if a taxable person customarily makes up accounts for that period.

Revenue's Notes for Guidance to the Finance Act 2008 indicate that the term should be read in the context of the amendments made under Section 94 of the Finance Act 2008 to Section 12 of the VAT Act. The amendments deal with the situation where a taxpayer is only entitled to a proportion of VAT incurred as a deduction. **[2–04]**

[2-05] This new definition was necessary because of the introduction of the CGS under Section 98 of the Finance Act and contained in Section 12E of the amended VAT Act. The term *"accounting year"* is used in the definition of the second interval arising under the CGS. (See the analysis of Section 12E further on in this chapter. See also Chapter 3 in relation to the CGS.)

[2-06] Provision is made in Regulation 21A of S.I. No. 548 of 2006 – VAT Regulations 2006 (inserted by S.I. No. 238 2008 – VAT (Amendment) Regulations 2008) for situations where the CGS owner changes the end date of his/her accounting year. (See Chapter 3 for more detail.)

Capital goods

[2-07] The amended Section 1 states that *"capital goods means developed immovable goods and includes refurbishment within the meaning of Section 12E and a reference to a capital good includes a reference to any part thereof and the term capital good shall be construed accordingly."*

[2-08] The term *"capital goods"*, therefore, means immovable property, or any part thereof, which has been developed as defined for VAT purposes. It includes refurbishment, which is defined in Section 12E(1) as *"development on a previously completed building, structure or engineering work"*.

[2-09] Inherent in this definition is the concept that, if immovable goods are not "developed" as defined, they are not capital goods as defined. Consequently, the definition of development is as fundamental under the new system as it was under the old system. (Development is considered in more detail in Chapter 4. The concept of refurbishment is considered in more detail in Chapter 3.)

Completed

[2-10] The term *"completed"* refers to immovable goods and should be read in the context of Section 88 of the Finance Act 2008, which introduced the new Section 4B. The Section 1 definition simply states that the term *"has the meaning assigned to it by Section 4B"*.

The concept of completion is dealt with in greater detail in Chapter 4.

Exempted Activity

[2-11] The old Section 1 stated that the term *"exempted activity"* meant *(inter alia)* *"a supply of immovable goods in respect of which pursuant to Section 4(6) tax is not chargeable"*.

[2-12] Amendments to the definition of the term *"exempted activity"* were introduced under Section 83(e) of the Finance Act 2008 and Schedule 6 of the Finance (No. 2) Act 2008.

As a result, part (a) of the term *"exempted activity"* now refers to *"a supply* **[2–13]** *of immovable goods in respect of which pursuant to Sections 4(6) and 4B(2) and subsections (2) and (6)(b) of Section 4C tax is not chargeable"*.

Under Section 86 of the Finance Act 2008, Section 4(6) would cease to **[2–14]** have application from 1 July 2008 onwards. Section 4(6) was the provision which dealt with exempt supplies of immovable goods.

The amended definition exempts certain supplies of property exempt **[2–15]** under both the transitional and the new property rules. (These are examined in more detail in Chapters 4 and 5.)

Freehold Equivalent Interest

The new term *"freehold equivalent interest"* is also defined and is referred **[2–16]** to subsequently in the new Section 4C, which was introduced under Section 88 of the Finance Act 2008 to deal with transitional measures for the supply of immovable goods.

A freehold equivalent interest is defined as meaning *"an interest in* **[2–17]** *immovable goods, other than a freehold interest the transfer of which constitutes a supply of goods in accordance with section 3"*.

Section 3 of the VAT Act deals with supplies of goods and the cross- **[2–18]** reference is to the new Section 3(1C), which deals with supplies of goods *"in the case of immovable goods"*.

Section 3(1C) as introduced under the Finance Act 2008 originally stated **[2–19]** the following:

> *"For the purposes of this Act in the case of immovable goods, 'supply' in relation to goods shall be regarded as including:*
>
> (a) *the transfer in substance of the right to dispose of immovable goods as owner or the transfer in substance of the right to dispose of immovable goods and*
> (b) *transactions where the holder of an estate or interest in immovable goods enters into a contract or agreement with another person in relation to the creation, establishment, alteration, surrender, relinquishment or termination of rights in respect of those immovable goods, apart from mortgages, and consideration or payments which amount to 50% or more of the open market value of the immovable goods at the time the contract or agreement is concluded are payable pursuant to or associated with the contract or agreement or otherwise either before the making of the contract or agreement or within 5 years of the commencement of such contract or agreement."*

[2–20] However, the second part of the definition was removed under the Finance (No. 2) Act 2008, which was enacted on 24 December 2008.

[2–21] Section 3(1)(a) of the VAT Act provides that *"transfer of ownership of the goods by agreement"* is a supply of goods for VAT purposes. Section 3(1C) was introduced to ensure that from a VAT perspective the grant of a very long leasehold interest (a *"freehold equivalent interest"* FEI) is also a supply of goods from a VAT perspective. But for Section 3(1C), the grant of a very long leasehold interest might have been considered to be a supply of a letting service.

[2–22] Revenue has clarified in its *VAT on Property Guide* from April 2008 (see Appendix 1) that the term *"in substance"* in Section 3(1C) "is taken to mean not only the freehold of a property but also other interests in the property that amount to effective ownership". Revenue uses the example of apartment owners, who typically do not hold the freehold of the property, but generally have a very long interest in the property: for instance, a 99- or 999-year lease. Under Section 3(1C), this would be regarded as a freehold equivalent interest. When a freehold equivalent interest is granted, typically the consideration is a premium equal to the value of the property with a nominal rent payable annually thereafter.

[2–23] Revenue has confirmed in its e-brief 37/2008: FAQs 2008 VAT on Property (see Appendix 2) that, in relation to the meaning of FEIs, the length of the lease is not of great importance. The amount of the payment and the nature of the payment(s) would be the most significant issues. Revenue takes the view that, as a very general rule of thumb, leases of 75 years duration or longer are likely to be considered to be FEIs. (Note: this interpretation has no legislative standing.)

Joint Option for Taxation

[2–24] The amended Section 1 merely states that this *"has the meaning assigned to it by Section 4B"*. This is a reference to the joint option to tax whereby the parties to the transfer of a freehold or freehold equivalent interest in immovable goods would jointly opt to make the supply subject to VAT in circumstances where it would otherwise be exempt.

Landlord's Option to Tax

[2–25] Again, the amended Section 1 states that this *"has the meaning assigned to it by Section 7A"*. The new Section 7A of the VAT Act deals with the unilateral option to tax a lease which may be available to the lessor subject to conditions. Again, it is dealt with in more detail in Section 7A and in Chapter 6.

Change to the existing definition of "Surrender"

Revenue's Notes for Guidance state that the definition of a "surrender" **[2–26]**
in relation to an interest in immovable goods has been qualified. Under
the old regime, a surrender of an interest arose if, for instance, the lessee
returned the interest in the property to the landlord before the term of
the lease had expired. The failure of the lessee to exercise an option
contained in the lease to extend the term of the lease was also regarded
as a surrender.

Section 83(i) of the Finance Act amended Section 1 of the VAT Act in **[2–27]**
relation to the definition of "surrender". The previous definition stated
that:

> *"surrender, in relation to an interest in immovable goods, means the
> surrender by a person (hereafter referred to in this definition as 'the
> lessee') of an interest in those goods or any part of those goods to
> the person (hereafter referred to in this definition as 'the lessor') who
> at the time of the surrender retains the reversion on the interest in
> those goods and also includes the abandonment of that interest by
> the lessee and the failure of the lessee to exercise any option of the
> type referred to in subsection (1)(b) of section 4 in relation to that
> interest and surrender of an interest also includes the recovery by
> the lessor of that interest in those goods by ejectment or forfeiture
> prior to the date and that interest would, but for its surrender, have
> expired."*

The new text is added after the words *"have expired"* and continues the **[2–28]**
sentence to say: *"but in the case of an interest in immovable goods created on
or after 1 July 2008, the failure of the lessee to exercise any option of the type
referred to in subsection (1)(b) of Section 4 in relation to that interest does not
constitute a surrender."*

According to Revenue's Notes for Guidance, this amendment provides **[2–29]**
that where an interest in property is created on or after 1 July 2008 and
the lessee fails to exercise an option to extend the term of the lease,
as provided for in the lease, the resulting early return of the interest
to the landlord no longer constitutes a surrender for VAT purposes.
The amendment was a necessary consequence of the new property
provisions which revised the VAT treatment of leases. Surrenders arising
on interests created prior to 1 July 2008 remain taxable if the lessee
was entitled to deductibility on the acquisition or development of the
property that is the subject of the lease.

The original definition indicated that the surrender of a lease is what one **[2–30]**
might expect it to be – i.e. a formal surrender back to the lessor of the

leased property – but it also stipulated that abandonment by the tenant, ejection of the tenant or forfeiture by the tenant of the leasehold property also constituted surrenders.

[2–31]   The option referred to in Section 4(1)(b) was an option to extend a lease to a period of at least 10 years. Under the old definition, failure to exercise such an option would have constituted a surrender. For this to make sense, one has to bear in mind that the grant of a short lease (i.e. a lease of less than 10 years in duration) which contained an option to extend to a period of at least 10 years (i.e. a long lease) would have been treated as the grant of a long lease for VAT purposes. The tenant in that case had an interest in the leasehold property and, if the tenant did not ultimately exercise the option to extend, the old definition deemed a surrender to take place, with the VAT consequences provided for under the old regime.

[2–32]   The change to the definition stipulates that if a landlord grants a new lease after 1 July 2008 and it contains an extension clause of the kind referred to in Section 4(1)(b) and the lessee does not exercise the extension clause, this will not constitute a surrender.

Section 3

[2–33]   Section 85 of the Finance Act 2008 introduced three changes to Section 3 of the VAT Act, which deals with the supply of goods. Two of these changes are relevant from a VAT and property perspective.

[2–34]   Paragraph (a) inserts the word *"movable"* before the word *"goods"*, which effectively confines the self-supply rule in Section 3(1)(e) to movable goods.

[2–35]   The old subsection 1(e) included in the definition of the supply of goods *"the application (otherwise than by way of disposal to another person) by a person for the purposes of any business carried on by him of the goods, **being goods** which were developed, constructed, assembled, manufactured, produced, extracted, purchased [imported or otherwise acquired] by him or by another person on his behalf, except where tax chargeable in relation to the application would, if it were charged, be wholly deductible under Section 12."*

[2–36]   This is one of the provisions in the VAT Act that deals with self-supplies. Section 85 introduces the word *"movable"* before "goods" (see words in italics in paragraph **2–34** above). The intention is to ensure that where immovable goods are diverted from a taxable use to an exempt use, the transaction is not considered to be a supply of goods but is dealt with under the capital goods scheme.

The reason for this amendment is that under the pre-Finance Act 2008 [2-37]
rules, a lease of 10 years or longer was a supply of goods for VAT purposes. Post 1 July 2008, leases are not categorised as goods (unless they
are freehold equivalent interests) so the self-supply of a leasehold interest in property cannot be a self-supply of goods.

This is to be differentiated from the position regarding non-taxable/pri- [2-38]
vate use of immovable goods, which was amended under Section 93 of
the Finance Act 2008. Section 93 introduced changes to Section 10 of the
VAT Act (see paragraphs **2–196** to **2–199**).

The ECJ case of *Lennartz v. Finanzamt Muenchen III* (C-97/90) is also relevant in relation to the diversion of property to a non- or partly-taxable
use or an exempt use. It provides that a person who acquires goods
partially for business purposes is entitled to take a deduction for the full
amount of input VAT incurred in relation to the acquisition and is
obliged to account for VAT on the value of the subsequent appropria-
tion of the goods to non-business use.

Section 85 of the Finance Act 2008 also introduced a new Section 1C into [2-39]
Section 3 in relation to freehold equivalent interests. See the analysis of
this legislation earlier in the chapter under the amendments made to
Section 1 of the VAT Act.

Section 4

Section 86 of the Finance Act 2008 inserts a new subsection (11) into [2-40]
Section 4 of the VAT Act. Under the old legislation, Section 4 contained
most of the provisions relating to the supply of immovable goods.

According to Revenue's Notes for Guidance, from 1 July 2008 onwards, [2-41]
Section 4 was no longer necessary, apart from some provisions which
will continue to apply to transitional properties.

The new subsection (11) provides that: [2-42]

> *"Subject to Section 4C, the other provisions of this section, **apart from**
> **subsections (9) and (10)**, shall not apply as regards –*
>
> *(a)   a disposal of an interest in immovable goods, or*
> *(b)   a surrender of possession of immovable goods,*
>
> *which occurs after 1 July 2008. Subsection (9) shall apply only as
> respects a reversionary interest created prior to 1 July 2008. Subsection
> (10) shall apply only as respects an interest which is disposed of prior to
> 1 July 2008."*

[2-43] The new Section 4C (to which this new provision is subject) deals with transitional measures in relation to supplies of immovable goods. The transitional measures would apply in a case where a taxable person had acquired/developed immovable goods prior to 1 July 2008 and had granted a long lease as defined under the old legislation prior to that date (see the new Section 4C(1)(a) and (b)).

[2-44] **Subject to Section 4C,** none of the provisions of Section 4 applies (except subsections (9) and (10)) after 1 July 2008 in relation to supplies of immovable goods or surrenders of immovable goods.

[2-45] Subsection (9) relates to the supply of the reversionary interest in property. Under the existing legislation, if the lessor of property disposes of his/her interest in the property having first granted a long lease, then the supply of this reversionary interest is not subject to VAT unless the property has been developed *"by, on behalf of, or to the benefit of"* the lessor between the grant of the original lease and the disposal of the reversionary interest. The new Section 4(11) provides that this continues to be the case from 1 July 2008 onwards, but only if the lessor granted the long lease prior to 1 July 2008.

[2-46] Section 4(10) deals with the circumstances in which a VAT input credit is available to the lessor in relation to post-letting expenses. This subsection continues to apply from 1 July 2008 onwards if a taxable long lease is granted prior to that date.

[2-47] Finally, Section 4C(7), which deals with surrenders and assignments of legacy leases, provides that Section 4(8) [i.e. a provision of the original Section 4] would apply to VAT arising on same.

[2-48] Section 4(8)(c)(ii) provides that a "document" would issue to the landlord or the assignee.

[2-49] Section 4C(8)(a) provides that when a taxable surrender or assignment takes place in relation to a legacy lease, then "the person who makes the assignment or surrender shall issue a document to the person to whom the interest is being assigned or surrendered". Section 4C(8)(a) goes on to set out the information which such a document would be required to provide.

[2-50] After the enactment of the Finance Act 2008, in cases where there was a taxable assignment or surrender of a legacy lease, Sections 4(8)(c)(ii) and 4C(8)(a) both provided for the "document". However, Schedule 6(4) of Finance (No. 2) Act 2008 clarifies the position and provides that Section 4(8)(c)(ii) *"shall not apply where the person who makes the surrender* *or assignment is obliged to issue a document in accordance with Section 4C(8)(a) to the person to whom that surrender or assignment is made".*

This provision avoids possible perceived duplication between Section 4(8)(c)(ii) and Section 4C(8)(a).

Section 4A

Section 4A of the VAT Act was repealed with effect from 1 July 2008 under Section 87 of the Finance Act 2008. Section 4A set out the mechanism whereby a lessor could pass the responsibility for accounting for the VAT in respect of a long lease to the lessee. As leases are no longer supplies of goods to be taxed when a supply takes place, this section is now redundant. **[2-51]**

Section 4B

Section 88 of the Finance Act 2008 inserted two new Sections 4B and 4C into the VAT Act. Section 4B deals with the new rules for taxing supplies of immovable goods. Section 4C deals with the rules for transitional properties which were taxed under the "old" rules. **[2-52]**

The new Section 4B contains the new rules on how property transactions are to be treated for VAT purposes. In particular, it provides for exemption of certain supplies of immovable goods and a joint option for taxation of those exempt supplies. (Section 4B is dealt with in more detail in Chapter 4.) **[2-53]**

Section 4B(1) contains definitions for the terms *"completed"* and *"occupied"*. These are significant because the taxation or exemption of a supply of property will be determined in most cases on the basis of the time the supply occurs by reference to the time the property was completed and the length of time it has been occupied. **[2-54]**

The term *"completed"* in respect of immovable goods is defined as meaning *"that the development of those goods has reached the state, apart from only such finishing or fitting work that would normally be carried out by or on behalf of the person who will use them, where those goods can effectively be used for purposes for which those goods were designed, and the utility services required for those purposes are connected to those goods."* **[2-55]**

This means that immovable goods are not completed until all of the development work except finishing and fitting work has been done **and** the services have been connected.

[2-56] (See also, however, *Tax Briefing,* Issue 69, in Appendix 3 in relation to Revenue's interpretation of the term *"completed"* with regard to residential property that is short-term let).

[2-57] The existing definition of *"development"* has been retained although there has been some modification in relation to the *de minimis* provisions (see the new Sections 4B and 4C, below).

[2-58] The term *"occupied"* in respect of immovable goods is defined as meaning the following:

> *"(a) occupied and fully in use following completion where that use is one for which planning permission for the development of the goods was granted, and*

> *(b) where those goods are let, occupied and fully in such use by the tenant."*

Whether the immovable goods are being used by an owner-occupier or a tenant, they are consequently **not** "occupied" as defined if they are being used for a purpose other than that for which planning permission was obtained.

[2-59] Section 4B(2) deals with the supply of immovable goods, i.e. the freehold or the freehold equivalent, as defined. It contains the main provisions for exempting the supply of a property from VAT. It is subject to subsections of (3), (5) and (7) of Section 4B(2) and Section 4C(6)(a). Subsection (3) is the new anti-avoidance section to replace the old Section 4(5), subsection (5) is the subsection dealing with the joint option to tax supplies of immovable goods and subsection (7) deals with supplies of residential property. Section 4C(6)(a) deals with the surrender or assignment of a taxable legacy lease.

[2-60] The importance of the terms *"completed"* and *"occupied"* is clear from the wording.

[2-61] Subject to the subsections outlined above, Section 4B(2) provides that VAT does not arise on supplies of immovable goods:

> *"(a) that have not been developed within 20 years of that supply…"* [i.e. supplies of immovable goods which have not been developed in the previous 20 years are exempt].

> *(b) "being completed immovable goods, the most recent completion of which occurred more than 5 years prior to that supply, and those goods have not been developed within that 5-year period…"* [i.e. supplies of

immovable goods if the most recent development of the property was more than five years earlier].

(c)   *"being completed immovable goods that have not been developed since the most recent completion of those goods, where that supply –*

    (i)   *occurs after the immovable goods have been occupied for an aggregate of at least 24 months following the most recent completion of those goods, and*

    (ii) *takes place after a previous supply of those goods on which tax was chargeable and that previous supply –*

        (I)   *took place after the most recent completion of those goods, and*

        (II) *was a transaction between persons who were not connected within the meaning of section 7A…"*

[i.e. a supply of a completed property which has been occupied as defined for at least 24 months **in aggregate** since its most recent development, if a previous taxable supply of the property between unconnected parties had taken place since that development. The term *"in aggregate"* indicates that the 24-month qualifying period can be made up of different non-continuous periods of occupancy by different occupiers].

(d)   *"being a building that was completed more than 5 years prior to that supply and on which development was carried out in the 5 years prior to that supply where –*

    (i)   *such development did not and was not intended to adapt the building for a materially altered use, and*

    (ii) *the cost of such development did not exceed 25% of the consideration for that supply"*

[i.e. a supply of a property which was completed more than five years before the supply, but further "minor" development on that property has been carried out since then. The supply will still be exempt if the further development does not adapt the property for materially altered use **and** the cost of the development does not exceed 25% of the sale price. If the property is either materially altered or the cost exceeds 25% of the sale price, then the property is taxable because the development is not minor.] If the property is materially altered, then it is developed for VAT purposes and the 25% threshold is not relevant.

"or

    (e) *being a building that was completed within the five years prior to that supply where –*

        (i) *the building had been occupied for an aggregate of at least 24 months following that completion,*

        (ii) *that supply takes place after a previous supply of the building on which tax was chargeable and that previous supply –*

            (I) *took place after that completion of the building, and*

            (II) *was a transaction between persons who were not connected within the meaning of Section 7A,*

    and

        (iii) *if any development of that building occurred after that completion –*

            (I) *such development did not and was not intended to adapt the building for a materially altered use, and*

            (II) *the cost of such development did not exceed 25% of the consideration for that supply."*

(This is similar to paragraph (d) but deals with a supply of property which would normally be exempt under the "two-year rule" where minor development has taken place.)

[2-62] Section 4B(3) provides that:

"Where a person supplies immovable goods to another person and in connection with that supply, a taxable person enters into an agreement with that other person or with a person connected with that other person to carry out a development in relation to those immovable goods, then –

    (a) *the person who supplies the goods shall, in relation to that supply, be deemed to be a taxable person,*

    (b) *the supply of the said immovable goods shall be deemed to be a supply of those goods to which section 2 applies, and*

    (c) *subsection (2) does not apply to that supply."*

[2-63] This subsection brings the anti-avoidance rule in Section 4(5) of the VAT Act into the new property regime. It prevents the application of an exemption to the supply of a site that is to be developed where the site is sold in connection with an agreement to develop that site. The exemption provisions provided for in Section 4B(2) do not apply.

The combination of Sections 4B(2)(a) and 4B(3) ensure that the supply of [2–64] "building land" is taxed in the same way under the new regime as it was under the old regime. The VAT treatment of undeveloped land (e.g. farm land) will not be affected. Land sold in connection with a contract to develop it will continue to be taxable.

> *Example – sale of property sold in connection with an agreement to develop the property*
>
> Anne Farmer owns a field which she has not developed. Dun Limited is a property developer. Jack and Jill sign a contract to buy the field from Mrs Farmer and a building agreement with Dun Limited to build a house for them. Jack and Jill's contract with Mrs Farmer is contingent on their performing the contract with Dun Limited.
>
> The sale of the field by Mrs Farmer to Jack and Jill is subject to VAT as it is connected with an agreement to develop it.

Section 4B(4) stipulates that *"Section 8(3) does not apply in relation to* [2–65] *a person who makes a supply of immovable goods"*. In other words, the registration thresholds do not apply to property transactions. This is modelled on the old Section 4(7) of the VAT Act.

Section 4B(5) states that: [2–66]

> *"Where a taxable person supplies immovable goods to another taxable person in circumstances where that supply would otherwise be exempt in accordance with subsection (2), or subsection (2) or 6(b) of Section 4C, then tax shall, notwithstanding subsection (2), or subsection (2) or 6(b) of Section 4C, be chargeable on that supply, where the supplier and the taxable person to whom the supply is made enter an agreement in writing no later than the fifteenth day of the month in which that supply occurs to opt to have tax chargeable on that supply (in this Act referred to as a 'joint option for taxation')."*

Subsection (5) provides for an option to tax a supply which is *prima facie* [2–67] exempt in accordance with the other provisions mentioned if both parties to the transaction agree. The option to tax the supply must be made in writing within the time frame outlined. Whether or not the option to tax the sale is exercised has implications for the supplier under the CGS.

The option to tax clause is not to be confused with a standard VAT clause and both may be required.

[2-68]   Section 4B(6) states that:

> *"Where a joint option for taxation is exercised in accordance with subsection (5) then –*
>
> *(a)   the person to whom the supply is made shall, in relation to that supply, be an accountable person and shall be liable to pay the tax chargeable on that supply as if that person supplied those goods, and*
>
> *(b)   the person who made the supply shall not be accountable for or liable to pay the said tax."*

[2-69]   This provides that, where the joint option to tax a supply of immovable goods is exercised in accordance with subsection (5), then the tax is accounted for by the purchaser on a reverse-charge basis. Paragraph (a) provides that the purchaser will be accountable for the tax and paragraph (b) provides that the seller will not be accountable.

[2-70]   In relation to claiming a deduction for input VAT credit, Revenue has clarified that the purchaser would rely on the option to tax document provided for in Section 4B(5). Section 12(1)(a)(iiic) provides that an accountable person would, insofar as the property would be used for the purposes of its taxable supplies/qualifying activities, be entitled to deduct the VAT chargeable under the Section 4B(6) reverse-charge procedure.

Residential property

[2-71]   Section 4B(7) provides that the first supply of **residential property** by a person in the business of developing property, or a person connected to that person, is not exempt, even if otherwise the transfer would seem to meet the exemption criteria in subsection (2). The supply of houses and apartments – whether by the sale of the freehold or via a very long lease (a "freehold equivalent interest") – for residential purposes will continue to be taxable at 13.5%. The first sale of houses and apartments by property developers and builders will continue to be taxable if the property is sold during the adjustment period.

The section states that:

> *"(a)   Where a taxable person supplies immovable goods to another person in circumstances where that supply would otherwise be exempt in accordance with subsection (2), tax shall, notwithstanding subsection (2), be chargeable on that supply where –*
>
> *(i)   the immovable goods are buildings designed or capable of being used as a dwelling,*

(ii) *the person who makes that supply is a person who developed the immovable goods in the course of a business of developing immovable goods or a person connected with that person, within the meaning of Section 7A, and*

(iii) *the person who developed those immovable goods was entitled to a deduction under Section 12 for tax chargeable to that person in respect of that person's acquisition or development of those immovable goods."*

Paragraph (a) describes the conditions under which the supply of residential properties by developers and builders is taxable, regardless of the time when the supply takes place, i.e. regardless of the two-year/five-year "rules".

Example – disposal of residential property by a property developer

O Limited, a property development company, buys an undeveloped site for €350,000. It acquires full planning permission and in 2009 builds a substantial dwelling at a cost of €2.5 million plus VAT of €337,500. O Limited, anticipating a VAT-able sale of the property, claims back the input VAT on costs. However, it is unable to sell the property immediately and in fact it lies idle for approximately six years.

Notwithstanding the five-year rule, Section 4B(7) provides that the sale in 2015 is subject to VAT in the normal manner, i.e. O Limited is required to charge the purchaser VAT at 13.5%.

It is likely that Section 4B(7) was introduced for anti-avoidance purposes. Purchasers of residential property are not generally entitled to recover input VAT. Without this section there might have been an incentive for developers to postpone sales to qualify for the exemption. **[2-72]**

In reality, it would be highly unlikely that a developer could keep a completed property on the books for that length of time without generating some kind of income from it. In the circumstances outlined in the example above, one might expect O Limited to find a tenant for the house pending sale. Under Section 7A, a letting of residential property cannot be subject to the option to tax and consequently the property would pass to an exempt use, albeit perhaps only for a few years. The letting of residential property by a property developer ("*a person who developed the immovable goods in the course of a business of developing immovable goods or a person connected with that person, within* **[2-73]** *the meaning of Section 7A")* is dealt with in Section 4B(7)(b), which continues as follows:

> "(b) *In the case of a building to which this subsection would apply if the building were supplied by the taxable person at any time during the capital goods scheme adjustment period for that building –*
>
> (i) *Section 12E(6) shall not apply, and*
>
> (ii) *Notwithstanding Section 12E(4) the proportion of total tax incurred that is deductible by that person shall be treated as the initial interval proportion of deductible use."*

[2–74] Paragraph (b) has the effect that the developer will pay back 1/20 of its input VAT deduction at the end of the second interval and each subsequent interval. It does this by disapplying Section 12E(6), which would, in the absence of the disapplication, clawback all of the VAT when the developer makes an exempt letting.

[2–75] In addition, sub-paragraph (ii) provides that the proportion of the "total tax incurred" deductible by the developer (i.e. 100% VAT deducted on the acquisition or development of the property) is treated as the "initial interval proportion of deductible use" (see Chapter 3 in relation to the CGS). This has the effect of disapplying the full adjustment that would be required in accordance with Section 12E(4) as the use for the initial interval is deemed to be 100% taxable.

[2–76] Effectively, where residential properties are let by a property developer prior to the first supply, the adjustment under the CGS is the annual adjustment. The letting is treated as a temporary arrangement that does not take the first supply out of the VAT "net".

[2–77] Revenue's Tax Briefing, Issue 69 (see Appendix 3) dated September 2008 outlines Revenue's approach to the VAT treatment of property developers who rent out residential properties. (The Tax Briefing is considered in more detail in Chapters 4 and 5.)

Section 4C

[2–78] The new Section 4C was introduced under Section 88 of the Finance Act 2008 and amended by Schedule 6(4)(d) of the Finance (No. 2) Act 2008. It deals with the measures which apply to transitional properties, i.e. those which have been subject to tax under the "old rules" and are disposed of or let under the "new rules".

Section 4C(1) says that:

"This section applies to –

(a) *immovable goods which are acquired or developed by a taxable person prior to 1 July 2008, being completed immovable goods before 1 July 2008, and have not been disposed of by that taxable person prior to that date, until such time as those goods have been disposed of by that taxable person on or after that date, and*

(b) *an interest in immovable goods within the meaning of section 4, other than a freehold interest or a freehold equivalent interest, created by a taxable person prior to 1 July 2008 and held by a taxable person on 1 July 2008 and the reversionary interest, within the meaning of section 4(9), on that interest until that interest is surrendered after 1 July 2008."*

Paragraph (a) provides that Section 4C applies to immovable goods acquired or developed by a taxable person prior to 1 July 2008 and not disposed of by that taxable person before that date.   **[2-79]**

Paragraph (b) provides that the section also applies to an interest in immovable goods within the meaning of Section 4 **other than** a freehold interest or a freehold equivalent interest created by the taxable person prior to 1 July 2008 and held by that person on 1 July 2008. This is a reference to long leases (not being freehold equivalent interests) as defined under the "old" legislation, i.e. leases of a term of 10 years or more, including the reversionary interest thereon until such time as it is surrendered after 1 July 2008.   **[2-80]**

Section 4C(1A) provides that: **[2-81]**

"Where an interest to which subsection (1)(b) applies is surrendered, then, for the purposes of the application of section 12E in respect of the immovable goods concerned –

(a) *the total tax incurred shall include the amount of tax chargeable on the surrender in accordance with subsection (7) and shall not include tax incurred prior to the creation of the surrendered interest, and*

(b) *the adjustment period shall consist of the number of intervals specified in subsection (11)(c)(iv) and the initial interval shall begin on the date of that surrender."*

When a taxable legacy lease is surrendered, which is not a freehold equivalent interest, then the amount of VAT arising in relation to the surrender is calculated using a formula set out in Section 4C(7).   **[2-82]**

Section 4C(1A), above, provides that VAT incurred before the original long lease was granted is not taken into account in the formula. In addition, the adjustment period under the CGS is to be determined using the provisions set out in Section 4C(11)(c)(iv) (see subsequently in this chapter and also in Chapter 5).

[2-83]   Section 4C(2) states that

> *"In the case of a supply of immovable goods to which subsection (1)(a) applies, being completed immovable goods within the meaning of Section 4B –*
>
> (a)   *where the person supplying those goods had no right to deduction under section 12 in relation to the tax chargeable on the acquisition or development of those goods prior to 1 July 2008, and*
>
> (b)   *if any subsequent development of those immovable goods occurs on or after 1 July 2008 –*
>
> > (i)   *that development does not and is not intended to adapt the immovable goods for a materially altered use, and*
> >
> > (ii)   *the cost of that development does not exceed 25% of the consideration for that supply,*
>
> *then, subject to Section 4B(3), that supply is not chargeable to tax but a joint option for taxation may be exercised in respect of that supply in accordance with Section 4B(5) and that tax is payable in accordance with Section 4B(6)."*

[2-84]   This subsection provides that, where a person was not entitled to deduct the tax chargeable on the acquisition or the development of transitional properties, and where those goods were not subsequently developed on or after 1 July 2008, other than "minor" development as outlined, then the supply is not automatically chargeable to VAT, but a joint option for taxation (as defined in subsection 4B(5)) may be exercised and tax is then payable by the purchaser on the reverse-charge basis.

[2-85]   Section 4C(3) states that:

> *"Where a person referred in subsection (1) –*
>
> (a)   *acquired, developed or has an interest in immovable goods to which this section applies,*
>
> (b)   *was entitled to deduct tax, in accordance with Section 12 on that person's acquisition or development of those goods, and*
>
> (c)   *makes a letting of those immovable goods to which paragraph (iv) of the First Schedule applies,*

then, that person shall calculate an amount in accordance with the formula in Section 4(3)(ab) and that amount shall be payable as if it were tax due by that person in accordance with Section 19 for the taxable period in which that letting takes place."

Subsection (3) provides that where a taxable person acquired, developed or has an interest in a transitional property and was entitled to deduct tax charged on the acquisition or development of that property and creates an exempt letting, then that person is required to calculate an amount in accordance with the formula in Section 4(3)(ab) of the VAT Act (the deductibility adjustment provisions) and that amount is payable as if it were tax due in the taxable period in which that letting takes place. **[2–86]**

The clawback treatment set out in Section 4C(3) applies to transitional property, i.e. property which was completed as defined before 1 July 2008. **[2–87]**

Effectively, the same clawback was provided for under the "old" rules, i.e. under Section 4(3)(ab) of the VAT Act, with effect from 1 May 2005, a deductibility adjustment clawback arose if a person who had reclaimed input VAT in relation to a property put it into exempt lettings, s/he suffered a lump sum clawback of VAT in the same manner. **[2–88]**

When the property is not transitional, i.e. is **both** completed **and** rented out in an exempt letting on or after 1 July 2008, Section 4B(7)(b) provides that an interval-based adjustment only would arise as opposed to a lump sum clawback calculated using Section 4(3)(ab). **[2–89]**

On the face of it, the VAT treatment applicable to exempt lettings of non-transitional property would appear to be a good deal more favourable than the VAT treatment applicable to transitional property. **[2–90]**

However, Revenue confirms in its Tax Briefing, Issue 69, dated September 2008 (see Appendix 3) that it is prepared to accept that a **residential** property may be regarded as not having been completed until it has been rented out. Revenue specifies that this approach would be confined to the cases referred to in the Tax Briefing. To reconsider briefly the definition of the term "completed", Section 4B(1) provides that in respect of immovable goods, the term completed means that: **[2–91]**

"… development has reached the state, apart from only such finishing or fitting work that would normally be carried out by or on behalf of the person who will use them, where those goods can effectively be used for the purposes for which those goods were designed, and the utility services required for those purposes are connected to those goods."

[2-92] Revenue's view has been welcomed by practitioners and yet it seems quite a leap of logic to consider that property would not be completed until it has been rented out. Effectively, the understanding is that the VAT adjustment in relation to exempt short-term letting of transitional properties could be the same as the treatment for non-transitional properties. However, in the examples given in the Tax Briefing, Revenue does not illustrate this viewpoint in relation to transitional properties. It would therefore appear prudent under the circumstances to examine each case on its own merits, bearing in mind that tax briefings are not a substitute for legislation.

In relation to the subsequent sales of such properties following exempt lettings, please see Chapters 4 and 5.

[2-93] Section 4C(4) states that:

> "An assignment or surrender of an interest in immovable goods to which subsection (1)(b) applies is deemed to be a supply of immovable goods for the purposes of this Act for a period of 20 years from the creation of the interest or the most recent assignment of that interest before 1 July 2008, whichever is the later."

[2-94] Subsection (4) provides that where an assignment or surrender of a long lease occurs within 20 years of the creation of the last assignment, it is deemed to be a supply of immovable goods.

[2-95] Section 4C(5) states that:

> "If a person makes a supply of immovable goods to which this section applies and tax is chargeable on that supply and that person was not entitled to deduct all the tax charged to that person on the acquisition or development of those immovable goods that person shall be entitled to make the appropriate adjustment that would apply under Section 12E(7)(a) as if the capital goods scheme applied to that transaction."

Subsection (5) provides for a refund of input VAT in cases where there is a taxable supply of immovable goods and the vendor was not entitled to deduct all of the input VAT when purchasing/developing the property. This is similar to the provisions of the "old" Section 12(5) of the VAT Act (see also Chapter 5 below for additional detail).

[2-96] Section 4C(6) states that:

> "In the case of an assignment or surrender of an interest in immovable goods referred to in subsection (4) –
>
> (a)   tax shall be chargeable if the person who makes the assignment or surrender was entitled to deduct in accordance with Section 12 any

of the tax chargeable on the acquisition of that interest, or the development of those immovable goods, and

(b) *tax shall not be chargeable where the person who makes the assignment or surrender had no right to deduction under section 12 on the acquisition of that interest or the development of those immovable goods, but a joint option for taxation of that assignment or surrender may be exercised."*

Subsection 6(a) provides that where a person was entitled to deduct tax on the acquisition or development of transitional property, a charge to tax will arise in the case of an assignment or surrender of an interest in that property. [2–97]

Subsection 6(b) provides that tax will **not** arise on an assignment or surrender where no right to deductibility arose on the acquisition or the development of transitional property. However, it also provides that a joint option for taxation may be exercised in such a case. [2–98]

Section 4C(7) states the following: [2–99]

"(a) *Notwithstanding section 10, the amount on which tax is chargeable on a taxable assignment or surrender to which sub-section (6) applies shall be the amount calculated in accordance with the formula in paragraph (b) divided by the rate as specified in section 11(1)(d) expressed in decimal form."*

Section 4C(7)(a) provides that the amount on which VAT is chargeable on a taxable assignment or surrender of transitional property is calculated using a formula set out in paragraph 4C(7)(b), divided by the reduced VAT rate referred to in Section 11(1)(d) of the VAT Act, as expressed in decimal form. At the time of writing, the VAT rate is 13.5%. Section 10 of the VAT Act, which deals with the amount on which VAT is chargeable, does not apply under these circumstances.

Section 4C(7) continues as follows: [2–100]

"(b) *The amount of tax due and payable in respect of a taxable assignment or surrender to which subsection (6) applies is an amount calculated in accordance with the following formula:*

$$T \times N/Y$$

where –

T is the total tax incurred referred to in subsection (11)(d), except for the amount of tax charged in respect of any development by the person who makes the assignment or surrender following the acquisition of this interest,

> *N is the number of full intervals plus one, that remain in the adjustment period referred to in subsection (11)(c), at the time of the assignment or surrender,*
>
> *Y is total number of intervals in that adjustment period for the person making the assignment or surrender,*
>
> *And section 4(8) shall apply to that tax."*

[2–101]   In relation to T, Section 4C(11)(d) provides that *"the amount of tax charged, or the amount of tax which would have been chargeable but for the application of sections 3(5)(b)(iii) or 13A, to the person treated as the capital goods owner on the acquisition of, or the development of, the capital goods shall be treated as the total tax incurred".* In other words, T is the total VAT arising (*"the total tax incurred"*) rather than the amount of VAT to which the capital goods owner was actually entitled to reclaim. However, any input VAT which may have been incurred on development work undertaken by the assigning or surrendering tenant is not included. This is because such development work would have constituted refurbishment, as defined in Section 12E(1), and the tenant would be the capital goods owner in respect of same (see Chapter 3).

[2–102]   N is a reference to the number of intervals remaining in the adjustment period at the time of the surrender/assignment. Y is a reference to the total length of the adjustment period.

[2–103]   In relation to surrenders/assignments of what Revenue terms "legacy leases", Section 4C(7)(b) specifies that the reverse-charge rule provided for under the old Section 4(8) is to apply.

> ### Example – assignment of transitional property where the assignor was not entitled to recover input VAT
>
> BlingBank acquired a 25-year lease from HoldCo on 1 January 2005. HoldCo charged BlingBank VAT of €500,000. BlingBank was not entitled to recover same because it was engaged in solely exempt supplies.
>
> On 1 January 2009, BlingBank assigns its lease to CompuTech Inc, which is engaged in fully taxable supplies. BlingBank has already

suffered the VAT on the lease and is not obliged to charge output VAT on the assignment. However, it could jointly opt with Compu-Tech to tax the assignment. If BlingBank were to do this, it would be entitled under Section 4C(5) to recover approximately 16/20 of the input VAT suffered when it was granted the lease, calculated using the formula set out in Section 12E(7)(a) of the VAT Act, i.e.: $E \times N/T$.

E = the non-deductible amount, i.e. €500,000.
N = the number of full intervals plus one in the adjustment period i.e. 16.
T = the total number of intervals in the adjustment period, i.e. 20.

Consequently the VAT recovery claim would be €500,000 × 16/20 = €400,000.

Example – assignment of a taxable transitional property where the assignee was entitled to recover input VAT

Mr Tee acquired a 25-year leasehold interest in a commercial property on 1 March 2003. VAT of €300,000 arose on the capitalised value under the "old" rules. The lessor obtained a VAT 4B and passed responsibility for accounting for the VAT on the lease to Mr Tee as tenant. Mr Tee accounted for the VAT on the reverse-charge basis. Mr Tee intended to use the property for the purpose of his fully taxable supplies. Consequently he was entitled to claim an input credit which matched the VAT on the lease and did not suffer any net VAT cost. Nonetheless he was still **entitled** to input VAT credit on his acquisition. As a result, output VAT would arise if he assigns the lease during the adjustment period.

Section 4C(7)(a) provides that the amount on which VAT is chargeable on a taxable assignment or surrender of transitional property is calculated using a formula set out in paragraph 4C(7)(b), divided by the reduced VAT rate referred to in Section 11(1)(d) of the VAT Act, as expressed in decimal form. At the time of writing, this is 13.5%. Section 10 of the VAT Act, which deals with the amount of which VAT is chargeable, does not apply under these circumstances.

The formula set out in Section 4C(7)(b) is:

$$\frac{T \times N}{Y}$$

T = the total tax incurred.

N = the number of full intervals plus one remaining in the adjustment period at the time of the assignment or surrender.

Y − is the total number of intervals in the adjustment period, i.e. generally 20.

Mr Tee assigns the lease on, say, 1 August 2009, the formula would apply as follows:

T = €300,000.

N = 14 (the total number of intervals in the adjustment period is 20, not 25. The lease was granted initially on 1 March 2003. Six years and four months later, on 1 August 2009, Mr Tee assigns the lease. There are 13 years and 8 months left in the lease term. N = the number of full intervals remaining plus one, i.e. 14).

Y = 20 (not 25. Although the original lease term was 25, the total number of intervals in the adjustment period cannot exceed 20).

Applying these figures to the formula would give the following outcome:

$$€300,000 \times 14/20 = €210,000.$$

This gives the amount of VAT payable in respect of the assignment. The amount on which VAT is chargeable as referred to in Section 4C(7)(a) is this VAT figure divided by 0.135 = €1,555,555 approx.

[2-104]   Finally, Section 4C(7)(b) provides that the VAT arising is to be accounted for under Section 4(8) of the VAT Act. Section 4(8) is one of the provisions of the old Section 4 which may apply under Section 4(11) subject to Section 4C.

[2-105]   Section 4C(8) states that:

"(a) Where an interest in immovable goods referred to in subsection (6) is assigned or surrendered to a taxable person during the adjustment period and tax is payable in respect of that assignment or surrender, then the person who makes the assignment or surrender shall issue a document to the person to whom the interest is being assigned or surrendered containing the following information:

(i)   the amount of tax due and payable on that assignment or surrender, and

(ii) the number of intervals remaining in the adjustment period, as determined in accordance with subsection (11)(c)(iv)".

Example – assignor's documentary obligations when assigning a taxable legacy lease

In the case of Mr Tee, when assigning the lease, he is required to issue a "document" to the assignee showing that the amount of VAT due and payable on the assignment is €210,000. The "document" must also confirm the number of intervals remaining in the adjustment period. It would appear that, in the above example, this would have to be 14, even though the legislation is not quite clear on this point. See the example below in relation to the assignee's position.

Section 4C(8) continues that: [2-106]

"(b) *Where paragraph (a) applies, the person to whom the interest is assigned or surrendered shall be a capital goods owner for the purpose of Section 12E in respect of the capital goods being assigned or surrendered, and shall be subject to the provisions of that section and for this purpose –*

(i) *the adjustment period shall be the period referred to in subsection (11)(c) as correctly specified on the document referred to in paragraph (a),*

(ii) *the total tax incurred shall be the amount of tax referred to in subsection (11)(d) as correctly specified in the document referred to in paragraph (a) and*

(iii) *the initial interval shall be a period of 12 months beginning on the date on which the assignment or surrender occurs."*

Subsection 4C(8)(a) is not dissimilar to the old Section 4(8) in that it provides that where an interest in transitional property is assigned or surrendered, then the person who makes the assignment or surrender must issue a document to the person to whom the interest is assigned or surrendered showing the amount of tax due and payable and the number of intervals remaining in the adjustment period. [2-107]

Subsection 4C(8)(b) provides that, where paragraph (a) applies, the person to whom the interest in immovable goods is assigned or surrendered is to be regarded as a capital goods owner and the provisions of the CGS set out in Section 12E apply. [2-108]

The adjustment period to be used is that set out in Section 4C(11)(c) and from the wording of paragraph (i) it seems that, if the document provided for under Section 4C(8)(a) misstates the adjustment period, then the "correct" adjustment period as calculated in accordance with Section 4C(11)(c) would prevail. [2-109]

Similarly, the VAT incurred in relation to the assignment/surrender is that calculated under the provision of subsection (11)(d).

[2–110]   Given that the assignee/lessor is now a capital goods owner, paragraph (iii) provides for the commencement date of the new capital goods owner's initial interval for CGS purposes.

> *Example – assignee's position in relation to surrender of a taxable legacy lease*
>
> In the above example, it is assumed that the assignee will use the property for the purpose of 100% VAT-able supplies. On taking over the assigned property, s/he self-accounts for VAT by including the VAT amount on the "document" in both the input and output VAT sections of the VAT return for the period in which s/he takes the assignment. The net VAT "cost" to the assignee is therefore "nil".

[2–111]   The legislation provides that the assignee also becomes a capital goods owner and must commence maintaining a capital goods record. If the property is acquired on, say, 13 September 2009, then this is the first date of the assignee's initial interval. The legislation provides that the initial interval would run for a 12-month period from 13 September 2009. It would therefore end on 12 September 2010. Section 4C(11)(c)(iii) provides that in most cases the assignee's adjustment period would be *"the period remaining in that interest at the time of the assignment ... or 20 years, whichever is the shorter"*. In this case, the *"period remaining"* is 14 intervals from 13 September 2009.

[2–112]   Subsection 4C(9) provides that:

> *"(a)   Where a person cancels an election to be an accountable person in accordance with section 8(5A) then, in respect of the immovable goods which were used in supplying the services for which that person made that election, section 12E does not apply if those immovable goods are held by that person on 1 July 2008 and are not further developed after that date."*

[2–113]   Where a person who has elected to register in respect of a holiday home wishes to cancel that election, the old rules continue to apply, provided that the holiday home is owned by that person on 1 July 2008 and is not further developed after that date.

[2–114]   Section 110 of the Finance Act 2000 introduced a new Section 8(5A) into the VAT Act. Section 8(5A) provided that if a person who had elected to register for VAT in respect of holiday lettings cancelled his/her election within 10 years of electing to register, then Revenue would be entitled to claw back a percentage of the VAT recovered in respect of the acquisition/development of the holiday home. If the trader remained registered for 10 years or more, then no clawback arose on a subsequent cancellation.

Example – cancellation of election to register for VAT in respect of holiday home – old rules

Mary purchased a holiday home in Kerry in March 2003 and elected to register for VAT with effect from that date. She reclaimed VAT of €60,000 in relation to her purchase and subsequently accounted for VAT on rental income. Mary then cancelled her election with effect from 1 March 2008. A clawback of VAT arose as follows, using the formula set out in Section 8(5A):

$$\frac{A \times (10-5)}{10}$$

A = the total amount of VAT reclaimed.

B = the number of full years (continuous period of 12 months) during which the property was used for the purposes of holiday lettings.

Consequently the formula gives the following result:

$$\frac{€60,000 \times (10-5)}{10} = €30,000$$

Upon cancellation of her election, Mary would have been liable to pay a clawback of VAT amounting to €30,000.

Provided that Mary does not develop her holiday home on or after 1 July 2008, the Section 8(5A) formula would still apply if she cancelled her election on or after 1 July 2008. The clawback period provided for under Section 8(5A) would expire 10 years after Mary elected to register. She could cancel her election on, say, 1 March 2015 without suffering a clawback.

Example – cancellation of election to register for VAT in respect of holiday home on or after 1 July 2008 – property acquired pre-1 July 2008 and developed after that date

Mary had a new sunroom constructed in her holiday home in Autumn 2008. All the work was completed by 1 March 2009. She spent €30,000 on the works net of VAT and claimed back purchase VAT of €4,050.

The property has now been refurbished, as defined for VAT purposes. Mary therefore has two capital goods: the original "transitional property" and a new capital good, with an adjustment period of 10 years, commencing on 1 March 2009.

If Mary cancels her election on 1 March 2012, Revenue has confirmed that the provisions of Section 8(5A) would apply to the **original** acquisition, i.e. she would be cancelling her election within the 10-year period and a clawback would arise using the formula set out above.

Revenue has also confirmed that, upon the cancellation, the development work which was completed in March 2009 would be subject to a separate clawback under Section 12E(7)(b).

Assuming Mary sells the property to a taxable person, she could opt to tax the sale and avoid both clawbacks.

[2-115]   Section 4C(10) states that:

> *"In the application of section 12E to immovable goods and interests in immovable goods to which this section applies, subsections (4)(5) and (6) of that section shall be disregarded in respect of the person who owns those immovable goods or holds an interest in those immovable goods on 1 July 2008, but if that person develops the immovable goods and that development is a refurbishment, within the meaning of section 12E, that is completed on or after 1 July 2008, then these subsections shall not be disregarded in respect of that refurbishment."*

[2-116]   This subsection provides that certain subsections of the CGS do not apply to transitional properties, namely:

- Section 12E(4), which contains provisions that require a CGS adjustment at the end of the first 12 months in certain circumstances.

- Section 12E(5), which requires that any change in the business use of a property during each year of the adjustment period when compared with the initial business use during the first year following acquisition is required to be adjusted for on an annual basis.

- Section 12E(6), which contains rules to deal with big percentage changes in business use and rules for dealing with letting of properties.

[2-117]   However, insofar as the capital goods owner refurbishes the property on or after 1 July 2008, then Sections 12E(4), (5) and (6) would continue to apply in relation to the refurbishment. If a transitional property is

refurbished, therefore, the interval-based adjustments provided for in Sections 12E(4), (5) and (6) above would apply in relation to the refurbishment but not in relation to the underlying capital good.

Section 4C(11) states that: [2–118]

"For the purposes of applying section 12E to immovable goods, or interests in immovable goods to which this section applies –

(a)   *any interest in immovable goods, to which this section applies shall be treated as a capital good,*

(b)   *any person who has an interest in immovable goods to which this section applies shall be treated as a capital goods owner, but shall not be so treated to the extent that the person has a reversionary interest in those immovable goods if those goods were not developed by, on behalf of, or to the benefit of that person,*

(c)   *the period to be treated as the adjustment period in respect of immovable goods or interests in immovable goods to which this section applies is –*

    (i)   *in the case of the acquisition of the freehold interest or freehold equivalent interest in those immovable goods, 20 years from the date of that acquisition,*

    (ii)   *in the case of the creation of an interest in those immovable goods, 20 years or, if the interest when it was created was for a period of less than 20 years, the number of full years in that interest when created, whichever is the shorter, or*

    (iii)   *in the case of the assignment or surrender of an interest in immovable goods prior to 1 July 2008 the period remaining in that interest at the time of the assignment or surrender of that interest or 20 years, whichever is the shorter, and*

    (iv)   *in the case of –*

        (I)   *the surrender or first assignment of an interest in immovable goods on or after 1 July 2008, the number of full years remaining in the adjustment period as determined in accordance with subparagraphs (ii) and (iii), plus one, or*

        (II)   *the second or subsequent assignment of an interest in immovable goods after 1 July 2008, the number of full intervals remaining in the adjustment period as determined in accordance with clause (I), plus one,*

and this number shall thereafter be the number of intervals remaining in the adjustment period,

but where the immovable goods have been developed since the acquisition of those immovable goods or the creation of that interest, 20 years from the date of the most recent development of those goods,

(d)   the amount of tax charged, or the amount of tax that would have been chargeable but for the application of section 3(5)(b)(iii) or 13A, to the person treated as the capital goods owner on the acquisition of, or development of, the capital goods shall be treated as the total tax incurred,

(e)   the total tax incurred divided by the number of intervals in the adjustment period referred to in paragraph (c) shall be treated as the base tax amount,

(f)   each year in the adjustment period referred to in paragraph (c) shall be treated as an interval,

(g)   the first 12 months of the adjustment period referred to in paragraph (c) shall be treated as the second interval,

(h)   the second year of the adjustment period referred to in paragraph (c) shall be treated as the second interval, but in the case of an interest which is assigned or surrendered on or after 1 July 2008, the second interval of the adjustment period shall have the meaning assigned to it by section 12E,

(i)   each year following the second year in the adjustment period referred to in paragraph (c) shall be treated as a subsequent interval,

(j)   the amount which shall be treated as the total reviewed deductible amount shall be the amount of the total tax incurred as provided for in paragraph (d) less –

    (i)   any amount of the total tax incurred which was charged to the person treated as the capital goods owner but which that owner was not entitled to deduct in accordance with section 12,

    (ii)   any amount accounted for in accordance with section 12D(4) by the person treated as the capital goods owner in respect of a transfer of the goods to that owner prior to 1 July 2008,

    (iii)   any tax payable in accordance with subsection (3) or section 4(3)(ab) by the person treated as the capital goods owner, and

    (iv)   where an adjustment of deductibility has been made in respect of the capital good in accordance with subsection (3) or section 4(3)(ab), the amount "T" in the formula in section 4(3)(ab),

(k)   the amount referred to in paragraph (d) less the amount referred to in paragraph (j) shall be treated as the non-deductible amount,

*and for the purposes of applying paragraphs (f),(h) and (i) "year"
means each 12 month period in the adjustment period, the first of
which begins on the first day of the initial interval referred to in
paragraph (g)."*

Section 4C(11) applies, as appropriate, the various CGS definitions for   **[2–119]**
the purposes of the transitional measures.

Paragraph (a) provides that even though a property may be transitional,
it will be referred to as a capital good where it meets the new definition.

Paragraph (b) provides that a person who owns a capital good as defined   **[2–120]**
will be treated as a capital goods owner, notwithstanding that the relevant property may be transitional. However, that person will **not** be
treated as a capital goods owner if s/he retains only the reversionary
interest in the property, provided that the property has not been developed by, on behalf of, or to the benefit of the owner of the reversionary
interest (presumably since the date on which the long lease in the property was granted).

In other words, a person who granted a VAT-able long lease as defined   **[2–121]**
under the old VAT and property legislation has effectively disposed of
his/her VAT-able interest in the property. Unless the property is subsequently developed "by, on behalf of or to the benefit of" the owner, then
a disposal by the owner of the remaining interest is not subject to VAT.

This is the same treatment as was available under Section 4(9) under the
"old" rules.

**Example – disposal of reversionary interest in transitional
property**

Declan acquired a commercial premises in November 2007 and
reclaimed input VAT. He was granted a taxable 20-year lease on
15 November. The VAT 4A/B procedure was used and the tenant
accounted for VAT on the capitalised value of the lease. On
15 October 2012 Declan sells his interest in the property. The tenant
remains *in situ*. This is a disposal of a reversionary interest in transitional property and provided the property has not been developed, the disposal is not subject to VAT.

Paragraph 4C(11)(c) deals with the adjustment period to apply to   **[2–122]**
transitional property.

Paragraph (i) provides that the adjustment period for transitional freehold   **[2–123]**
or freehold equivalent interests is 20 years from acquisition date.

[2-124] Paragraph (ii) provides that when the interest consists of a legacy lease, then the adjustment period will be 20 years or a shorter period if the legacy lease had a term of less than 20 years. Even if a legacy lease had a term of 25 years at grant, it would have a maximum adjustment period of 20 years.

[2-125] Paragraph (iii) provides that in the case of leases surrendered or assigned prior to 1 July 2008, the adjustment period would be the period remaining in the lease term at assignment or surrender, or 20 years, whichever is shorter.

[2-126] Paragraph (iv)(I) provides that the adjustment period in relation to a leasehold interest which is subject to surrender or a first assignment on or after 1 July 2008 is determined in accordance with (ii) or (iii) above, as appropriate, plus one.

[2-127] Paragraph (iv)(II) provides that the adjustment period in relation to a leasehold interest subject to a second assignment or surrender on or after 1 July 2008 is determined in accordance with (iv)(I) above, plus one.

[2-128] Revenue has confirmed that the adjustment period for a capital good is established at the point when the capital good is acquired or developed to completion.

Example – surrender of legacy lease

1 May 2006   L grants a 25-year lease to T. Total tax incurred by T is €400,000.

1 July 2009   T surrenders the lease.

Section 4C(7) provides that the amount of VAT chargeable on the surrender is calculated by reference to the original VAT charged on the creation of the lease, i.e. €400,000. The VAT chargeable is calculated by T as follows:

$$T \times \frac{N}{Y}$$

Section 4C(11)(c)(iv)(I) provides that in this case (the surrender of an interest in immovable goods on or after 1 July 2008) the adjustment period is *"the number of full years remaining in the adjustment period as determined in accordance with subparagraphs (ii) and (iii), plus one"*. The adjustment period for L is therefore 17 intervals.

$N = 16 + 1 = 17.$

Y = total number of intervals in the T's adjustment period (20, even though the original lease term was 25).

The amount of VAT on the surrender is therefore €340,000, being:

$$\text{€400,000} \times \frac{17}{20}$$

If the immovable goods have been developed, the last paragraph of Section 4C(11) provides that the adjustment period will be 20 years from the most recent development of the property. Revenue has confirmed that this last paragraph is interpreted as meaning developed to completion. In other words, if I purchase an undeveloped site in 1995 and develop a building on it to completion in 2000, then the adjustment period for the capital good is 20 years from 2000. If I carry out a further development in 2006 (completed in that year), it is a refurbishment and has its own adjustment period of 10 years.   **[2–129]**

However, if I buy a completed building in 1985 and VAT is charged on the acquisition, the adjustment period for the building is 20 years from 1985. Any subsequent development is treated as a separate capital good (refurbishment) and has an adjustment period of 10 years.

Paragraph (d) provides that the amount of input VAT arising (even if not actually charged because of the operation of Sections 3(5)(b)(iii) or 13A) is to be treated as the total VAT incurred in relation to transitional properties.   **[2–130]**

Example – amount of input VAT arising – transitional property

Donal bought a pub business on 1 November 2006. His acquisition included the pub licence, stock, fixtures and fittings and goodwill, as well as the pub premises. He did not pay VAT on his acquisition since under Section 3(5)(b)(iii) of the VAT Act, it was deemed not to be a supply. Donal's total purchase consideration was €2 million. The market value of the pub at the time of acquisition was €1 million. When Donal acquired the pub it would have constituted developed property. In other words, if Section 3(5)(b)(iii) had not applied, Donal would have paid VAT at 13.5%, being €135,000. For the purposes of the CGS, the amount of input VAT arising is €135,000.

Paragraph (e) provides that the total tax incurred as defined at (d) will be divided by the number of intervals in the adjustment period as defined at (c) to give the base tax amount. Under the capital goods   **[2–131]** scheme, the base tax amount is the annualised VAT incurred amount before any CGS adjustment. In Donal's case, above, the base tax amount would therefore be €135,000 divided by 20 intervals = €6,750.

[2–132] Paragraph (f) provides that, in relation to transitional properties, each year in the adjustment period is to be treated as a CGS interval. In relation to the second interval, this is a slight departure from the definition of the term "interval" used in Section 12E.

[2–133] Paragraph (g) provides that in relation to transitional properties, the first 12 months of the adjustment period as defined at (c) above is to be treated as the initial interval.

In the above example therefore, Donal's first interval would end on 31 October 2007.

The initial interval for transitional properties is, therefore, the same as the initial interval for non-transitional properties (see paragraph **2–218**).

[2–134] Paragraph (h) provides that, in relation to transitional properties, the second year of the adjustment period as defined at (c) above is to be treated as the second interval. In the case of Donal, above, the second interval would end on 31 October 2008.

[2–135] However, paragraph (h) also stipulates that in the case of a legacy lease which is assigned or surrendered on or after 1 July 2008, the second interval of the adjustment period shall have the meaning assigned to it by Section 12E.

To summarise, for non-transitional properties and for legacy leases assigned or surrendered on or after 1 July 2008, the second interval ends at the end of the capital goods owner's accounting year in the year in which the second interval begins. This means that the second interval could potentially be shorter than 12 months. However, for transitional properties **other than** legacy leases assigned or surrendered on or after 1 July 2008, the second interval is the second **year** of the adjustment period, i.e. the second interval will prima facie be 12 months long.

[2–136] Paragraph (i) provides that in relation to transitional properties, each year following the second year in the adjustment period is to be regarded as a subsequent interval. This provision is the same for transitional as non-transitional properties.

In the above example, Donal's third interval would end on 31 December 2009.

Paragraph (j) refers to the total reviewed deductible amount. The total **[2-137]** reviewed deductible amount is defined in the new Section 12E(2) as the total tax incurred (see above) adjusted to reflect the proportion of VAT-able use to which the property is put.

Paragraph (j) specifies that in the case of transitional properties, the total **[2-138]** reviewed deductible amount will be the total tax incurred as defined above less:

- Any part of the total tax incurred which the CGS owner was not entitled to deduct under Section 12 of the VAT Act.

- Any amount of the total tax incurred which the CGS owner had actually suffered under Section 12D(4) of the VAT Act. This is a reference to a clawback that the CGS owner might have suffered, for example, on the acquisition of a property under Section 3(5)(iii)(b) of the VAT Act.

- Any amount of the total tax payable which the CGS owner might already have had to repay under Section 4C(3) or Section 4(3)(ab).

In the above example, assuming that the pub is used for 100% VAT-able activities, then the total reviewed deductible amount would be the same as the total tax incurred, i.e. €135,000.

Paragraph (k) provides that the amount referred to in paragraph (d) **[2-139]** (the total VAT incurred) less any amount deducted under paragraph (j) (total reviewed deductible amount) will be treated as the non-deductible amount. The non-deductible amount is mentioned subsequently in Section 12E in relation to subsequent disposals of the property.

Finally, Section 4C(11) provides that for the purposes of applying para- **[2-140]** graphs (f), (h) and (i), all of which use the term "year", a "year" is to be taken as meaning a 12-month period in the adjustment period, the first of which begins on the first day of the initial interval referred to in paragraph (g).

Section 4C(12) states that: **[2-141]**

> *"Where a taxable person acquires immovable goods on or after 1 July 2007, then, notwithstanding subsection (10), section 12E(4) shall apply and, notwithstanding subsection (11)(j), the total reviewed deductible amount shall have the meaning assigned to it by section 12E. However this subsection does not apply where a taxable person has made an adjustment in accordance with Section 12(4)(f) in respect of those goods."*

This subsection deals with transitional properties acquired on or after 1 July 2007. It recognises that from 1 July 2008, Section 12(4) (which sets out the normal VAT deductibility rules for partly-exempt businesses) no longer applies to immovable goods. The section applies to any properties acquired or developed after 1 July 2007 which have not been subject to an adjustment in accordance with Section 12(4)(f). Such properties are subject to Section 12E(4) and an adjustment of deductibility taken on the acquisition or development of a property will arise in accordance with that section in certain circumstances.

Section 5

[2-142] Section 89 of the Finance Act 2008 introduced two changes to Section 5 of the VAT Act, which deals with the supply of services.

Section 5 is amended:

(a) in subsection (3)(a) by inserting *"other than immovable goods"* after the *"use of goods"*; and

(b) by inserting the following after subsection (3A):

"(3B) The use of immovable goods forming part of the assets of a business –

(a) for the private use of an accountable person or of such person's staff, or

(b) for any purpose other than those of the accountable person's business, is a taxable supply of services if –

(i) that use occurs during a period of 20 years following the acquisition or development of those goods by the accountable person, and

(ii) those goods are treated for tax purposes as forming part of the asset of the business at the time of their acquisition or development."

[2-143] Paragraph (a) excludes immovable goods from the definition of "supply of services" in the provisions of Section 5(3)(a). These provisions deal with the taxation of services which a taxpayer provides for his own use, for his staff's personal use or for other business purposes where the VAT on the goods to which the services relate is fully or partially deductible. In any event, the regulations required to give effect to Section 5(3)(a) have not yet been introduced (except in relation to staff canteen services).

Paragraph (b) provides that the private and non-business use of **[2–144]** immovable goods which form part of the assets of a business will instead be dealt with under a new Section 5(3B). The new subsection provides that, if VAT deductibility is claimed by a business on the acquisition or development of immovable property, then the private or non-business use of that property is a taxable supply of the services for a period of 20 years. The taxable amount is based on the amount of VAT charged to the accountable person at the time of the acquisition or development of the property. Under Section 10(4D) introduced by Section 93 of the Finance Act 2008, a clawback would occur in each bi-monthly VAT period during which the self-supply continues.

Revenue clarified in its e-brief 37/2008 (reproduced in Appendix 2) that **[2–145]** the provisions in Section 5(3B) are independent of the CGS. The rules for adjusting deductibility in the capital goods scheme relate to diversions to exempt use (see Section 12E and Chapter 3 of this book). In relation to Section 5(3B), 20 years is the period over which the taxpayer must account for the VAT where a deduction has been taken and the property is subsequently diverted to a non-business use in accordance with Section 5(3B). The amount on which VAT is chargeable as a result of this supply is based on this same 20-year period in accordance with Section 10(4D). See also Regulation 21B of S.I. No. 548 2006 – VAT Regulations 2006 (inserted by S.I. No. 238 of 2008 – VAT (Amendment) Regulations 2008).

See example in relation to Section 10(4D) later in this chapter at paragraph [2–198].

Section 7

Section 90 of the Finance Act 2008 introduced changes to Section 7 of **[2–146]** the VAT Act, which deals with the waiver of exemption in relation to short-term lettings of immovable property. It is amended:

(a) by inserting in Section 7(3) *"or in accordance with section 7B(3)"* after *"at the request of a person"* (see below), and

(b) by inserting the following after Section 7(4):

> *"5(a) No waiver of exemption from tax in accordance with this section shall commence on or after 1 July 2008.*
>
> *(b) Any waiver of exemption from tax which applies under this section shall not extend to any letting of immovable goods where those goods are acquired or developed on or after 1 July 2008.*

> (c)   *For the purpose of applying paragraph (b), a waiver of exemption,*
> *which is in place on 18 February 2008 in respect of the letting of*
> *immovable goods which are undergoing development on that day by*
> *or on behalf of the person who has that waiver, may extend to a letting*
> *of those immovable goods."*

[2–147]   Section 21 of the Finance Act 2009 also amended Section 7(3). Following
both amendments it reads:

> *"Provision may be made by regulations for the cancellation, at the request*
> *of a person or in accordance with subsection **(3)(7) or (9) of section 7B***
> *of a waiver made by him under subsection (1) and for the payment by him*
> *to the Revenue Commissioners as a condition of cancellation of such sum*
> *(if any) as when added to the total amount of tax (if any) due by him in*
> *accordance with section 19 …".*

The reference to subsection (3) of section 7B was introduced under the
Finance Act 2008, whereas the references to subsections (7) and (9) of
section 7B were introduced under the Finance Act 2009.

[2–148]   Provision is therefore retained for the cancellation by the taxable person
of his/her waiver, but there is now also provision for the cancellation
of the waiver by the operation of the new Section 7B(3) (7) or (9).

Section 7B(3) provides that a waiver of exemption in existence as at
1 July 2008 ceases to apply with effect from that date if the connected
person's restrictions provided for in Section 7A(2) apply (see below).
In other words, following the amendment, the taxable person can
either choose to cancel a pre-existing waiver of exemption on or after
1 July 2008 or, if a connected person's restriction applies, then the
waiver will in any event be deemed to be cancelled.

Subsections (7)(8)(9) and (10) were included in the VAT Act under the
Finance Act 2009 (see below).

Section 7B(7) VAT Act 1972 applies where:

- the landlord owned a property, which was subject to his or her waiver
  of exemption on 1 July 2008; and

- The landlord does not own any property, which is subject to the
  waiver of exemption on 3 June 2009.

Where this provision applies, the landlord's waiver of exemption is
deemed to be cancelled on 3 June 2009 and the landlord is obliged to
pay the waiver cancellation amount. (Finance Act 2009 was enacted on
3 June 2009, hence the date reference.)

Section 7B(9) VAT Act 1972 applies where:

- the landlord has a waiver of exemption in place on 3 June 2009;

- The landlord owns a property which is subject to the waiver of exemption on 3 June 2009; and

- The landlord at any time on or after this date ceases to own (or have an interest in) any such property.

When this provision applies, the landlord's waiver of exemption is deemed to be cancelled on the date that the landlord ceases to own (or have an interest in) property which is subject to his or her waiver of exemption.

Further examination of Section 7(B)(7)(8)(9) and (10) is set out subsequently in this chapter and in Chapter 6.

It is worth noting that if a landlord **elects** to cancel his/her waiver, then the "old" rules apply and the cancellation would apply to all short-term lettings subject to the waiver of exemption. If the waiver is deemed to be cancelled because a certain letting fails the connected persons test, then the cancellation would apply only to that letting. See examples below in relation to Section 7B(3).

[2–149] Under the Finance act 2008, a new subsection 5 is introduced after the existing subsection 4 of Section 7. The new Section 7(5)(a) provides that no new waiver can be put in place after 1 July 2008. Revenue has confirmed separately that subject to Regulation 4 of the VAT Regulations 2006, a back-dated waiver of exemption would still be available if sought on or after 1 July 2008 in relation to a period prior to this date.

[2–150] The new Section 7(5)(b) provides that no waiver of exemption in place on 1 July 2008 can extend to any letting of immovable goods where the goods are acquired or developed on or after 1 July 2008. Revenue has confirmed that this provision is to be interpreted as meaning that where the immovable goods were developed to completion before 1 July 2008 (or where developed to completion after 1 July 2008 in cases to which Section 7(5)(c) applies) then the waiver continues to apply to such immovable goods. Any subsequent development of these completed immovable goods after 1 July 2008 does not cause a pre-existing waiver to be cancelled.

The new Section 7(5)(c) also provides that pre-existing waivers can extend to lettings where the relevant properties are developed on or after that date **provided that** the waiver was already in place at 18 February 2008 **and** the development work was also in progress on that date.

Finally, Finance Act 2009 introduces a new subsection (6) in Section 7. It reads:

> "When a person cancelled his or her waiver of exemption before 1 July 2008 then, for the purposes of applying Section 12E, the adjustment period (within the meaning of that section or, as the context may require, the period to be treated as the adjustment period in accordance with section 4C(11)) in relation to any capital good the tax chargeable on that person's acquisition or development of which that person was obliged to take into account when that person made that cancellation, shall be treated as if it ended on the date on which that cancellation had effect."

This means that where a landlord who has a waiver of exemption in place cancels that waiver and subsequently sells a property (which has been subject to that landlord's waiver of exemption) then the CGS adjustment period for that property ends on the date the waiver is cancelled.

Section 7A

[2-151]　Section 91 of the Finance Act 2008 inserted two new sections into the VAT Act after Section 7. These are the new Sections 7A and 7B. Both were subsequently amended under the Finance (No. 2) Act 2008.

[2-152]　Section 7A contains the new rules on how the letting of property is to be treated for VAT purposes. It deals with situations where leases are granted on or after 1 July 2008. Short lettings already in existence at 1 July 2008 are dealt with under the new Section 7B.

[2-153]　Section 7A(1) is quite lengthy and is broken down as follows:

> "(a)　Tax shall be chargeable in accordance with this Act on the supply of a service to which paragraph (iv) of the First Schedule relates (in this section referred to as a 'letting') where, subject to subsections (2) and (4), the supplier (in this section referred to as a 'landlord') opts to make that letting so chargeable, and a landlord who exercises this option (referred to in this Act as a 'landlord's option to tax') shall, notwithstanding Section 8(3), be an accountable person and liable to account for the tax on that letting in accordance with this Act, and that letting shall not be a supply to which section 6 applies."

Paragraph (a) provides that tax is chargeable on rents where the landlord opts to tax the letting. Where the option is exercised the landlord is an accountable person in respect of the letting and is liable to account for the VAT on the rents.

Section 7A(1) continues: **[2–154]**

"(b) *Where a taxable person is entitled to deduct tax on the acquisition or development of immovable goods on the basis that the goods will be used for the purpose of a letting or lettings in respect of which a landlord's option to tax will apply, then –*

 (i) *that person shall be treated as having exercised the landlord's option to tax in respect of any lettings of those immovable goods, and*

 (ii) *that option shall be deemed to continue in place until that person makes a letting in respect of which neither of the conditions of paragraph (c) are fulfilled."*

Paragraph (b) provides that a person who is entitled to deduct the VAT incurred on the acquisition or development of a property, on the basis that the letting of that property will be taxed, will be treated as having exercised the landlord's option to tax and that option will remain in place until such time as it is clear that the procedures provided for in paragraph (c) have not been carried out.

Paragraph (c) reads as follows: **[2–155]**

"(c) *A landlord's option to tax in respect of a letting is exercised by –*

 (i) *a provision in writing in a letting agreement between the landlord and the person to whom the letting is made (in this section referred to as a 'tenant') that tax is chargeable on the rent, or*

 (ii) *the issuing by the landlord of a document to the tenant giving notification that tax is chargeable on the letting."*

This provides that a landlord's option to tax is exercised either by including a provision for the taxation of the rents in the letting agreement or by the landlord's issuing a letter or similar to the tenant notifying him/her that tax is chargeable on the letting.

The option to tax clause is not to be confused with a standard VAT clause and both may be required.

Section 7A(1)(d) reads as follows: **[2–156]**

"(d) *A landlord's option to tax in respect of a letting is terminated –*

 (i) *in the case of an option exercised in accordance with paragraph (b) by making a letting of the immovable goods referred to in that paragraph in respect of which neither of the conditions of paragraph (c), is fulfilled,*

(ii) *in the case of an option exercised in accordance with paragraph (c), by –*

    (I) *an agreement in writing between the landlord and tenant that the option is terminated and specifying the date of termination, which shall not be earlier than the date of that agreement, or*

    (II) *the delivery to the tenant of a document giving notification that the option has been terminated and specifying the date of termination, which shall not be earlier than the date that notification is received by the tenant,*

    (III) *when the landlord and tenant become connected persons,*

(iii) *when the landlord or a person connected with the landlord occupies the immovable goods that are subject to that letting whether that person occupies those goods by way of a letting or otherwise, or*

(iv) *when the immovable goods that are subject to that letting are used or to be used for residential purposes within the meaning of subsection (4)."*

[2-157] Section 7A(1)(d) sets out the manner in which an option to tax is terminated.

Section 7A(1)(d)(i) provides that despite the assumption set out in paragraph (b) in relation to the entitlement to input credit, if the landlord subsequently fails to meet the documentary requirements set out in paragraph (c) (i.e. notifying the tenant in writing that VAT will apply to that particular letting), then the option to tax is automatically terminated.

[2-158] Section 7A(1)(d)(ii) provides that in cases where the documentary requirements **are** met, the option to tax can be terminated either by agreement in writing between landlord and tenant or unilaterally, if the landlord notifies the tenant in writing and specifies the date from which the option is to be terminated.

[2-159] Section 7A(1)(d)(iii) provides that the option to tax will terminate automatically when the landlord and **tenant** become connected persons. Section 7A(3) contains a broad definition of the term "connected persons" (see below). However, the automatic termination does not arise if the connected person is entitled to at least 90% input VAT recovery. (See the "90%" tenant concession contained in Section 7A(2)(b) below.)

Section 7A(1)(d)(iv) provides that the option to tax will also terminate automatically if the landlord or a person connected with the landlord (see Section 7A(3) in relation to the term "connected") **occupies** the property. The basis on which the occupant might be *in situ* is not relevant, i.e. the occupant might have a sub-lease or a licence, etc. An occupant does not therefore have to have a formal letting/subletting to fall foul of this provision. Mere occupancy would trigger the termination. However, again, Section 7A(2)(c) provides that the automatic termination of the option to tax would not arise if the connected occupant is entitled to at least 90% input VAT recovery. [2–160]

Section 7A(1)(d)(v) provides for termination of the option to tax if the property is used for residential purposes, as defined in Section 7A(4). See Section 7A(4) at paragraph **2–174** below for more detail on this point. [2–161]

It is important to be aware that Section 7A(1)(d)(iii) and (iv) apply to the automatic termination of the option to tax when landlord and tenant/occupant **become** connected during the course of an **existing** lease. A different provision (Section 7A(2)) deals with restrictions in relation to connected parties when the option to tax is being considered in relation to a **new** lease. [2–162]

In relation to new leases and connected tenants/occupants, Section 7A(2) as amended under the Finance (No. 2) Act 2008, is worded as follows: [2–163]

"(a) Subject to paragraphs (b) and (c), a landlord may not opt to tax a letting –

(i)   Where that landlord and the tenant in respect of that letting are connected persons, or

(ii)   where the landlord, whether or not connected to the tenant, or a person connected to the landlord, occupies the immovable goods that is subject to that letting whether that landlord or that person occupies those goods by way of letting or otherwise.

(b)   Paragraph (a)(i) and subsection (1)(d)(iii) shall not apply where the immovable goods which are the subject of the letting are used for the purposes of supplies or activities which entitle the tenant to deduct at least 90% of the tax chargeable on the letting in accordance with section 12. However, where a landlord has exercised a landlord's option to tax in respect of a letting to which paragraph (a)(i) would have applied but for this paragraph, paragraph (a)(i) shall apply from the end of the first accounting year in which the goods are used

> *for the purposes of supplies or activities which entitle the tenant to deduct less than 90% of the said tax chargeable.*
>
> (c)   *Paragraph (a)(ii) and subsection (1)(d)(iv) shall not apply where the occupant (being any person including the landlord referred to in that paragraph or that subsection) uses the immovable goods which are the subject of a letting for the purpose of making supplies which entitle that occupant to deduct, in accordance with section 12, at least 90% of all tax chargeable in respect of goods or services used by that occupant for the purpose of making those supplies. However, where a landlord has exercised a landlord's option to tax in respect of a letting to which paragraph (a)(ii) would have applied but for this paragraph, paragraph (a)(ii) shall apply from the end of the first accounting year in which the immovable goods are used for the purpose of making supplies which entitle that occupant to deduct less than 90% of the said tax chargeable."*

[2–164]   Section 7A(2) essentially deals with the position where a landlord is granting a **new** letting or similar and is connected with the tenant/occupant.

Paragraph (a) provides that the option to tax may not be exercised where either the tenant or the occupant are connected with the landlord. However, paragraph (a) is subject to paragraphs (b) and (c).

[2–165]   Paragraph (b) provides that an option to tax a lease can still be exercised when landlord and tenant are connected, provided that the tenant is entitled to at least 90% input VAT recovery. The 90% rule is letting specific in that it refers to the extent to which a particular tenant puts the let property to a VAT-able use. For example, a bank may carry out exempt banking functions in one property but engage in 100% VAT-able finance lease activities in another property. Paragraph (b) also provides that an existing option to tax may remain in place (see Section 7A(1)(d)(iii)) when landlord and tenant become connected, provided that the tenant is entitled to at least 90% input VAT recovery.

[2–166]   Paragraph (c) deals with connected occupants (as opposed to connected tenants). It provides that the option to tax can still be exercised when the occupant is connected with the landlord at the commencement of a lease. It also provides that an existing option to tax may remain in place (see Section 7(a)(d)(iv)) when landlord and occupant become connected, provided that the occupant is entitled to at least 90% input VAT recovery.

[2–167]   In summary, the option to tax may be exercised at the outset of a new letting and may remain in place in relation to an existing letting, even if the landlord is or becomes connected with the tenant or occupant, provided that the tenant or occupant is entitled to at least 90% input VAT recovery.

Note: the 90% rule is only relevant when the parties are connected. If there is no connection between the parties, the recovery percentage of the tenant/occupant is not relevant and the option to tax is available to the landlord unless prohibited under some other provision, e.g. the property is residential. Provided that the landlord observes the prescribed notification procedures, there is no need to obtain the tenant's **permission** to exercise the option to tax. As a separate matter, an exempt tenant might of course object to an option to tax on the basis that would not be entitled to recover VAT on rents. This is a commercial issue to be agreed between the parties. **[2-168]**

Moving on to Section 7A(3), Revenue's Notes for Guidance in relation to the Finance Act 2008 merely state that the subsection *"defines connected persons for the purposes of this section"*. However, the definition provided is very wide-ranging indeed. Section 7A(3)(a) states that: **[2-169]**

> *"(a) For the purposes of this section, any question of whether a person is connected with another person shall be determined in accordance with the following:*
>
> *(i) a person is connected with an individual if that person is the individual's spouse, or is a relative, or the spouse of a relative, of the individual or of the individual's spouse."*

Consequently, a husband is connected with his wife and vice versa. One is also connected with one's relatives and the spouses of one's relatives, as defined. The term "relative" is defined in Section 7A(3)(b) as meaning a brother, sister, ancestor or lineal descendant. It would therefore appear that aunts, uncles, nieces and nephews are not relatives. Nor would the partners in a co-habiting couple be connected for this purpose. **[2-170]**

> *"(ii) A person is connected with any person with whom he or she is in partnership, and with the spouse or a relative or any individual with whom he or she is in partnership."*

The reference here is of course to business partners and to the spouse or relatives (as defined) of business partners.

> *"(iii) Subject to clauses (IV) and (V) of subparagraph (v), a person is connected with another person if he or she has control over that other person, or if the other person has control over the first-mentioned person, or if both persons are controlled by another person or persons."*

[2-171]   The term "control" as used above and in Section 7A(3)(b) is contained in the existing Section 8(3B) of the VAT Act.

> "(iv) A body of persons is connected with another person if that person, or persons connected with him or her, have control of that body of persons, or the person and person connected with him or her together have control of it,
>
> (v) A body of persons is connected with another body of persons –
>
> > (I)   if the same person has control of both or a person has control of one and persons connected with that person or that person and persons connected with that person have control of the other,
> >
> > (II) if a group of 2 or more persons has control of each body of persons and the groups either consist of the same persons or could be regarded as consisting of the same persons by treating (in one or more cases) a member of either group as replaced by a person with whom he or she is connected,
> >
> > (III) if both bodies of persons act in pursuit of a common purpose,
> >
> > (IV) if any person or any group of persons having a reasonable commonality of identity have or had the means or power, either directly or indirectly, to determine the activities carried on or to be carried on by both bodies of persons, or
> >
> > (V)   if both bodies of persons are under the control of any person or group of persons or groups of persons having a reasonable commonality of identity."

[2-172]   These provisions are especially widely defined, in particular subparagraphs (III), (IV) and (V). For the moment it is not known precisely how the terms "common purpose" and "reasonable commonality of identity" might be applied. However, it does seem clear that certain VAT planning structures which might previously have been legally permissible are now in many cases likely to fall foul of the "connected persons" provisions.

> "(vi) a person in the capacity as trustee of a settlement is connected with –
>
> > (I)   any person who in relation to the settlement is a settler, or
> >
> > (II) any person who is a beneficiary under the settlement."

Section 7A(3)(b) goes on to state that: [2-173]

"In this subsection –

'control', in the case of a body corporate or in the case of a partnership, has the meaning assigned to it by section 8(3B);

'relative' means a brother, sister, ancestor or lineal descendant."

Finally, Section 7A(4) states that: [2-174]

"A landlord's option to tax may not be exercised in respect of all or part of a house or apartment or other similar establishment to the extent that those immovable goods are used or to be used for residential purposes, including any such letting –

(a)   *governed by the Residential Tenancies Act 2004,*

(b)   *governed by the Housing (Rent Books) Regulations 1993 (S.I. No. 146 of 1993,)*

(c)   *governed by Section 10 of the Housing Act 1998,*

(d)   *of a dwelling to which Part II of the Housing (Private Rented Dwellings Act) 1982 applies, or*

(e)   *of accommodation which is provided as a temporary dwelling for emergency residential purposes,*

and a landlord's option to tax, once exercised, shall immediately cease to have effect to the extent that the immovable goods which are the subject of the letting to which the option applies, come to be used for a residential purpose."

This simply provides that an option to tax cannot apply if the property is used for residential purposes, whether it is a new option or whether a property subject to a letting/option comes to be used for residential purposes during the lease. This is broadly in keeping with the waiver of exemption provisions which were introduced as a result of the Finance Act 2007.

Section 7B

Section 7B contains the transitional measures for lettings to which the   [2-175]
waiver of exemption applies.

Section 7B(1) states that:

"This section applies to an accountable person who had waived his or her right to exemption from tax in accordance with section 7 and who had not

cancelled that waiver before 1 July 2008 (hereafter in this section referred to as a 'landlord')."

The section therefore covers landlords who have a waiver of exemption in place before 1 July 2008.

[2–176] Following Finance Act 2008 and amendments made under Finance (No. 2) Act 2008, Section 7B(2) reads as follows:

"Section 12E does not apply to a landlord to the extent that tax relating to the acquisition or development of immovable goods has been or would be taken into account in calculating, in accordance with section 7(3), the sum, if any, due by that landlord as a condition of the cancellation of a waiver."

Finance Act 2009 replaced subsection (2) completely. With effect from 3 June 2009 it reads as follows:

"For the purposes of applying section 12E, the adjustment period (within the meaning of that section or, as the context may require, the period to be treated as the adjustment period in accordance with section 4C(11)) in relation to a capital good the tax chargeable on the landlord's acquisition or development of which that landlord was obliged to take into account when that landlord cancelled his or her waiver of exemption, shall end on the date on which that cancellation had effect".

Section 7B(2) used to state that the CGS did not apply if a landlord had a property subject to the waiver of exemption. Now it provides instead that the adjustment period for that property ends on the date that the waiver is cancelled.

[2–177] Section 7B(3) states that:

"Where a landlord makes or has made a letting and, were that letting not already subject to a waiver, that letting would be one in respect of which the landlord would not, because of the provision of section 7A(2), be entitled to exercise a landlord's option to tax in accordance with section 7A, then the landlord's waiver of exemption shall, subject to subsection (4), immediately cease to apply to that letting, and –

(a) that landlord shall pay the amount, as if it were tax due by that person in accordance with section 19 for the taxable period in which the waiver ceases to apply to that letting and the amount shall be the sum, if any, which would be payable in accordance with section 7(3) in respect of the cancellation of a waiver as if that landlord's waiver applied only to the immovable goods or the interest in immovable goods or the interest in immovable goods subject to that letting to which the waiver has ceased to apply, and

> (b) the amounts taken into account in calculating that sum, if any, shall be disregarded in any future cancellation of that waiver."

Section 7B(3)(a) and (b) deal with lettings between connected parties. Paragraph (a) provides that if a waiver is already in place at 1 July 2008 but the letting is one which would not satisfy the "connected" persons criteria set out in Section 7A(2), then it will be deemed cancelled on 1 July 2008. See references to Section 7A(2) above. **[2–178]**

If the Section 7A(2) criteria are not satisfied and the waiver of exemption is cancelled, then Section 7B(3)(a) provides for a clawback of VAT as calculated under Section 7(3) but a fundamental difference is that the waiver ceases to apply only as far as the **particular** "non-qualifying" property is concerned. The cessation would consequently not affect other properties subject to a pre-existing waiver, provided of course that the lettings satisfied the conditions set out in Section 7A(2). **[2–179]**

Section 7B(3)(b) provides that if a landlord does repay VAT as a result of the operation of paragraph (a) and subsequently cancels his/her waiver of exemption in the normal manner, the original "per property" clawback amount would be disregarded. It seems that the intention of paragraph (b) may have been to ensure that a landlord cancelling a waiver of exemption would not have to repay the same clawback twice. However, the wording of paragraph (b) would allow the opposite inter-pretation. If the clawback is later "disregarded", would it not have to be paid again under a subsequent Section 7(3) cancellation? Revenue's Notes for Guidance in relation to the Finance Act 2008 do not offer any clarification of this point. Readers concerned about falling foul of this provision should contact Revenue on a case-by-case basis. **[2–180]**

Section 7B(4)(a) states the following: **[2–181]**

> "Subject to paragraph (c), where a landlord has a letting to which subsection (3) would otherwise apply, the provisions of that subsection shall not apply while, on the basis of the letting agreement in place, the tax that the landlord will be required to account for, in equal amounts for each taxable period, in respect of the letting during the next 12 months is not less than the amount calculated at that time in accordance with the formula in subsection (5)."

Subsection (3) deals with the cancellation of a pre-existing waiver of exemption in regard to a particular letting, should that letting fail to satisfy the option to tax criteria set out in Section 7A(2), i.e. should the parties to the letting/occupancy be connected, with the tenant/occupant not meeting the 90% recovery criterion. **[2–182]**

[2-183]   Subsection 7B(4) therefore provides that despite failing to satisfy the option to tax criteria, the pre-existing waiver would continue to apply to a particular letting (subject to Section 7B(4)(c)) provided that under the terms of the letting agreement already in place at 1 July 2008, the landlord would be required to account for a certain amount of VAT in the 12-month period following 1 July 2008. This amount would be calculated under a formula set out in Section 7B(5). The reference to "equal instalments" was clarified at a meeting of the Taxes Administration Liaison Committee (TALC) in May 2008. It seems that, despite the wording of the legislation, there would be no need to account for the VAT in equal bi-monthly instalments if the letting provided, for example, that the rent was to be paid less frequently, e.g. quarterly or annually. Nor would the rent actually have to be paid by the tenant to the landlord, although the VAT on the rent would have to be accounted for by the landlord. The VAT amount calculated under the formula would, however, have to be paid by reference to the year commencing 1 July 2008. The first adjustment should appear in the landlord's July/August 2008 VAT return.

[2-184]   Section 7B(4)(b) states:

> "Where the conditions in paragraph (a) fail to be satisfied because of a variation in the terms of the lease or otherwise or if the tax paid at any time in respect of the letting is less than the tax payable, this subsection shall cease to apply."

This appears to provide that a variation or similar in the lease cannot be used subsequently so that a lease initially meets the VAT repayment threshold and is later varied so as to reduce the VAT repayable. Interestingly, the second part of the paragraph allows Revenue to cancel the waiver if the landlord repays less than the VAT required under Section 7B(5). This provision adds a further dimension to VAT audits.

[2-185]   Section 7B(4)(c) states that:

> "This subsection applies to a letting referred to in paragraph (a) –
>
> (i)   where a landlord has a waiver in place on 18 February 2008 and –
>
>   (I)   on 1 July that letting had been in place since 18 February 2008, or
>
>   (II)   the immovable goods subject to the letting are owned by that landlord on 18 February 2008 and are in the course of development by or on behalf of that landlord on that day,
>
> or

(ii)   *where a landlord holds an interest, other than a freehold interest or a freehold equivalent interest in the immovable goods subject to the letting, acquired between 18 February 2008 and 30 June 2008 from a person with whom the landlord is not connected, within the meaning of Section 7A, in a transaction which is treated as a supply of goods in accordance with section 4."*

Section 7B(4) is only relevant to landlords in a position where a waiver in existence at 1 July 2008 would be cancelled due to the "connected persons"/90% rule but for the threshold provided in Section 7B(5). Not only must such a landlord meet the threshold amount, s/he must also satisfy the provisions set out in Section 7B(4), i.e. even if the threshold is met, the waiver would only continue in respect of a particular letting if: **[2–186]**

The letting had been in place on 18 February and was still in place at 1 July 2008 **or** the relevant interest had already been owned by the landlord on 18 February 2008 and s/he was in the process of developing it on that date.

Alternatively, the waiver can continue if Section 7B(5) is satisfied and the landlord is, in respect of the relevant property, the lessee in a long lease where his/her landlord is an unconnected person and the long lease in question was granted between 18 February and 1 July 2008.   **[2–187]**

Section 7B(5) sets out the formula for calculating the minimum amount of tax payable on a letting between connected persons for the purposes of allowing a waiver to continue to apply. It states that: **[2–188]**

"The formula to be used for the purposes of subsection (4) is:

$$\frac{A - B}{12 - Y}$$

where –

A   *is the amount of tax that would be taken into account for the purpose of section 7(3) in respect of the acquisition or development of the immovable goods, if the waiver were being cancelled at the time referred to in subsection (4),*

B   *is the amount of tax chargeable on the consideration by the landlord in respect of the letting of those immovable goods and paid in accordance with section 19 that would be taken into account for the purposes of section 7(3) if the waiver were being cancelled at that time, and if that letting were the only one to which that waiver applied, and*

Y   *is 11, or the number of full years since the later of –*

> (i)   *the date of the first letting of those goods, and*
>
> (ii)   *the date on which the landlord waived exemption, where that number is less than 11 years."*

'A' would be the total input VAT credit claimed by a landlord in respect of the acquisition/development of a particular property.

'B' would be the amount of output VAT for which the landlord had accounted in respect of the relevant letting.

[2–189] Section 7B(4) cross-references to Section 7B(3), which provides that the clawback of VAT would be done on a per letting basis. In every other way the 'A – B' figure corresponds to the clawback calculation provided for in Section 7(3).

[2–190] The number '12' in the formula is constant. The second number will either be 11 **or** a number less than 11, if either the number of full years since the letting commenced or the number of full years since the landlord waived exemption is less than 11. In such a case, the figure to be used instead of 11 in the formula will be the number of full years since either of these events occurred and if one period is shorter than the other, the shorter number of years will be used.

[2–191] The premise of Section 7B(5) is that in any event the input VAT arising in respect of a letting would have to be repaid to Revenue no later than 12 years from 1 July 2008, and in most cases the repayment period will be somewhat shorter.

Chapter 6 contains a detailed example in relation to the continuation of a pre-existing waiver of exemption when there is a landlord/tenant connection and the tenant fails the 90% test.

[2–192] A new Section 7B(6) was introduced in Finance No. 2 (Act) 2008, enacted on 24 December 2008. It provides that:

> *"Where a landlord has a letting to which subsection (3) or (4) applies and that landlord becomes a person in a group within the meaning of section 8(8) on or after 1 July 2008 and the person to whom that letting is made is a person in that group, then the person referred to in section 8(8)(a)(i)(I) in respect of that group shall be liable to pay the amount as specified in subsection (3)(a) as if it were tax due in accordance with Section 19 –*
>
> (a)   *in the case of a landlord who became a person in that group before the date of passing of the Finance Act 2009, in the taxable period in which that Act is passed or,*

(b)   *in the case of a landlord who became a person in that group after the date of passing of the Finance Act 2009, in the taxable period during which that landlord became a person in that group."*

Revenue's Notes for Guidance in relation to this amendment state that   **[2–193]**
"it ensures that the landlord cannot avoid the liability imposed in subsection (3) simply by being part of a VAT group with the tenant".

No VAT would arise in relation to lettings of property granted by one member of a VAT group to another. This is because under the VAT group provision, no supply takes place between VAT group members and VAT would not, in any event, be charged on rents even when the waiver of exemption continues to apply.

Section 7B(6) provides that if a pre-existing waiver of exemption would   **[2–194]**
not qualify for continued application to a particular letting under the connected persons provisions referred to in Section 7B(3)/(4), then a clawback of VAT still arises under the CGS.

Revenue's e-brief 37/2009 dated 5 June 2009 refers to relevant guidance   **[2–194A]**
material which has been published in Chapter 7B.1 of the VAT Manual on the subject of Section 7B(6). The guidance material clarifies as follows:

"Section 70 of the Finance (No. 2) Act 2008 introduced a new subsection (6) into section 7B of the VAT Act 1972 (as amended). This deals with situations where a landlord who has a letting of less than ten years with a waiver in place to a connected tenant becomes a member of a VAT group (where the tenant is a member of that group) on or after 1 July 2008. In such cases, the subsection provides for two separate scenarios –

(1)   Where the landlord enters the group between 1 July 2008 and the date of passing of the Finance (No. 2) Act 2008 (i.e. 24 December 2008), a waiver cancellation adjustment is triggered and the person in the group liable to account for VAT (the group remitter) is liable to pay the cancellation amount as if it were tax due in the taxable period in which the Act is passed (i.e. Nov/Dec 2008).

(2)   Where the landlord enters the group after the date of passing of the Finance (No. 2) Act 2008 (i.e. 24 December 2008), a waiver cancellation adjustment is triggered and the person in the group liable to account for VAT (the group remitter) is liable to pay the cancellation amount as if it were tax due in the taxable period in which the landlord enters the VAT group.

This rule ensures that connected persons cannot use the grouping provisions to avoid the rules in section 7B VAT Act 1972 (as amended) for lettings between connected persons where a waiver of exemption has been exercised. This rule will not apply where the underlying use of the property is for other than exempt purposes and the property is used by the group for the purpose of making supplies that entitle that group to deduct at least 90% of the VAT incurred by it in relation to those supplies.

...

In relation to cases where (1) above applies, Revenue are willing to accept that the cancellation amount may be accounted for in the return for the taxable period following the passing of the Finance (No. 2) Act 2008, i.e. Jan/Feb 2009 return. This is to take account of the fact that there is a very short time period between the passing of the Act and the end of the taxable period (Nov/Dec).

...

Revenue are willing to accept that where a landlord applies to leave the VAT group before the end of February 2009, the landlord can keep the waiver in place by availing of the 12-year rule. In order for this to be acceptable the landlord must –

(1)   Apply in writing to their local Revenue Office to leave the group and specify that the reason they wish to leave is to avail of this concessional treatment.

(2)   Ensure that VAT accounted for in respect of the rents charged to the connected tenant meets the minimum amount in accordance with the formula in section 7B(5) VAT Act 1972 (as amended)."

[2–194B]   As indicated above, Finance Act 2009 also introduced new subsections (7) (8)(9) and (10) to Section 7B. In relation to the meaning of "relevant date" and "relevant immovable goods" as used in the new subsections, see the definitions given in the new subsection (10) (below).

Subsection (7) reads as follows:

"(a)   This subsection applies where —

(i)   on 1 July 2008 a landlord had an interest in relevant immovable goods,

(ii)   on the relevant date the landlord did not have an interest in any relevant immovable goods, and

   (iii) *that landlord's waiver of exemption had not been cancelled on or before the relevant date in accordance with section 7(3).*

(b)   *Where this subsection applies –*

   (i)   *the landlord's waiver of exemption shall be treated as if it were cancelled in accordance with section 7(3) on the date of the passing of the Finance Act 2009, and*

   (ii) *that landlord shall pay an amount, being the amount payable in accordance with section 7(3) in respect of the cancellation of that waiver, as if it were tax due by that landlord for the taxable period beginning on 1 May 2009."*

Revenue's guidance material published in Chapter 7B.1 of the VAT Manual, as announced by e-brief 37/2009 on 5 June 2009, clarifies the new subsection as follows:

"Section 7B(7) VAT Act 1972 applies where –

- The landlord owned a property, which was subject to his or her waiver of exemption on 1 July 2008, and

- The landlord does not own any property, which is subject to the waiver of exemption on 3 June 2009.

Where this provision applies, the landlord's waiver of exemption is deemed to be cancelled on 3 June 2009 and the landlord is obliged to pay the waiver cancellation amount. The example below illustrates how this operates in practice.

Example

ABC Ltd purchases a property on 19 September 2005 on which VAT of €1,000,000 is chargeable. ABC waives its exemption from VAT and is entitled to deduct all of the VAT.

ABC Ltd grants a three-year lease from 1 October 2005 and charges VAT at the standard rate (at the time 21%) on the rent of €200,000 per annum. On 30 September 2008 the tenant's lease expires and the tenant vacates the property. ABC sells the property on 1 November 2008. It did not cancel its waiver prior to the sale. There was no liability for ABC to pay the CGS claw-back in accordance with Section 12E(7)(b) VAT Act 1972 by virtue of the wording of Section 7B(2) VAT Act 1972 prior to it being amended by the Finance Act 2009 with effect from 3 June 2009.

> As ABC owned a waiver property on 1 July 2008 but on 3 June 2009 no longer owns any properties which are subject to the waiver, ABC's waiver of exemption is deemed to be cancelled on 3 June 2009 and ABC is liable to pay the waiver cancellation amount, which is the excess of VAT deducted (€1,000,000) over the VAT paid on the rents (€126,000), which, in this case is €874,000."

Subsection (8) reads as follows:

"(a) *This subsection applies where —*

(i) *in the period from 1 July 2008 to the relevant date, a landlord made a supply of relevant immovable goods during the adjustment period (within the meaning of section 12E or, as the context may require, the period to be treated as the adjustment period in accordance with section 4C(11)) in relation to those goods, and*

(ii) *tax was not chargeable on that supply.*

(b) *Where this subsection applies, then for the purposes of sections 4B(5), 12E(3)(d) and 12E(7)(b) the supply of the relevant immovable goods is treated as if it was made on the date of the passing of the Finance Act 2009.*

(c) *Paragraph (b) shall not apply where —*

(i) *the landlord's waiver of exemption has been cancelled in accordance with subsection (7), or*

(ii) *the landlord cancels his or her waiver of exemption in accordance with section 7(3) before 1 July 2009."*

Revenue's guidance material published in Chapter 7B.1 of the VAT Manual, as announced by e-brief 37/2009 on 5 June 2009, clarifies the new subsection as follows:

"Section 7B(8) VAT Act 1972 applies where:

- The landlord has a waiver in place on 1 July 2008,

- The landlord sells a property, which was subject to the waiver of exemption, between 1 July 2008 and 3 June 2009 in a situation where the sale is exempt from VAT, and

The landlord owns other property/(ies) which is/are subject to the waiver of exemption on 3 June 2009.

Where this provision applies, the sale of the property is treated as if it occurred on 3 June 2009. The effect of this provision is outlined in the example below.

Example

Ms E. is a landlord who owns four properties (all acquired before 1 July 2008), which are subject to her waiver of exemption.

One of these properties owned by Ms E was purchased on 3 December 2005 and VAT of €2,000,000 was chargeable on this acquisition. This VAT was deducted on the basis that Ms E has a waiver of exemption in place and was going to rent out the property short-term.

Ms E granted a three-year lease in this property from 1 January 2006 and charged VAT at the standard rate (at the time 21%) on the rent. On 31 December 2007 the tenant's lease expires when the tenant vacates the property. Ms E sells the property on 3 November 2008. She did not cancel her waiver prior to the sale. There was no liability for her to pay the CGS clawback in accordance with Section 12E(7)(b) VAT Act 1972 by virtue of the wording of Section 7B(2) VAT Act 1972 prior to it being amended by Finance Act 2009 with effect from 3 June 2009.

Ms E sold a waiver property (the one that was acquired on 3 December 2005) between 1 July 2008 and 3 June 2009 and owns other properties on 3 June 2009, which are subject to the waiver. For the purposes of the clawback provisions in the CGS, the sale (which occurred on 3 Nov 2008) is treated as if it had occurred on 3 June 2009. The sale is exempt from VAT and this triggers a clawback of VAT from Ms E calculated as follows:

$$\frac{B \times N}{T}$$

$$\frac{2,000,000 \times 17}{20}$$

= €1,700,000 which is payable by Ms E for the taxable period May/June 2009.

It is worth noting that had the CGS clawback arisen when the actual sale occurred, Ms E would have had to pay a higher amount than the amount calculated as above. The waiver of exemption is allowed to continue in relation to her three remaining properties that are subject to that waiver.

Note: The CGS clawback will not apply if Ms E cancels her waiver of exemption before 1 July 2009 or if she (in conjunction with the person who purchased the property) jointly opts to tax the sale in accordance with Section 4B(5)."

Subsection (9) reads as follows:

"(a) This subsection applies where –

(i) on or after the date of the passing of the Finance Act 2009 a landlord has an interest in relevant immovable goods,

(ii) the landlord ceases, whether as a result of disposing of such goods or otherwise, to have an interest in any such goods, and

(iii) on the date when that landlord ceases to have any such interest, that landlord's waiver of exemption has not been cancelled in accordance with section 7(3).

(b) Where this subsection applies –

(i) the landlord's waiver of exemption shall be treated as if it were cancelled on the date referred to in paragraph (a)(iii), and

(ii) that landlord shall pay an amount, being the amount payable in accordance with section 7(3) in respect of the cancellation of that waiver, as if it were tax due by that landlord for the taxable period in which the waiver of exemption is so treated as cancelled."

Revenue's guidance material published in Chapter 7B.1 of the VAT Manual, as announced by e-brief 37/2009 on 5 June 2009, clarifies the new subsection as follows:

"Section 7B(9) VAT Act 1972 applies where:

- The landlord has a waiver of exemption in place on 3 June 2009,

- The landlord owns a property which is subject to the waiver of exemption on 3 June 2009, and

- The landlord at any time on or after this date ceases to own (or have an interest in) any such property.

When this provision applies the landlord's waiver of exemption is deemed to be cancelled on the date that the landlord ceases to own (or have an interest in) property which is subject to his or her waiver of exemption. The example below illustrates how this provision operates in practice.

Example

Mr B. purchased a property on 19 September 1995 on which VAT of €75,000 was chargeable. Mr. B waived his exemption from VAT and was entitled to deduct all of the VAT.

Mr B rented the property out to various tenants between September 1995 and 4 June 2010 when he sold the property on. The total VAT paid on the rents during this period was €46,000.

Unless Mr B and the purchaser exercise the joint option to tax the sale (see Note below), the sale is exempt from VAT and the normal CGS rules apply (as the waiver has not been cancelled prior to the sale) which result in a claw-back of some of the VAT deducted, as follows.

$$B \times \frac{N}{T}$$

$$= 75,000 \times \frac{6}{20}$$

€22,500 VAT payable by Mr B.

As Mr B has no more properties, which are subject to the waiver, the waiver is automatically deemed to be cancelled and the cancellation sum must be paid. This is the difference between the VAT deducted and the VAT paid on the rents.

75,000 − 46,000 = €29,000

The VAT payable on the CGS claw-back may be offset against this liability –

29,000 − 22,500 = €6,500.

Total VAT payable for the taxable period where sale occurs (May/June 2010) is €22,500 + €6,500 = €29,000

Timeline of events

[2-194C]   The sequence of events is that the property is first sold. When this happens the following is triggered:

1. A CGS clawback, as it is an exempt sale of a property.

2. The waiver is automatically cancelled.

Although both the sale and the waiver cancellation occur on the same day, the sequence of events is very clear: it is the sale (on which the CGS clawback arises) that triggers the waiver cancellation. The offset of the CGS amount against the waiver cancellation ensures there is no double taxation.

If Mr B and the purchaser did jointly opt to tax the sale, VAT would be chargeable. When the property is sold, the provisions of Section 7B(9) would apply to Mr B, as he no longer owns any property that is subject to his waiver of exemption. As a result, his waiver would be automatically deemed to be cancelled and Mr B would be obliged to pay the cancellation sum (if any). The amount of VAT chargeable on the sale would be taken into account when calculating the cancellation amount. For example, if the VAT chargeable on the sale were €300,000, then the cancellation amount would be nil, since there is no excess in the VAT deducted (€75,000) over the VAT paid on the rents plus the VAT chargeable on the sale (€46,000 + €300,000 = €346,000)."

Subsection (10) reads as follows:

"(10) In this section –

'relevant immovable goods' means immovable goods the tax chargeable on the acquisition or development of which a landlord would be obliged to take into account in accordance with section 7(3) in relation to the cancellation of that landlord's waiver of exemption;

'relevant date' means the date immediately before the date of the passing of the Finance Act 2009."

Section 10

[2-195]   Section 93 of the Finance Act 2008 introduced three changes to Section 10 of the VAT Act, which deals with the amount on which VAT is chargeable. Only two of these changes are relevant to the new VAT and property rules.

Section 10 is amended – [2–196]

(a) by inserting, with effect from 1 July 2008, the following after subsection (4C):

"(4D)(a)   The amount on which tax is chargeable in relation to a supply of services referred to in section 5(3B) in any taxable period shall be an amount equal to one sixth of one twentieth of the cost of the immovable goods used to provide those services, being –

   (i)   the amount on which tax was chargeable to the person making the supply in respect of that person's acquisition

   or development of the immovable goods referred to in section 5(3B), and

   (ii)   in the case where section 3(5)(b)(iii) applied to the acquisition of the immovable goods, the amount on which tax would have been chargeable but for the operation of that section,

adjusted to correctly reflect the proportion of the use of the goods in that period.

(b)   The Revenue Commissioners may make regulations specifying methods which may be used –

   (i)   To identify the proportion which correctly reflects the extent to which immovable goods are used for the purposes referred to in section 5(3B), and

   (ii)   To calculate the relevant taxable amount or amounts."

Section 5(3B) provides that the diversion of immovable goods to non-business use is considered to be a supply of a taxable service if an input VAT credit was available in relation to the acquisition/development of the property and the diversion takes place during the adjustment period. [2–197]

Section 10(4D)(a) specifies that the capital goods owner would calculate an amount of output VAT in relation to this deemed taxable service in each bi-monthly VAT period in which the diversion continues. The amount on which the VAT on the service would be chargeable would be based on the cost on which VAT had originally been recovered, divided by 20 (to reflect the 20 intervals in the CGS) and divided by six (to reflect six bi-monthly VAT periods in a year). [2–198]

Example – "self-supply" of property

Moving Limited acquired a four-floor commercial property for €4 million net on 1 January 2009 and recovered input VAT of €540,000. It intended to use the property for the purpose of its fully taxable supplies. On 1 November 2011, Mr Moved, the managing director, began using the second floor of the property free of charge to store his personal effects following the sale of his residence and pending the completion of his new residence. This floor had previously been used to store stock for the business. However, it was possible to squeeze the stock into another area on a temporary basis. Mr Moved's new house was ready on 1 May 2012. On that date, he moved his personal property into his new house. The second floor of the premises was again used to store stock for Moving Limited.

Between 1 November 2011 and 30 April 2012, the fourth floor was diverted to Mr Moved's personal use and Section 5(3B) deems this diversion to be the provision of a taxable service. Although Mr Moved does not pay for the service, Moving Limited is required to calculate a corresponding output VAT liability and pay this to the Collector General under the provisions of Section 19 of the VAT Act.

The amount on which VAT is chargeable in this case would be calculated as follows:

- €4,000,000 divided by 4 (the building has four floors) = €1,000,000.

- €1,000,000 divided by 20 (reflecting the 20 intervals in the adjustment period) = 5 €50,000.

- €50,000 divided by six, to reflect six bi-monthly VAT periods in each interval = €8,333.33.

This is the "amount on which tax is chargeable" in each bi-monthly VAT period between 1 November 2011 and 30 April 2012. The standard VAT rate would apply, i.e. 21.5% (with effect from 1 December 2008). Consequently, Moving Limited would be required to include output VAT of €1,792 (€8,333.33 × 21.5%) in each VAT 3 filed for the bi-monthly periods November-December 2011, January-February 2012 and March-April 2012.

Since VAT would probably have been reclaimed at 13.5%, the diversion of the property to personal use is therefore dealt with relatively harshly.

A final paragraph (c) of Section 93 states that Section 10 of the VAT Act   [2-199]
is to be further amended as follows:

"(a) in subsection (9)(i) –

by inserting the following after paragraph (b):

"(ba) Subsections (a) and (b) apply in respect of transactions
which take place prior to 1 July 2008.",

and

(ii) with effect from 1 July 2008 in paragraph (c), by substituting
"value" for "price" in both places where it occurs."

The first amendment provides that the old capitalised value rule for
long leases does not apply under the new regime. The amendment at (ii)
appears to have been made for the sake of consistency throughout the
legislation.

Section 12

Section 94 of the Finance Act 2008 and the technical amendments intro-   [2-200]
duced under the Finance (No. 2) Act 2008 amended Section 12 of the
VAT Act, which deals with deductions for VAT borne or paid and the
various circumstances under which an accountable person may or may
not claim back VAT when calculating the amount of VAT which is
payable at the end of a taxable period. It is amended:

(a) In subsection (1)(a) –

(i) in paragraph (iiic) with effect from 1 July 2008 by substituting
"section 4B(6)(a) or 4(8) ..."

Post-amendment, Section 12(1)(a)(iiic) provides that an accountable   [2-201]
person may, subject to criteria provided for in Section 12(1)(a), deduct
"the tax chargeable during the period, being tax for which the accountable
person is liable by virtue of section 4B(6) or Section 4(8)". Prior to the
amendment, only Section 4(8) was mentioned, i.e. there was no cross-
reference to the reverse-charge provisions contained in relation to the
option to tax introduced in the new Section 4B(6). This is therefore a
technical amendment to ensure that the normal deductibility entitlement applies in the case of joint options for taxation.

[2–202] Section 12(4)(a) was amended to the following:

> *"'dual-use' inputs means movable goods or services (other than goods or services on the purchase or acquisition of which, by virtue of subsection (3), a deduction of tax shall not be made) or services related to the development of immovable goods that are subject to the provisions of section 12E".*

As a result of the amendments to Section 12(4)(a) it now provides that the term "dual-use inputs" applies to movable goods only and consequently not to immovable goods. Any change in the use of immovable goods is now dealt with under the CGS.

[2–203] Section 12(4)(f) was also amended to provide consistency throughout the legislation. It now reads:

> *"the proportion of tax deductible as calculated by an accountable person for a taxable period shall be adjusted in accordance with regulations, if, for the accounting year in which the taxable period ends, that proportion does not correctly reflect the extent to which the dual-use inputs are used for the purposes of that person's deductible supplies or activities or does not have due regard to the range of that person's total supplies and activities."*

[2–204] Under paragraph (c) of Section 94 of the Finance Act 2008, Section 12(5) of the VAT Act was deleted. This section, which dealt with adjustments of deductibility in relation to immovable goods, is no longer necessary because of the new VAT and property provisions introduced in the Finance Act.

Section 12D

[2–205] Section 97 of the Finance Act 2008 amended Section 12D of the VAT Act. Section 12D dealt with the adjustment of deductible VAT when property was transferred in the context of a transfer of business. Section 97 of the Finance Act provided for the inclusion of a new subsection (5) after Section 12D(4) and this states that *"This section does not apply to a transfer of an interest in immovable goods which occurs on or after 1 July 2008".*

In relation to such transfers taking place on or after 1 July 2008, the provisions set down in the new VAT on property provisions replaced Section 12D.

Section 12E

Section 98 of the Finance Act 2008 inserted a new Section 12E into the VAT Act after the existing Section 12D. The new Section 12E deals with the capital goods scheme (CGS). [2–206]

Section 12E(1) states that:

"This section applies to capital goods –

(a)   on the supply or development of which tax was chargeable to a taxable person, or

(b)   on the supply of which tax would have been chargeable to a taxable person but for the application of section 3(5)(b)(iii)."

This section provides that the scheme applies to capital goods on which VAT was chargeable to a "taxable person". A taxable person is defined in Section 1 of the VAT Act as *"a person who independently carries out any business in the State"*. A taxable person can be an exempt person for VAT purposes, i.e. s/he is not necessarily also an *"accountable person"*. Accountable persons are defined in Section 8(1) of the VAT Act as taxable persons who engage in taxable supplies. In other words, accountable persons are, in a manner of speaking, a subset of taxable persons.

Section 12E(2) contains a number of definitions necessary to set out the provisions of the scheme. These are referred to consistently in the many formulae throughout Section 12E. The various definitions given in Section 12E(2) are as follows: [2–207]

"'adjustment period' in relation to a capital good, means the period encompassing the number of intervals as provided for in subsection (3)(a) during which adjustments of deductions are required to be made in respect of a capital good."

The adjustment period in basic terms is a type of VAT life in relation to a capital good. The "adjustments of deductions" referred to are the potential periodic repayments/clawbacks of VAT which may arise as a result of changes in the extent to which the property is put to a taxable use in the course of the adjustment period. [2–208]

Section 12E(2) continues as follows: [2–209]

"'base tax amount', in relation to a capital good, means the amount calculated by dividing the total tax incurred in relation to that capital good by the number of intervals in the adjustment period applicable to that capital good."

[2-210]   The various definitions are presented in alphabetical order. However, in this case it might have made more sense to give the definition of "total tax incurred" before that of the term *"base tax amount"*. The base tax amount is the total tax incurred divided equally over the number of "intervals" in the adjustment period. The definition of the total tax incurred is provided in Section 12E(3)(b). In brief, it is the total input VAT **arising** in relation to the acquisition/development of an immovable good. Consequently, neither the total tax incurred nor the base tax amount necessarily correspond to the amount of VAT which the capital goods owner might actually be entitled to recover in relation to acquisition/development.

[2-211]   Section 12E(2) continues:

> *"'capital goods owner' means –*
>
> (a)   *except where paragraph (b) applies, a taxable person who incurs expenditure on the acquisition or development of a capital good,*
>
> (b)   *in the case of a taxable person who is a flat-rate farmer, means a taxable person who incurs expenditure to develop or acquire a capital good other than a building or structure designed and used solely for the purposes of a farming business or for fencing, drainage or reclamation of land, and which has actually been put to use in such business."*

[2-212]   The capital goods owner would, therefore, be whichever party incurred expenditure in relation to the acquisition/development of a capital good. In the case of developed property that is leased out to a tenant, the lessor is the capital goods owner to the extent that the lessor *"incurs expenditure on the acquisition or development"* of the capital good. A lessee will only acquire a capital good if the interest it acquires is a freehold equivalent interest (see Chapter 4). If the lessee is granted a lease which is not a freehold equivalent interest, then s/he is not a capital goods owner, even if s/he pays a substantial upfront premium, because s/he is not acquiring the underlying capital good. If the lessee carries out development work, then s/he is a capital goods owner to the extent that s/he incurs expenditure on refurbishment work.

[2-213]   Paragraph (b) provides that the CGS would not apply to acquisitions of capital goods acquired by flat-rate farmers if used for the farming business but would apply should a flat-rate farmer acquire a capital good and use it for a non-farming purpose.

[2-214]   One of the definitions contained in Section 12E is that of the term "refurbishment". Refurbishment is defined as *"development on a previously*

completed building, structure or engineering work". Note that refurbishment is still development.

"Deductible supplies or activities" is stated to be *"as defined in Section 12(4)"*, **[2–215]** bearing in mind that Section 94 of the Finance Act 2008, amended Section 12(4)(a) to provide that the term "dual-use inputs" now applies to movable goods only rather than to immovable goods.

Section 12E also defines the terms *"interval"*, *"initial interval"*, *"second* **[2–216]** *interval"* and *"subsequent interval"*. Although the strict alphabetisation of the definitions separates these terms in the legislation, it makes sense to consider them together in a legislative analysis.

The term "interval" is defined as *"the initial, second or subsequent interval* **[2–217]** *in an adjustment period, whichever is appropriate"*.

> *"'Initial interval' in relation to a capital good, means a period of 12 months beginning on the date when a capital good is completed or, in the case of a capital good that is supplied following completion, the initial interval for the recipient of that supply is the 12-month period beginning on the date of that supply."*

The term "completed" is defined in the amended Section 1 of the VAT **[2–218]** Act. Under the legislation, the initial interval in an adjustment period will always be 12 months long but it can commence on the date the capital good is completed as defined **or** on the date it is supplied, if the date of supply is later. This wording covers both owner-occupier situations and situations where a builder/developer disposes of an interest in a building following completion.

Capital goods owners will have certain administrative responsibilities at **[2–219]** the end of each interval under the CGS (see below). At a TALC meeting in May 2008, Revenue agreed that capital goods owners could, if they considered it necessary, approach their local tax office with a view to allowing the first interval end on the last day of the accounting year, as defined, rather than on the first 12-month anniversary of the date of completion or supply, as provided for in the legislation. (See "second interval" in relation to the definition of the term "accounting year".) Each case submitted will, it seems, be reviewed on its own merits.

The term "initial interval" under Section 12E is not to be confused with **[2–220]** the same term as used in Section 4C(8). This section provides that, in relation to surrenders and assignments of "legacy leases", *"initial interval shall be a period of 12 months beginning on the date on which the assignment or surrender occurs"*.

> *"'Second interval' in relation to a capital good, means the period beginning on the day following the end of the initial interval in the adjustment period applicable to that capital good and ending on the final day of the accounting year during which the second interval begins."*

[2-221] The term "accounting year" is important in relation to the definition of the second interval. Its definition was inserted in Section 1 of the VAT Act under Section 83 of the Finance Act 2008. Revenue's Notes for Guidance to the Finance Act 2008 clarify that the term "accounting year" means a period of 12 months ending on 31 December but can be a period of 12 months ending on another fixed date if a taxable person customarily makes up accounts for that period.

The second interval will, therefore, usually be less than 12 months in duration.

[2-222] The term "subsequent interval" is defined as follows:

> *"'Subsequent interval' in relation to a capital good, means each accounting year of a capital goods owner in the adjustment period applicable to that capital good, which follows the second interval."*

Each interval following the second interval will be 12 months long and will always end on the last day of the accounting year, as defined.

[2-223] The new definition of the term "accounting year" and its interaction with the various intervals as defined is an area where capital goods owners might encounter operational difficulties. Businesses are already accustomed to using the term "accounting year" to describe the 12-month period for which the business accounts are prepared. For some businesses the partial exemption calculation is a major task performed once a year, whereas the application of the CGS might require partial exemption calculations throughout the year.

[2-224] Revenue has clarified in e-brief 37/2008 (reproduced in Appendix 2) that there may be some flexibility in relation to the practical application of the CGS in relation to intervals as defined. It has indicated that submissions may be made on a case-by-case basis to the local tax office if, for example, a taxable person wants the first interval to correspond with the business accounting year in which the capital good is acquired and the second interval to correspond with the second accounting year.

[2-225] Regulation 21A of S.I. No. 548 2006 - VAT Regulations 2006 (inserted by S.I. No. 238 2008 – VAT (Amendment) Regulations 2008) provides for situations where a capital goods owner changes the end date of his/her accounting year during a subsequent interval of the adjustment period. It also provides for non-correspondence of transferor and transferee accounting years in cases where capital goods change ownership under Section 3(5)(b)(iii) transfers of trade. (For greater detail, see Chapter 3 in relation to the CGS.)

Section 12E(3)(a) of the VAT Act provides that: [2–226]

"In relation to a capital good, the number of intervals in the adjustment period during which adjustments of deductions are required under this section to be made, is –

(i)   *in the case of refurbishment, 10 intervals.*

(ii)   *In the case of a capital good to which paragraph (c) or (d) of subsection (6) applies, the number of full intervals remaining in the adjustment period applicable to that capital good plus one as required to be calculated in accordance with the formula in subsection (7)(b), and*

(iii) *in all other cases, 20 intervals."*

The term "refurbishment" is defined in Section 12E(2) as *"development on*   [2–227]
a previously completed building, structure or engineering work". The adjustment period for refurbishment is 10 intervals in length.

The reference in paragraph (ii) is to the duration of the new adjustment   [2–228]
period which commences when a landlord either cancels an option to tax a letting or exercises an option to tax in respect of a letting which was previously exempt.

Finally, paragraph (iii) provides for the standard 20-year adjustment   [2–229]
period for buildings.

A number of terms are also defined in Section 12E relating to the amount   [2–230]
of input VAT recoverable and the manner in which an adjustment arises at the end of each interval.

The terms "total tax incurred" and "base tax amount" have already been   [2–231]
examined to some extent.

In greater detail, the "**total tax incurred**" in relation to a capital good is defined in Section 12E(3)(b) as:

"(i)   the amount of tax charged to a capital goods owner in respect of that owner's acquisition or development of a capital good,

(ii)   *in the case of a transferee where a transfer of ownership of a capital good to which section 3(5)(b)(iii) applies –*

(I)   *where such a transfer would have been a supply but for the application of section 3(5)(b)(iii) and that supply would have been exempt in accordance with section 4B(2) or subsection (2) or (6)(b) of Section 4C, then the total tax incurred that is required to be included in the copy of the capital good record that is required to be furnished by the transferor in accordance with subsection (10), and*

(II)   *where such a transfer is not one to which clause (I) applies, then the amount of tax that would have been chargeable on that transfer but for the application of sections 3(5)(b)(iii) and 13A."*

[2-232]   According to paragraph (i), the total tax incurred can therefore be the VAT actually charged to a capital goods owner in respect of acquisition/development of a capital good.

[2-233]   Alternatively, under paragraph (ii) (I) and (II) the total tax incurred can also be the VAT which might arise on a transfer of capital goods but for the operation of transfer of business relief under Section 3(5)(b)(iii) of the VAT Act.

[2-234]   Sub-paragraph (I) deals with this type of transfer when Section 12E(10) applies, i.e.:

- There is a transfer of immovable goods under Section 3(5)(b)(iii) and

- The disposal of the immovable goods would in any event be exempt under the two- or five-year rules contained in Section 4B(2) or the disposal would be exempt under Section 4C(2) because the vendor had had no right of deduction under Section 12 or the disposal, constituting the assignment or surrender of a legacy lease, would be exempt under Section 4C(6)(b) because the person assigning or surrendering the interest had no right of deduction under Section 12.

[2-235]   The vendor cannot practically opt to tax the sale of the immovable property since Section 3(5)(b)(iii) deems that a property transferring as part of a transfer of a business is not a supply for VAT purposes. Under normal circumstances, if a property is "old" and yet is sold during the adjustment period and the vendor does not opt to tax the sale, s/he would suffer a proportional clawback of input VAT in relation to the property.

[2-236]   However, the effect of Section 12E(3)(b)(ii)(I) is that the vendor in such circumstances does not suffer a clawback of VAT but passes his/her responsibilities under the CGS to the transferee. Consequently the total tax incurred by the transferee would be **deemed** to be that incurred originally by the vendor, allowing for any adjustments which the vendor should have made in his/her ownership. The transferee also "inherits" the remainder of the adjustment period. (An example of how this operates in practice is set out in Chapter 3 on the CGS.)

Sub-paragraph (II) deals with a normal transfer of immovable prop- [2–237] erty where VAT arises but is not payable due to the operation of Section 3(5)(b)(iii) or Section 13A of the VAT Act. The amount of VAT which would have arisen on the sale (but does not arise because of the relieving provisions outlined) is the "total tax incurred" for the purpose of the CGS.

In summary, in relation to the terms "total tax incurred" and "base tax [2–238] amount", the tax above amount is simply the total tax incurred, divided up over the number of intervals in the adjustment period. The capital goods owner's deductibility entitlement has no relevance here.

Other terms defined in Section 12E are "initial interval proportion of [2–239] deductible use", "total reviewed deductible amount", "non-deductible amount", "reference deduction amount", "proportion of deductible use" and "interval deductible amount". It is in considering these terms that the entitlement to deductibility becomes relevant.

These terms are dealt with at this point not because they occur in this [2–240] order in the legislation, but because it makes sense to consider them together. They cannot be examined meaningfully without keeping an eye to the meaning of the terms "total tax incurred" and "base tax amount". (Chapter 3 on the CGS contains practical examples of how the terms apply.)

The "**initial interval proportion of deductible use**" in relation to a [2–241] capital good means *"the proportion that correctly reflects the extent to which a capital good is used during the initial interval for the purposes of a capital goods owner's deductible supplies or activities"*. The proportion is likely to be a percentage or similar reflecting deductibility entitlement as reviewed at the end of the initial interval.

The "**total reviewed deductible amount**", in relation to a capital good, [2–242] is defined as *"the amount calculated by multiplying the total tax incurred in relation to that capital good by the initial interval proportion of deductible use in relation to that capital good."*

The total reviewed deductible amount is therefore the amount of input [2–243] VAT to which the capital goods owner is entitled based on the initial interval proportion of deductible use. The total reviewed deductible amount is calculated at the end of the initial interval. Any difference between the total reviewed deductible amount and the total tax incurred is referred to as the "non-deductible amount".

[2-244]   The "**non-deductible amount**" means *"the amount which is the difference between the total tax incurred in relation to that capital good and the total reviewed deductible amount in relation to that capital good".*

[2-245]   The "**reference deduction amount**" in relation to a capital good is *"the amount calculated by dividing the total reviewed deductible amount in relation to that capital good by the number of intervals in the adjustment period applicable to that capital good".*

To make sense of this definition, it is necessary to refer to the definition of the term "adjustment period" as contained in Section 12E(3)(a). This provides that:

"In relation to a capital good, the number of intervals in the adjustment period during which adjustments of deductions are required under this section to be made, is –

(i)   in the case of refurbishment, 10 intervals.

(ii)   In the case of a capital good to which paragraph (c) or (d) of subsection (6) applies, the number of full intervals remaining in the adjustment period applicable to that capital good plus one as required to be calculated in accordance with the formula in subsection (7)(b), and

(iii)   in all other cases, 20 intervals."

[2-246]   Paragraphs (i) and (iii) are straightforward in that the adjustment period for refurbishment is to be 10 intervals, whereas in most other cases it is 20 intervals. Again, bear in mind the different definition for the term "adjustment period" provided for in Section 4C(8) of the legislation in relation to surrenders/assignments of legacy leases.

[2-247]   Paragraph (ii) refers to Section 12E(6)(c) and (d). These paragraphs refer to cases in which the landlord's option to tax is cancelled. The number of intervals remaining in the adjustment period (plus one) would apply in such cases rather than a full 20-year adjustment period.

[2-248]   To return to the meaning of the term "reference deduction amount", it therefore denotes the total amount of input VAT to which a capital goods owner is entitled on the acquisition/development of a capital good divided over the appropriate number of intervals in the adjustment period.

The term "**proportion of deductible use**" in relation to a capital good [2–249] for an interval other than the initial interval, means "*the proportion that correctly reflects the extent to which a capital good is used during that interval for the purposes of a capital goods owner's deductible supplies or activities*".

It is similar to the initial interval proportion of deductible use but reflects the use to which a capital good is put in intervals other than the initial interval.

Finally, the "**interval deduction amount**" in respect of the second and [2–250] each subsequent interval means "*the amount calculated by multiplying the base tax amount in relation to that capital good by the proportion of deductible use for that capital good applicable to the relevant interval*".

If the interval deduction amount is less or greater than the reference deduction amount (see above), then an adjustment would be required under the CGS. That adjustment could represent a clawback of input VAT or a reclaim of input VAT, depending on whether the proportion of deductible use had exceeded or fallen below the initial interval proportion of deductible use.

Section 12E(3)(a) and (b) define the terms "adjustment period" and "total [2–251] tax incurred". As these definitions have already been considered in the analysis of Section 12E(2) above, they are not re-examined at this point.

Section 12E(3)(c) provides that:

"*Where a capital goods owner acquires a capital good –*

(i) *by way of a transfer, being a transfer to which section 3(5)(b)(iii) applies other than a transfer to which subsection (10) applies, on which tax would have been chargeable but for the application of section 3(5)(b)(iii), or*

(ii) *on the supply or development of which tax was chargeable in accordance with section 13A,*

then, for the purposes of this section, that capital goods owner is deemed to have claimed a deduction in accordance with section 12 of the tax that would have been chargeable –

(I) *on the transfer of that capital good but for the application of section 3(5)(b)(iii), less any amount accounted for by that owner in respect of that transfer in accordance with subsection (7)(d), and*

(II) *on the supply or development of that capital good but for the application of section 13A.*"

[2-252]   This provision deals with situations where a property was subject to VAT at acquisition but VAT was not actually charged because of Section 3(5)(iii)(b) or Section 13A of the VAT Act. The capital goods owner is nonetheless **deemed** to have claimed an input VAT credit. This is an important point in relation to the VAT history of the property for subsequent transfers. Clearly it also has implications in relation to the operation of the capital goods scheme, i.e. VAT adjustments may arise even though the capital goods owner did not pay VAT at acquisition/development.

[2-253]   Section 12E(3)(d) provides that:

> *"Where a capital goods owner supplies or transfers by means of a transfer to which section 3(5)(b)(iii) applies a capital good during the adjustment period then the adjustment period for that capital good for that owner shall end on the date of that supply or transfer."*

Thus, Sections 12E(3)(c) and (d) together deal with the general rules applicable to both the acquisition and the disposal of a capital good.

[2-254]   Section 12E(4) (a) states that:

> *"Where the initial interval proportion of deductible use in relation to a capital good differs from the proportion of the total tax incurred in relation to that capital good which was deductible by that owner in accordance with Section 12, then that owner shall, at the end of the initial interval, calculate an amount in accordance with the following formula:*

$$A - B$$

> *where –*

> A   *is the amount of the total tax incurred in relation to that capital good which was deductible by that owner in accordance with section 12, and*

> B   *is the total reviewed deductible amount in relation to that capital good."*

This provision requires the capital goods owner to carry out a comparison exercise at the end of the first interval to calculate any difference between the total input VAT credit originally claimed in relation to acquisition/development and the actual input credit entitlement arising as a result of the use to which the property was put during the first interval.

[2-255]   Section 12E(4)(b) states that:

> *"Where in accordance with paragraph (a) –*

> (i)   *A is greater than B, then the amount calculated in accordance with the formula in paragraph (a) shall be payable by that owner as if it*

were tax due in accordance with section 19 for the taxable period immediately following the end of the initial interval or,

(ii)   B is greater than A, then that owner is entitled to increase the amount of tax deductible for the purposes of section 12 by the amount calculated in accordance with paragraph (a) for the taxable period immediately following the end of the initial interval."

This subsection provides for a repayment of input VAT or a further input VAT credit, depending on whether the proportion of deductible use has increased or decreased in the first interval. Any repayment of input VAT is payable according to Section 19 of the VAT Act, i.e. in general terms it is repayable no later than the 19th day of the month following the end of the bi-monthly VAT period in which the first interval ends.

The clawback/repayment amount provided for is effectively a lump sum.

Section 12E(4)(c) states that: [2–256]

"Where a capital good is not used during the initial interval then the initial interval proportion of deductible use is the proportion of the total input tax incurred that is deductible by the capital goods owner in accordance with section 12."

This subsection provides that no adjustment is necessary at the end of the initial interval if the capital good has not been used during the first interval, i.e. the original input VAT entitlement under Section 12 of the VAT Act stands.

Section 12E(5)(a)(i) states that: [2–257]

"Subject to subsection (6)(b), where in respect of an interval, other than the initial interval, the proportion of deductible use for that interval in relation to that capital good differs from the initial interval proportion of deductible use in relation to that capital good, then the capital goods owner shall, at the end of that interval, calculate an amount in accordance with the following formula:

$$C - D$$

where –

C   is the reference deduction amount in relation to that capital good, and

D   is the interval deductible amount in relation to that capital good."

This subsection deals with adjustments which may be required in relation to input VAT as a result of any changes of use of a property during any interval other than the initial interval.

[2–258]   In relation to 'C', the "reference deduction amount" is defined at the beginning of Section 12E as the amount calculated by dividing the "total reviewed deductible amount" by the number of intervals applicable. The "total reviewed deductible amount" is defined as the total tax incurred multiplied by the initial interval proportion of deductible use.

Consequently, 'C' in most cases is likely to be $\frac{1}{20}$ of the total input VAT to which the capital goods owner was entitled following the review carried out at the end of the first interval. In its Notes for Guidance, Revenue refers to this amount as the "benchmark figure".

[2–259]   In relation to 'D', the "interval deductible amount" is a term used only in relation to the second and subsequent interval and it is defined as the amount calculated by multiplying the "base tax" (total tax **incurred** ÷ no. of intervals) by the proportion of deductible use applicable to the interval in question.

[2–260]   The cross-reference making this subsection subject to subsection 6(b) means that Section 12E(5)(a)(i) would not apply if a change in taxable use of more than 50% had occurred in the interval.

[2–261]   Section 12E(5)(b)(ii) states that:

> *"Where in accordance with subparagraph (i) –*
>
> (I)   *C is greater than D, then the amount calculated in accordance with the formula in subparagraph (i) shall be payable by that owner as if it were tax due in accordance with section 19 for the taxable period immediately following the end of that interval, or*
>
> (II) *D is greater than C, then that owner is entitled to increase the amount of tax deductible for the purposes of section 12 by the amount calculated in accordance with the formula in subparagraph (i) for the taxable period immediately following the end of that interval."*

Depending on whether the proportion of deductible use has increased or decreased vis-à-vis the benchmark figure, then the capital goods owner will either repay VAT or will be entitled to additional input VAT credit.

[2–262]   Section 12E(5)(b) states that:

> *"Where for the second or any subsequent interval, a capital good is not used during that interval, the proportion of deductible use in respect of that capital good for that interval shall be the proportion of deductible use for the previous interval."*

This is similar to the corresponding Section 12E(4)(c) dealing with situations where capital goods are not used in the initial interval. Section 12E(5)(b) provides that if capital goods are not used in other intervals, the capital goods owner can rely on the proportion of deductible use which applied in the prior interval, i.e. the fact that the capital good is not used in a particular interval does not give rise to an adjustment. This might arise if the property was not occupied for a period of time.

Section 12E(6)(a)(i) states that: [2–263]

> "Where in respect of a capital good for an interval other than the initial interval the proportion of deductible use expressed as a percentage differs by more than 50 percentage points from the initial interval proportion of deductible use expressed as a percentage, then the capital goods owner shall at the end of that interval calculate an amount in accordance with the following formula:
>
> $$(C - D) \times N$$
>
> where –
>
> C   is the reference deduction amount in relation to that capital good,
>
> D   is the interval deductible amount in relation to that capital good, and
>
> N   is the number of full intervals remaining in the adjustment period at the end of that interval plus one."

Apart from the adjustment which may arise at the end of the initial interval, the other periodic adjustments are not calculated on a lump sum basis but are calculated on a "per interval" basis. However, what is provided for in Section 12E(6)(a)(i) is effectively a lump sum adjustment arising as a result of a significant swing in the deductible use to which a property is put in an interval other than the initial interval.

The first part of the formula is the same as that used in Section 12E(5)(a)   [2–264]
to calculate the standard adjustment at the end of the second and subsequent interval. However, the "x N" ensures that the adjustment will be made not just for the interval in question but for all remaining intervals in the adjustment period as well.

Example – "Big Swing" adjustment

Brain Limited is a management consultancy and training business. It buys a premises on 21 August 2011 for €3 million plus VAT at €405,000 (this is the "total tax incurred" as defined for the purposes of the CGS). The "base tax amount" for the purposes of the CGS is €405,000 divided by 20 intervals = €20,250.

Brain Limited's turnover is 30% management consultancy (taxable) and 70% training (exempt). Its accounting year ends on 31 March. When it purchases the building, Brain Limited recovers only 30% of the total tax incurred (30% of €405,000 = €121,500).

For the first few intervals, the taxable : exempt turnover ratio remains unchanged. At the end of the initial interval (20/08/2012) the initial interval proportion of deductible use is still 30%. No adjustment is required under the CGS. The total reviewed deductible amount is €121,500 (€405,000 × 30%). The reference deduction amount is €6,075 (€121,500 divided by 20).

In 2015, i.e. during the fifth interval, Brain Limited's turnover switches to 100% taxable, as it ceases the exempt training activity. The proportion of deductible use expressed as a percentage (100%) differs by more than 50% from the initial interval proportion of deductible use expressed as a percentage (30%). Consequently, at the end of the fifth interval, Brain Limited is required to calculate an amount as follows:

$$(C - D) \times N$$

C is the reference deduction amount (€6,075).

D is the interval deductible amount (€20,250, i.e. the base tax amount × 100%).

N is the number of full intervals remaining in the adjustment period at the end of that interval plus one, i.e. in this case 15 + 1 = 16.

Consequently the amount to be calculated is (€6,075 − €20,250) = (€14,175) × 16 = (€226,800).

Section 12E(6)(a)(ii) states that:

"Where in accordance with subparagraph (i)-

(I) C is greater than D, then the amount calculated in accordance with the formula in subparagraph (i) shall be payable by that owner as if it were tax due in accordance with section 19 for the taxable period immediately following the end of that interval, or

(II) D is greater than C, then that owner is entitled to increase the amount of tax deductible for the purposes of section 12 by the amount calculated in accordance with the formula in subparagraph (i) for the taxable period immediately following the end of that interval."

These paragraphs simply provide that the amount of additional input VAT payable or repayable is to be accounted for in the bi-monthly VAT period following the end of the interval in which the change in use occurred.

In the above case, D is greater than C and Brain Limited may reclaim an amount of €226,800 in its March–April 2015 VAT return.

Section 12E(6)(a)(iii) states that:

"The provisions of subparagraph (i) shall not apply to a capital good or part thereof that has been subject to the provisions of paragraphs (c) or (d) during the interval to which subparagraph (i) applies."

This provides that the "big swing" adjustment provided for in sub-paragraph (i) would not apply in the same interval as one in which the landlord's option to tax is either cancelled (paragraph (c)) or exercised (paragraph (d)).

Section 12E(6)(a)(iv) states that:

"Where a capital goods owner is obliged to carry out a calculation referred to in subparagraph (i) in respect of a capital good, then, for the purposes of the remaining intervals in the adjustment period, the proportion of deductible use in relation to that capital good for the interval in respect of which the calculation is required to be made shall be treated as if it were the initial interval proportion of deductible use in relation to that capital good and, until a further calculation is required under subparagraph (i), all other definition amounts shall be calculated accordingly."

The calculation referred to in subparagraph (i) is the lump sum VAT adjustment arising from a significant change in the use to which the property is put. Section 12E(6)(a)(iv) provides that at the end of intervals following such an adjustment, the subsequent adjustments will be made on the basis of appropriately revised definition amounts. Clearly the definition amounts would have to be adjusted if such a significant change in taxable use arose.

Following the "big swing" adjustment at the end of the fifth interval, Brain Limited has recovered the following input VAT:

$$€405,000 \times 4/20 \times 30\% = €24,300 \text{ plus}$$

$$€405,000 \times 16/20 \times 100\% = €324,000$$

$$\text{Total input VAT recovered} = €348,300.$$

This is the total tax incurred in relation to the remainder of the CGS.

Section 12E(6)(b) states that: *"Where the provisions of paragraph (a) apply to*   **[2–265]**
an interval then the provisions of subsection (5) do not apply to that interval."

[2-266]   If the "big swing" adjustment in Section 12E(6)(a) applies in a given interval, then the normal annual adjustment dealt with in Section 12E(5) does not apply in that interval. This provision simply clarifies that only one or other adjustment is required in a particular interval and presumably its intention is to avoid any duplication of adjustments.

[2-267]   Section 12E(6)(c) states that:

> "Where a capital goods owner who is a landlord in respect of all or part of a capital good terminates his or her landlord's option to tax in accordance with section 7A(a) in respect of any letting of that capital good, then –
>
> (i)   that owner is deemed, for the purposes of this section, to have supplied and simultaneously acquired the capital good to which that letting relates,
>
> (ii)   that supply shall be deemed to be a supply on which tax is not chargeable and no option to tax that supply in accordance with section 4B(5) shall be permitted on that supply, and
>
> (iii) the capital good acquired shall be treated as a capital good for the purposes of this section and the amount calculated in accordance with subsection (7)(b) on that supply shall be treated as the total tax incurred in relation to that capital good."

This subsection deals specifically with the capital goods scheme where the capital goods owner is a landlord. If the landlord terminates his/her option to tax, then an immediate lump sum VAT adjustment is triggered as calculated under the formula set out in Section 12E(7)(b).

[2-268]   Section 12E(6)(d) states that:

> "Where in respect of a letting of a capital good that is not subject to a landlord's option to tax in accordance with Section 7A(1), a landlord subsequently exercises a landlord's option to tax in respect of a letting of that capital good, then –
>
> (i)   that landlord is deemed, for the purposes of this section, to have supplied and simultaneously acquired that capital good to which that letting related,
>
> (ii)   that supply shall be deemed to be a supply on which tax is chargeable, and
>
> (iii) the capital good acquired shall be treated as a capital good for the purposes of this section, and –
>
> > (I)   the amount calculated in accordance with subsection (7)(a) shall be treated as the total tax incurred in relation to that capital good, and

> *(II)   the total tax incurred shall be deemed to have been deducted in*
> *accordance with section 12 at the time of that supply."*

The previous subsection dealt with situations in which a landlord   **[2–269]**
terminated his/her option to tax in respect of a particular letting.
Subsection (6)(d) deals with situations in which a landlord opts to tax a
letting during the course of that letting.

Initially, the landlord would not have claimed any input VAT in respect   **[2–270]**
of an "unopted" letting. However, when the landlord opts to tax a letting, s/he is deemed to have deducted input VAT. An actual credit is
provided for. This is because the provision deems the capital goods to
be supplied and immediately reacquired. As the supply is deemed to be
one on which VAT is chargeable, Section 12E(7)(a) applies. The owner is
therefore entitled to a VAT credit for the amount calculated in accordance with the formula contained in Section 12E(7)(a). (This point is
illustrated in Example 37 of Revenue's *VAT on Property Guide*, which is
reproduced in Appendix 1.)

Section 12E(7)(a) states that: **[2–271]**

> *"Where a capital goods owner supplies a capital good or transfers a capital*
> *good, being a transfer to which section 3(5)(b)(iii) applies, other than a*
> *transfer to which subsection (10) applies, during the adjustment period in*
> *relation to that capital good, and where –*
>
> *(i)   tax is chargeable on that supply, or tax would have been chargeable*
> *on that transfer but for the application of section 3(5)(b)(iii), and*
>
> *(ii)   the non-deductible amount in relation to that capital good for that*
> *owner is greater than zero or in the case of a supply or transfer*
> *during the initial interval, that owner was not entitled to deduct all*
> *of the total tax incurred in accordance with section 12,*
>
> *then that owner is entitled to increase the amount of tax deductible by*
> *that owner for the purposes of section 12 for the taxable period in which*
> *the supply or transfer occurs, by an amount calculated in accordance with*
> *the following formula:*

$$\frac{E \times N}{T}$$

> *where –*
> *E   is the non-deductible amount in relation to that capital good, or in the*
> *case of a supply before the end of the initial interval, the amount of the*
> *total tax incurred in relation to that capital good which was not*
> *deductible by that owner in accordance with section 12,*

N   is the number of full intervals remaining in the adjustment period in relation to that capital good at the time of supply plus one, and

T   is the total number of intervals in the adjustment period in relation to that capital good."

[2-272]   Section 12E(7) deals with the sale of capital goods. Section 12(7)(a) provides that where the sale is taxable and the seller was not entitled to claim credit in full or in part for the original input VAT s/he incurred, then a proportionate VAT credit is allowed when the property is sold. The formula given in the subsection is based on the number of intervals remaining in the adjustment period.

[2-273]   The cross-reference to subsection (10) is to a situation where in the circumstances specified therein, the transferee would take over the capital goods record from the transferor.

[2-274]   Section 12E(7)(b) states that:

"Where a capital goods owner supplies a capital good during the adjustment period applicable to that capital good and where tax is not chargeable on the supply and where either –

(i)   the total reviewed deductible amount in relation to that capital good is greater than zero, or

(ii)   in the case of a supply before the end of the initial interval where the amount of the total tax incurred in relation to that capital good which was deductible by that owner in accordance with section 12 is greater than zero,

then that owner shall calculate an amount which shall be payable as if it were tax due in accordance with section 19 for the taxable period in which the supply occurs in accordance with the following formula:

$$\frac{B \times N}{T}$$

where –

B   is the total reviewed deductible amount in relation to that capital good, or, in the case of a supply to which subparagraph (ii) applies, the amount of the total tax incurred in relation to that capital good which that owner claimed as a deduction in accordance with section 12,

N   is the number of full intervals remaining in the adjustment period in relation to that capital good at the time of supply plus one, and

T   is the total number of intervals in the adjustment period in relation to that capital good."

This subsection deals with the scenario in which a capital goods owner was entitled to input VAT credit upon acquisition/development of the property but the property when sold is not subject to VAT. (This situation could arise for example if the property is "old" when disposed of but is still within the adjustment period and the parties do not opt to tax the sale.) The capital goods owner would be required to calculate and repay a clawback of input VAT based, again, on the number of intervals remaining at the time the capital good is sold.

Section 12E(7)(c) states that: [2–275]

"Where a capital goods owner supplies or transfers, being a transfer to which section 3(5)(b)(iii) applies, part of a capital good during the adjustment period, then for the remainder of the adjustment period applicable to that capital good –

(i)   the total tax incurred,

(ii)   the total reviewed deductible amount, and

(iii)   all other definition amounts,

in relation to the remainder of that capital good for that owner shall be adjusted accordingly on a fair and reasonable basis."

Section 12E(7)(c) confirms that when part of a capital good is disposed of and the transaction is deemed not to be a supply because of the operation of the transfer of business relief contained in Section 3(5)(b)(iii), then the capital goods owner is required to adjust the various definition amounts in relation to the remaining property. No guidance is given as to how this adjustment is to be calculated, other than that it is to be done on a fair and reasonable basis.

Section 12E(7)(d) states that: [2–276]

"Where a transfer of ownership of a capital good occurs, being a transfer to which section 3(5)(b)(iii) applies, but excluding a transfer to which subsection (10) applies, and where the transferee would not have been entitled to deduct all of the tax that would have been chargeable on that transfer but for the application of Section 3(5)(b)(iii), then that transferee shall calculate an amount as follows:

$$F - G$$

where –
F   is the amount of tax that would have been chargeable but for the application of section 3(5)(b)(iii), and

> G   *is the amount of that tax that would have been deductible in accordance*
> *with section 12 by that transferee if section 3(5)(b)(iii) had not applied*
> *to that transfer,*
>
> *and that amount shall be payable by that transferee as if it were tax due*
> *in accordance with section 19 for the taxable period in which the transfer*
> *occurs and for the purposes of this section that amount shall be deemed to*
> *be the amount of the total tax incurred in relation to that capital good that*
> *the transferee was not entitled to deduct in accordance with section 12."*

As previously, the cross-reference to subsection (10) is to a situation where in the circumstances specified therein, the transferee would take over the capital goods record from the transferor.

[2-277]   Subsection (d) provides that the VAT-free acquisition under the transfer of business rules cannot be exploited by an entity which would not be entitled to full VAT deductibility. F is the amount of VAT which would have been charged in relation to the transfer but for the operation of Section 3(5)(b)(iii) and G is the amount of this input VAT which the transferee would have been entitled to deduct but for the operation of Section 3(5)(b)(iii). If there is a difference between these amounts, then the transferee has to repay a clawback of input VAT. These provisions are an important element preserving VAT neutrality in the CGS. Section 12E(7)(d) is comparable to Section 12D(4), which applied to similar transfers until 30 June 2008.

[2-278]   Section 12E(8)(a) states that:

> *"Where a tenant who has an interest other than a freehold equivalent*
> *interest in immovable goods is the capital goods owner in respect of a*
> *refurbishment carried out on those immovable goods, assigns or surrenders*
> *that interest, then that tenant shall calculate an amount in respect of that*
> *capital good which is that refurbishment in accordance with the formula*
> *in subsection (7)(b), and that amount shall be payable by that tenant as if*
> *it were tax due in accordance with section 19 for the taxable period in*
> *which the assignment or surrender occurs."*

This subsection deals with situations where a tenant, who is a capital goods owner in respect of a refurbishment of a property, assigns or surrenders a lease during the 10-year adjustment period associated with the refurbishment. Subsection 12E(8)(a) sets out the general rule. The tenant suffers a clawback of input VAT as per the formula set out in Section 12E(7)(b). The amount of the clawback is based on the total reviewed deductible amount and the number of intervals remaining in the adjustment period at the time when the assignment/surrender takes place.

Section 12E(8)(b) states that: [2-279]

"Paragraph (a) shall not apply where –

(i) *the total reviewed deductible amount in relation to that capital good is equal to the total tax incurred in relation to that capital good, or in relation to an assignment or surrender that occurs prior to the end of the initial interval in relation to that capital good the tenant was entitled to deduct all of the total tax incurred in accordance with section 12 in relation to that capital good,*

(ii) *the tenant enters into a written agreement with the person to whom the interest is assigned or surrendered, to the effect that that person shall be responsible for all obligations under this section in relation to the capital good referred to in paragraph (a) from the date of the assignment or surrender of the interest referred to in paragraph (a), as if –*

 (I) *the total tax incurred and the amount deducted by that tenant in relation to that capital good were the total tax incurred and the amount deducted by the person to whom the interest is assigned or surrendered, and*

 (II) *any adjustments required to be made under this section by the tenant were made,*

 and

(iii) *the tenant issues a copy of the capital good records in respect of the capital good referred to in paragraph (a) to the person to whom the interest is being assigned or surrendered."*

Section 12E(8)(b) is a relieving provision in relation to the general rule set out at paragraph (a). This means that paragraph (a) does not apply if the conditions set out in paragraph (b) are met. Where the tenant was entitled to deduct all of the VAT incurred on the refurbishment, then the person to whom the lease is being surrendered or assigned can take over the relevant obligations under the capital goods scheme and the tenant assigning/surrendering the lease does not suffer the clawback provided for in paragraph (a). This provision is subject to being agreed in writing between the parties.

Section 12E(8)(c) states that: [2-280]

"Where paragraph (b) applies the person to whom the interest is assigned or surrendered shall be responsible for the obligations referred to in paragraph (b)(ii) and shall use the information in the copy of the capital good record issued by the tenant in accordance with paragraph (b)(iii)

for the purposes of calculating any tax chargeable or deductible in accordance with this section in respect of that capital good by that person from the date of the assignment or surrender of the interest referred to in paragraph (a)."

[2-281] Under the relieving provisions the person to whom the interest is assigned or surrendered becomes the capital goods owner in relation to the refurbishment and is responsible for all of the obligations in relation to the capital goods record, based on the capital goods record furnished by the transferor.

[2-282] Section 12E(8)(d) states that:

"Where the capital good is one to which subsection (11) applies paragraphs (a), (b) and (c) shall not apply."

The cross-reference to subsection (11) means that if the refurbishment is destroyed, then no clawback applies and in addition the procedure whereby the tenant can pass the refurbishment to the assignee/landlord does not arise.

[2-283] Section 12E(9) states that:

"Where a capital goods owner –

(a)   supplies a capital good during the adjustment period applicable to that capital good, and where tax is chargeable on that supply, or

(b)   transfers, other than a transfer to which subsection (10) applies, a capital good during the adjustment period applicable to that capital good and tax would have been chargeable on that transfer but for the application of section 3(5)(b)(iii),

and where, at the time of that supply or transfer, that owner and the person to whom the capital good is supplied or transferred are connected within the meaning of section 7A, and where –

(i)   the amount of tax chargeable on the supply of that capital good,

(ii)   the amount of tax that would have been chargeable on the transfer of that capital good but for the application of section 3(5)(b)(iii), or

(iii)   the amount of tax that would have been chargeable on the supply but for the application of section 13A,

*is less than the amount, thereafter referred to as the "adjustment **amount**", calculated in accordance with the following formula:*

$$\frac{H \times N}{T}$$

where –

H   *is the total tax incurred in relation to that capital good for the capital goods owner making the supply or transfer,*

N   *is the number of full intervals remaining in the adjustment period in relation to that capital good plus one, and*

T   *is the total number of intervals in the adjustment period in relation to that capital good,*

then, that owner shall calculate an amount, which shall be payable by that owner as if it were tax due in accordance with section 19 for the taxable period in which the supply or transfer occurs, in accordance with the following formula:

$$I - J$$

where –

I   *is the adjustment amount, and*

J   *is the amount of tax chargeable on the supply of that capital good, or the amount of tax that would have been chargeable on the transfer of that capital good but for the application of section 3(5)(b)(iii), or the amount of tax what would have been chargeable on the supply but for the application of section 13A."*

Section 12E(9) is an anti-avoidance provision which applies to sales of   **[2–284]** properties between connected persons. In these circumstances, the capital goods owner is first required to calculate an adjustment amount as per the first formula. The adjustment amount is basically the amount of input tax incurred by the transferee when s/he acquired/developed the capital goods, reduced to reflect the number of intervals remaining at the time the goods are transferred to the connected person. If the VAT arising in relation to the transfer is less than the "adjustment amount", then a clawback of input VAT is payable by the transferor as per the I-J formula, i.e. the clawback amounts to the difference between the transferor's adjusted input VAT and the output the transferor would propose to account for in relation to the transfer of the property but for the operation of Section 12E(9).

The operation and application of Section 12E(9) is an anti-avoidance   **[2–285]** measure similar in operation to the economic value test which existed under Section 4(3A) of the VAT Act, which no longer has application after 30 June 2008. In the same manner as the economic value test, Section 12E(9) prevents VAT "leakage". Section 12D(9) applies to the transfer of a capital good, i.e. it has no application to lettings. The economic value test applied to the creation and transfer of long leases, as these were treated as the supply of goods under the VAT regime in place until 30 June 2008. (See example and further comment in Chapter 3 at paragraph **3–60**.)

[2-286] Section 12E(10) states that:

> "Where a capital goods owner transfers a capital good, being a transfer to which section 3(5)(b)(iii) applies and that transfer would have been a supply but for the application of section 3(5)(b)(iii), and where such supply would be exempt in accordance with section 4B(2) or subsection (2) or (6)(b) of Section 4C, then –
>
> (a)   the transferor shall issue a copy of the capital good record to the transferee,
>
> (b)   the transferee shall be the successor to the capital goods owner transferring the capital good and shall be responsible for all obligations of that owner under this section from the date of the transfer of that capital good, as if –
>
>   (i)   the total tax incurred and the amount deducted by the transferor in relation to that capital good were the total tax incurred and the amount deducted by the transferee, and
>
>   (ii)   any adjustments required to be made under this section by the transferor were made,
>
> and
>
> (c)   that transferee as successor shall use the information in the copy of the capital good record issued by the transferor in accordance with paragraph (a) for the purposes of calculating tax chargeable or deductible by that successor in accordance with this section for the remainder of the adjustment period applicable to that capital good from the date of transfer of that capital good."

[2-287] Subsection 10 deals with situations where a property is transferred as part of a transfer of a business during the adjustment period and the sale would (unless "opted") be exempt due to the operation of the two- or five-year rule or, if transitional property, because the person disposing of the interest in the property had not been entitled to deduct input VAT in relation to its acquisition. If Section 3(5)(b)(iii) did not apply in these circumstances, then the vendor would suffer a proportionate clawback of input VAT. However, the legislation provides that the transferee becomes the successor to the transferor and "takes over" the liabilities of the property under the scheme. The transferor is obliged to pass on the capital goods record for this purpose.

See example in Chapter 3 at paragraph **3-56**.

[2-288] Section 12E(11) states that:

> "If a capital good is destroyed during the adjustment period in relation to that capital good, then no further adjustment under this section shall be

made by the capital goods owner in respect of any remaining intervals in
the adjustment period in relation to that capital good."

This subsection is intended to provide that destruction of the capital good represents neither a supply nor a change in use.

Section 12E(12) states that: [2–289]

"A capital goods owner shall create and maintain a record (in this section
referred to as a 'capital good record') in respect of each capital good and
that record shall contain sufficient information to determine any
adjustments in respect of that capital good required in accordance with
this section."

This is reasonably self-explanatory. A separate record is to be kept for each capital good, bearing in mind that refurbishment for example is a separate capital good from the capital good which is refurbished. According to Revenue's Notes for Guidance, the capital good record will be checked by Revenue in audit situations. In addition, it must also be passed on to the transferee in certain circumstances (see for example Section 12E(10)).

Section 12E(13) states that: [2–290]

"The Revenue Commissioners may make regulations necessary for the
purposes of the operation of this section, in particular in relation to the
duration of a subsequent interval where the accounting year of a capital
goods owner changes."

These Regulations have since been issued (see S.I. No. 238 of 2008 – Value-Added Tax (Amendment) Regulations 2008). They will be considered in more detail in Chapter 3.

Chapter 3

The Capital Goods Scheme (CGS)

The purpose of the CGS

The CGS is provided for in Section 12E of the VAT Act. It is a mechanism for regulating VAT deductibility over the "VAT life" of immovable goods in a proportionate and equitable manner. [3–01]

The CGS contains a series of definitions and procedures which the capital goods owner is required to use in order to "track" changes in the taxable use of immovable goods. However, the CGS does not determine whether a supply of the property is subject to VAT. This matter is dealt with by other sections of the VAT Act. [3–02]

Input VAT deductibility will be allowed initially by reference to the first 12 months of full use. Subsequently the capital goods owner is required to carry out a review – usually annually – of the use to which the property is put (in terms of taxable or exempt use). Where there is a change in the proportion of VAT-deductible use, a VAT adjustment will be required. The adjustment will reflect the difference between the use in the initial 12 months and the use in the year being reviewed. Ultimately, the proportion of input VAT deducted will reflect the actual use of the property over the adjustment period. The adjustment period is comparable to a VAT "life" of an immovable property and is usually (though not always) approximately 20 years in duration. [3–03]

The adjustments do not apply unless there is a change in VAT-able use of a property. This means that for businesses whose entitlement to deduct VAT does not vary from year to year, the scheme has very little impact (for more detail and examples, see the section below on interval-based adjustments, paragraphs **3–10** to **3–14**). [3–04]

Once the adjustment period has expired, there are no further obligations under the CGS. [3–05]

[3–06]   Section 12E contains provisions to deal with periodic use-based adjustments, sales, lettings and refurbishment of immovable property.

How the CGS works

When does it apply?

[3–07]   The CGS applies to any person who is charged VAT on the acquisition or development of immovable property for a business purpose. Such persons are defined as capital goods owners under Section 12E(2). When a person acquires a property, s/he can be a capital goods owner even if s/he is not entitled to recover input VAT. For example, a doctor who suffers VAT on acquiring a building for use in a medical practice would not be entitled to recover input VAT when the building is acquired. However, if the property is sold during the adjustment period and if the sale is subject to VAT, then a proportion of the input VAT suffered may be taken as a credit at the time of the sale.

When does it not apply?

[3–08]   The CGS does not apply to private individuals or bodies established by statute that are not engaging in an economic activity. Nor does it apply to a taxable person who acquires or develops a property in a non-business capacity. Furthermore, it does not apply to any person who acquires a property on which VAT is not chargeable. The fact that VAT might not actually be disbursed would not necessarily put the property outside the VAT "net". When enquiring about the VAT status of a property, it is not uncommon to hear the owner reason that s/he "didn't pay any VAT" and therefore the property must be outside the VAT "net". However, a number of provisions in the VAT Act would give rise to non-disbursement. A property might, for example, change hands as part of the transfer of a business and hence fall within the provisions of Section 3(5)(b)(iii). Non-disbursement does not necessarily mean that a property is not in the VAT "net". It is always necessary to establish **why** no VAT may have been paid.

What is a capital good?

[3–09]   A capital good is defined in Section 1 of the VAT Act as developed immovable goods. For example, undeveloped land is not a capital good. A capital goods owner is defined in Section 12E(2) as *"a taxable person who incurs expenditure on the acquisition or development of a capital good"*. In the case of developed property that is leased out to a tenant, the lessor is the capital goods owner to the extent that the lessor *"incurs expenditure on the acquisition or development"* of the capital good. A lessee will only acquire a capital good if the interest is a freehold equivalent interest (see Chapter 4, paragraph **4–03**). If the lessee is granted a lease which is not a freehold equivalent interest, then it is not a capital goods owner, even if it pays a substantial up-front premium, because it is not acquiring the underlying capital good. If the lessee carries out development work, then it is a capital goods owner to the extent that it incurs expenditure on refurbishment work (see below, paragraphs **3-41** to **3-46** and also Chapter 4 in relation to refurbishment).

Intervals and the adjustment period

The adjustment period can be compared to the "VAT life" of the immov-   **[3-10]**
able goods. Most capital goods have an adjustment period of 20 intervals. An interval is usually 12 months in duration. However, the second
interval can be shorter than 12 months (see below, paragraph **3-14**).

In brief, the adjustment period is a period of time during which the   **[3-11]**
owner of a capital good must make periodic "adjustments" to his/her
VAT recovery position based on the extent to which the relevant capital
good is put to a VAT-able use. Once the adjustment period is over, no
further "adjustments" need to be made. In most cases, the use to which
a capital good is put remains unchanged over its lifetime and no
periodic adjustments would need to be made.

The adjustment period commences when the initial interval, as defined
in Section 12E(2), commences.

Under Section 12E(2), the initial interval is *"a period of 12 months*   **[3-12]**
beginning on the date when a capital good is completed ... [as defined in
Section 4B(1)] *... or, in the case of a capital good that is supplied following
completion, the initial interval ... is the 12-month period beginning on the date
of that supply."*

Example – initial interval and the start of the adjustment period

Surefire Insurance Corporation acquired the freehold interest in a
new property on 1 May 2010 for €10 million plus VAT at 13.5%
(€1,350,000). As the property was supplied on 1 May 2010, this is
the date when the initial interval commences and is also the date
when the 20-interval adjustment period commences.

If Surefire Insurance Corporation had the property constructed
itself as opposed to buying it from a developer, then the initial
interval and the 20-interval adjustment period would have
commenced on the date on which the property was completed.
Under Section 4B(1) of the VAT Act, the property would be completed when *"the development of those goods had reached the state, apart
from only such finishing or fitting work that would normally be carried*

out by or on behalf of the person who will use them, where those goods can effectively be used for the purposes for which those goods were designed, and the utility services required for those purposes are connected to those goods." Under this definition, the property would be "completed" and the initial interval would commence if the utilities had been connected, even if Surefire had not yet completed its internal finishing or fitting out work. For the purposes of this example, it is assumed that Surefire's completion date is 1 May 2010.

[3–13] Under Section 12E(1), the initial interval ends 12 months after it commences. Consequently, unless the capital goods owner disposes of the property during the initial interval, then the initial interval is always 12 months long. In the Surefire example above, the first interval would therefore end on 30 April 2011.

[3–14] The end of the initial interval would not necessarily correspond with the end of the capital goods owner's accounting year. The accounting year is defined in Section 1 of the VAT Act as *"a period of 12 months ending on 31 December, but if a taxable person customarily makes up accounts for periods of 12 months ending on another fixed date, then for such a person, a period of 12 months ending on that particular fixed date".*

Example – second interval

The second interval is defined in Section 12E(1) as *"the period beginning on the day following the end of the initial interval in the adjustment period applicable to that capital good and ending on the final day of the accounting year during which the second interval begins."*

In the case of Surefire, for example, the second interval would therefore commence on 1 May 2011. If it is assumed that Surefire normally makes up accounts to 31 December, then the second interval would run from 1 May 2011 to 31 December 2011, i.e. it would be nine months long rather than the full 12 months.

Example – subsequent interval

Under Section 12E(1), the subsequent interval is defined as *"each accounting year of a capital goods owner in the adjustment period applicable to that capital good, which follows the second interval".*

In the Surefire example, the first subsequent interval would commence on 1 January 2012. This would effectively be the start of the third interval. It would be 12 months long, i.e. it would end on 31 December 2012. All subsequent intervals in the CGS would end on 31 December, unless the property is subsequently sold mid-interval.

The CGS would end at the end of the 20th interval, i.e. in this case it would end on 31 December 2029. Alternatively, Surefire's CGS obligations would end before that date if it disposes of the property.

Changing the accounting year

As each interval from the second interval onwards ends on the same date as the capital goods owner's accounting year, some provisions were necessary to allow for changes of accounting year.

[3–15]

The Value-Added Tax (Amendment) Regulations 2008 introduced a new Regulation 21A into the Value-Added Tax Regulations 2006 to deal with changes to the capital goods owner's accounting year in *subsequent* intervals.

The first interval would also be 12 months long, i.e. it is independent of the accounting year. The second interval may not be 12 months long because it ends on the last day of the accounting year. However, Regulation 21A does not address changes of accounting year in the second interval. Revenue has acknowledged in e-brief 37/2008, FAQs published in July 2008 in relation to the new legislation that *"the practical application of the CGS may give rise in certain circumstances to some issues and some flexibility will be considered as these issues come to light"* (see Appendix 2).

[3–16]

In relation to subsequent intervals, i.e. intervals which are neither the first nor the second interval, Regulation 21A(1) provides that the general rule would be that *"the duration of that subsequent interval shall be a period of 12 months from the start date of that subsequent interval and in such circumstances, starting from and including the first day following the end of that subsequent interval, the remaining subsequent intervals in the adjustment period shall be consecutive periods of 12 months"*.

[3–17]

Example – changing the accounting year

In the case of Surefire above, the company's accounting year is initially 31 December. Consequently all intervals from the second interval inclusive onwards end on 31 December. If in the fifth interval Surefire changes its accounting year to, say, 31 March, then the general rule is that the subsequent intervals would then fall out of step with the accounting year, i.e. they would continue to follow the 31 December pattern.

However, Regulation 21A(b) provides for alternative procedures.

In the case of Surefire, the new accounting year ends on 31 March 2014, i.e. three months after it began on 1 January 2014. Regulation 21(A)(b)(ii) provides that if the accounting year ends less than 12 months from the start date of the relevant interval, then the capital goods owner may, instead of retaining the original interval end date (31/12/2014), extend the fifth interval to match the end of the new accounting year, i.e. in this case the interval would be extended to 31 March 2015. It would therefore be a 15-month interval and not a 12-month interval.

If Surefire's accounting year is to end on 31 March 2014, then the directors might also simply decide to extend the 2013 accounts, i.e. the accounting year would run from 1 January 2013 to 31 March 2014. The accounting year would be 15 months long, i.e. it would end on 31 March 2014, more than 12 months from the start date of the relevant interval (1 January 2013). This scenario is provided for in Regulation 21A(1)(b)(i). The capital goods owner has the option of extending the 4th interval to a duration of 15 months ending on 31 March 2014.

[3–18] Regulation 21A(2) refers to Section 12E(10) transfers, i.e. transfers of capital goods under Section 3(5)(b)(iii) of the VAT Act. Under Section 12E(10), the transferee takes over the transferor's responsibilities under the capital goods scheme. If such a transfer takes place in a subsequent interval and the transferee's accounting year does not match that of the transferor, the general rule is that the subsequent interval for the transferee will have a duration of 12 months from the date on which the transfer takes place. However, Regulation 21A(2)(b) also allows the interval to be extended in a manner similar to that outlined above.

Various interval-based adjustments

[3–19] Under Sections 12E(4) and (5) of the VAT Act, the capital goods owner is required to review the VAT deductibility position at the end of each interval and if necessary make a VAT adjustment. The adjustment may take the form of additional VAT payable or receivable.

The initial interval adjustment

[3–20] This is dealt with in Section 12E(4) and works slightly differently from most of the other interval-based adjustments.

In order to consider the initial interval adjustment, it is first necessary to consider what VAT the capital goods owner recovered at acquisition. This figure is the *"total tax incurred which was deductible by that owner in accordance with section 12"*, as referred to in Section 12E(4).

Section 12E(3)(b)(i) defines the total tax incurred as *"the amount of tax* **[3–21]** *charged to a capital goods owner in respect of that owner's acquisition or development of a capital good"*. However, depending on the extent to which the capital goods owner estimates the property will be put to a VAT-able use, the proportion of **deductible** VAT may be restricted.

Example – initial interval adjustment

In the case of Surefire, above, let us say that when the building is purchased on 1 May 2010, the directors estimate it will be used for 60% exempt purposes (insurance services) and 40% VAT-able purposes (e.g. administration services). Surefire does not reclaim the full €1,350,000 purchase VAT charged (the *"total tax incurred"*). Instead, it reclaims only 40%, i.e. €540,000 (€1,350,000 × 40%). This is the *"total tax incurred which was deductible ... in accordance with section 12"*, as referred to in Section 12E(4).

As the end of the initial interval approaches, Surefire would be required to review its business to establish whether the VAT deductibility percentages used at the outset have been accurate. If they have, then no VAT adjustment would be required at the end of the initial interval. However, let us say that the actual deductibility percentages at the end of the initial interval are 70% exempt and 30% VAT-able. The company's estimates of the proportion of VAT-able use at the outset were not correct, i.e. the *"initial interval proportion of deductible use ... differs from the proportion of the total tax incurred in relation to that capital good which was deductible ... in accordance with section 12"*. Section 12E(4) requires Surefire to apply the formula set out below to calculate a lump sum of VAT, i.e.:

$$A - B$$

A = the amount of total tax deducted and
B = the total reviewed deductible amount.
A in this case is the original €540,000 deducted. B is 30% of €1,350,000, i.e. €405,000. A − B = €135,000.

Under Section 12E(4)(b)(i), Surefire is required to repay the difference to thé Collector General *"in accordance with Section 19"*, i.e. via its VAT return for the taxable period in which the initial interval ends. In this case the initial interval ends on 30 April 2011. The March–April 2011 VAT 3 would be due for submission no later than 19 May 2011. Surefire would be required to include an

> additional amount of VAT due of €135,000. Although an excess of VAT was claimed at purchase, as long as the adjustment amount is paid promptly, Revenue would not impose an interest payment in these circumstances.
>
> The initial interval adjustment can also work the other way, e.g. Surefire might have found upon review that it had in fact used the building not for 60% exempt purposes but only for 50% exempt purposes. In that case, Section 12E(4)(b)(ii) would entitle it to reclaim a corresponding additional amount of input VAT in the March–April 2011 VAT 3.

[3–22]   There are some terminology points arising from the above that have relevance for the adjustments in future intervals.

Under Section 12E(2), the *"base tax amount"* is defined as the total tax incurred divided by the number of intervals. The base tax amount is therefore based on the amount of VAT which the capital goods owner is **charged** rather than the amount of VAT actually recoverable under Section 12. In this case, the base tax amount would be €1,350,000 divided by 20 = €67,500.

[3–23]   The *"non-deductible amount"* is the difference between the total tax incurred and the total reviewed deductible amount, i.e. in this case €945,000 (€1,350,000 minus 30% of €1,350,000 (€405,000)).

[3–24]   The *"total reviewed deductible amount"* is the total input VAT incurred (€1,350,000 in this case) multiplied by the *"initial interval proportion of deductible use"*, i.e. in this case 30%, so the total reviewed deductible amount is €405,000.

[3–25]   The *"reference deduction amount"* means the amount calculated by dividing the total reviewed deductible amount by the number of intervals in the adjustment period. In this case, the reference deduction amount would be €20,250 (€405,000 divided by 20).

[3–26]   The *"interval deductible amount"* in relation to the second or subsequent interval is the amount calculated by multiplying the **base tax amount** by the proportion of deductible use for that capital good applicable to the relevant interval. In the case of Surefire, let us say that the proportion of VAT-able use has fallen to 20% by the end of the second interval. The interval deductible amount would be 20% of the base tax amount (i.e. the total tax incurred divided by the total number of intervals). In the case of Surefire, the interval deductible amount would therefore be €13,500 (€1,350,000 divided by 20 intervals × 20%). At the end of the second interval, Section 12E(5) requires Surefire to compare the proportion of deductible use for that interval (20%) with the initial interval proportion of deductible use (30%). As there has been a further change in the proportion of deductible use, a VAT adjustment will be required. In this case, the adjustment will be that shown in the example below. It is important to be aware that the adjustment can be favourable or unfavourable, depending on whether the proportion of deductible use in the interval has increased or decreased.

Example – second or subsequent interval adjustment

Surefire's accounting year ends on 31 December. As outlined above, the second interval ends therefore on 31 December 2011.

Section 12E(5)(a)(i) provides that if the proportion of deductible use for the second or subsequent interval differs from the initial proportion of deductible use, then the capital goods owner is required to calculate an adjustment.

An adjustment would only be necessary if the proportion of deductible use for the second or subsequent interval is different from the initial interval proportion of deductible use. In the case of Surefire, for example, an adjustment would be necessary if, upon carrying out the interval review, it emerges that the VAT-able proportion of Surefire's activities taking place in the building is more or less than 30%. As above, let us say that by the end of the second interval, the proportion of deductible use has fallen to 20%. Surefire is required to calculate an adjustment in accordance with the following formula:

$$C - D$$

C = the reference deduction amount, i.e. in the case of Surefire €20,250.

D = the interval deductible amount. This is a percentage of the **base tax** amount (in this case 20% of €67,500 = €13,500).

$C - D$ = €20,250 − €13,500 = €6,750.

Because the proportion of deductible use has fallen from 30% to 20%, then Surefire would be required to repay VAT of €6,750 by 19 January 2012, i.e. by the 19th day of the month following the taxable period in which the second interval ends.

Interval-based adjustments for the subsequent intervals would be made as necessary in the same manner.

"Big Swing" Adjustments

Apart from the possible adjustment at the end of the initial interval, [3–27]
unless a capital good is being disposed of, interval-based adjustments

are based on the reference deduction amount, i.e. the maximum amount of VAT payable or repayable would generally be the base tax amount.

[3 28]   However, under Section 12E(6), if the percentage of VAT-able use differs more than 50 percentage points from the initial interval proportion of deductible use, then a full lump sum VAT adjustment arises. Under Section 12E(6), the VAT adjustment is not based on $\frac{1}{20}$ of the VAT incurred but is based on the total tax incurred, reduced proportionately by the number of intervals which have already expired in the adjustment period.

Example – "Big Swing" Adjustment

In the Surefire example above **(see paragraph 3–12)**, let us say that Surefire's business model changes in the sixth interval. The initial interval proportion of deductible use is 30%, i.e. 30% of Surefire's activities in relation to the capital good in question are VAT-able and this proportion remains constant until the sixth interval. On 1 July 2015, the business switches to administration services completely, i.e. it no longer engages in exempt supplies of insurance services. Surefire is now entitled to 100% input VAT credit in respect of the activities carried on at this property. Under Section 12E(6), the capital goods owner is required to calculate an amount of VAT in accordance with the following formula:

$$(C - D) \times N$$

C = the reference deduction amount, i.e. in the case of Surefire €20,250 (€1,350,000 × 30% divided by 20 intervals).

D = the interval deduction amount = €67,500 (base tax amount (€1,350,000 divided by 20 intervals) multiplied by the proportion of deductible use for the sixth interval, i.e. 100%).

N = the number of full intervals remaining in the adjustment period at the end of the interval in which the "big swing" takes place, plus one. In the case of Surefire, the change of use takes place on 1 July 2015, i.e. in the sixth interval. There are 20 intervals in total, so the number of full intervals remaining is 14. Adding 1 as per the formula, N = 15.

The VAT amount calculated under the formula is therefore:

$$(€20,250 - €67,500) \times 15 = (€708,750)$$

Because the capital good is now passing to 100% VAT-able use, Surefire will be entitled to recover an additional €708,750 of input VAT in the VAT return for the final bi-monthly VAT period in the sixth interval.

Following repayment of the €708,750, Surefire would be in a position where it would have recovered total input VAT of €1,113,750 (€405,000 (see total reviewed deductible amount, above) plus €708,750 under the "big swing" adjustment).

To cross-check this calculation, Surefire would have been entitled to recover five intervals at 30% of the €67,500 base tax amount (€101,250) plus the remaining 15 intervals at 100% of the €67,500 base tax amount (€1,012,500). €101,250 plus €1,012,500 = €1,113,500.

Under Section 12E(6)(a)(iv), following the "big swing" adjustment, the proportion of deductible use for the sixth interval would be treated as if it were the initial interval proportion of deductible use in this case, i.e. for future calculations, the initial interval proportion of deductible use would no longer be 30% but would be 100%. As the legislation indicates, *"all other definition amounts shall be calculated accordingly"*.

The CGS and the option to tax lettings

The letting of property is *prima facie* an exempt supply for VAT purposes. Since 1 July 2008, this *prima facie* exemption prevails regardless of the lease term. Under Section 7A of the VAT Act, a lessor may, subject to conditions, opt to tax a letting, i.e. to make the rents subject to VAT (this is not to be confused with the option to tax the **sale** of a property). Section 7A also provides for the termination of the option to tax a letting. Application or termination of the option to tax a letting would cause a property to pass in to or out of VAT-able use. Consequently, when one or other takes place, it would have potential implications for the CGS in relation to the relevant property.   [3–29]

The general rules for the above scenario are set out in Section 12E(6)(c) and (d) of the VAT Act. If a lessor terminates an option to tax a letting or exercises an option to tax a previously exempt letting, then the lessor is deemed for the purposes of the CGS to have supplied the property and immediately reacquired it. Where the lessor terminates the option to tax, the "supply" is deemed to be exempt, which gives rise to a withdrawal of deductibility already allowed.   [3–30]

Cancelling the option to tax

Under Section 12E(6)(c)(i), if a lessor cancels an option to tax, then the lessor is deemed to make an exempt sale of the property to itself and to immediately reacquire it. Paragraph (ii) provides that the option to tax provided for in Section 4B(5) cannot apply to the deemed sale, i.e. the lessor cannot use the provisions of Section 4B(5) to make the deemed sale taxable rather than exempt. Paragraph (iii) provides that a VAT   [3–31] lump sum on the deemed exempt disposal is to be calculated by the lessor using a formula set out in Section 12(7)(b). The lessor is to repay this to Revenue under the provisions of Section 19 of the VAT Act, i.e. by inclusion in the VAT return for the taxable period in which the option is cancelled.

Example – cancelling the option to tax

Clare acquires a commercial unit on 1 January 2015 for €1,500,000 plus VAT at 13.5% (€202,500). Clare recovers her input VAT and grants a 10-year lease to an alternative healthcare practice. She opts to tax the lease and charges the practice VAT on rents at the standard VAT rate. Towards the end of 2019, a change in VAT legislation exempts the supplies made by the alternative healthcare practice. The partnership will no longer be entitled to recover input VAT from 1 May 2020. The partners approach Clare to discuss this and she agrees to cancel the option to tax with effect from 1 May 2020.

Clare is deemed to make an exempt sale of the property on 1 May 2020, i.e. in the sixth interval of the CGS.

The formula in Section 12E(7)(b) is as follows:

$$\frac{B \times N}{T}$$

B = the total reviewed deductible amount (€202,500).
N = the number of full intervals remaining plus one, i.e. (15).
T = the total number of intervals in the adjustment period (20).

The clawback is therefore €202,500 × 15/20 = €151,875. Clare is required to return this in the May-June 2020 VAT return, which must be filed no later than 19 July 2020.

Under Section 12E(6)(c)(iii), for the purpose of the CGS, Clare's clawback of €151,875 is now deemed to be her *"total tax incurred"*. Her *"non-deductible amount"* is also €151,875, as none of the total tax incurred as defined is currently recoverable due to the exempt use of the property.

Section 12E(6)(c)(iii) expressly provides that Clare is deemed to have acquired a capital good on 1 May 2020. Logically a new "initial interval" would commence on that date. However, it is also possible that the existing interval and adjustment period would simply continue uninterrupted. This matter does not seem to be clear from the legislation.

Exercising the option to tax

[3–32] If a capital good is used for exempt lettings from the time it is acquired/developed, then the capital goods owner would not be entitled to recover any of the input VAT incurred in respect of the acquisition/development costs.

Example – exercising the option to tax

Let us say that Manny Limited acquires a commercial property on 1 February 2015 for €3,000,000 plus VAT at 13.5% (€405,000). It intends to let the property to a bank and has agreed not to exercise its option to tax, on the basis that the bank would not be entitled to recover VAT on rents. It grants a 20-year lease to Sand Bank on 1 February 2015. Manny Limited's total tax incurred is €405,000. This is also its non-deductible amount under the legislation.

At the end of the first interval, the total reviewed deductible amount is "nil", on the basis that the letting is exempt. In 2020 (i.e. in the sixth interval) Sand Bank informs Manny Limited that it intends to relocate its banking activities from 1 July. It will move its commercial leasing division into the property. Sand Bank has no objection to Manny Limited's opting to tax the lease from that date, as it would be entitled to recover VAT on rents in relation to the offices to be used by the commercial leasing division. Manny Limited makes up its accounts to 31 December.

If Manny Limited proceeds with the option to tax, it would be deemed to have deducted a proportion of the input VAT on the property to reflect the principle that it is now passing from an exempt to a VAT-able use. Under Section 12E(6)(d)(i) of the VAT Act, Manny Limited would be deemed to have supplied and simultaneously reacquired the property. Under paragraph (ii), the deemed sale would be considered to be subject to VAT. Under paragraph (iii)(I), the formula provided in Section 12E(7)(a) would be used to calculate Manny Limited's deemed total tax incurred, as defined.

The formula in Section 12E(7)(a) is as follows:

$$\frac{E \times N}{T}$$

E = the non-deductible amount (€405,000).
N = the number of full intervals remaining in the adjustment period plus one (15).
T = the total number of intervals in the adjustment period (20).

Manny Limited would therefore claim an input VAT credit of €405,000 × 15/20 = €303,750 via its July-August 2020 VAT 3.

Because Manny Limited is deemed to reacquire the property on 1 July 2020, then 1 July 2020 would appear to be the beginning of a "new" initial interval. However, as before, this matter is not dealt with in the legislation.

Under Section 12E(6)(d), the total tax incurred is €405,000. This is also the total reviewed deductible amount calculated at the end of the initial interval. If there are no further changes in the extent to which the property is put to a taxable use, then no interval-based adjustments should arise for the remainder of the adjustment period.

[3–33]   Revenue has confirmed in e-brief 37/2008: FAQs 2008 VAT on Property (see Appendix 2) that in its view, a refund of purchase VAT (a CGS positive adjustment) does **not** arise when a lessor had a short-term letting pre 1 July 2008 without a waiver and opts to tax it on or after 1 July 2008.

Periods of disuse

[3–34]   Periods of disuse of a capital good are almost inevitable, whether they arise from a delay moving into the completed property or a gap between tenants during the adjustment period.

The legislation provides that the capital goods owner does not suffer an input VAT clawback as a result of a period of disuse.

[3–35]   Section 12E(4)(c) deals with periods of disuse in the initial interval.

> "Where a capital good is not used during the initial interval then the initial interval proportion of deductible use is the proportion of the total input tax incurred that is deductible by the capital goods owner in accordance with section 12."

This subsection provides that no adjustment is necessary at the end of the initial interval if the capital good has not been used during the first interval, i.e. the original input VAT entitlement under Section 12 of the VAT Act stands. The capital goods owner will effectively be able to rely on deductibility under Section 12 of the VAT Act based on his/her *intended* use for the property.

Example – period of disuse in the initial interval

High Hopes Limited engages a builder to develop a new head office for its property management business. The business gives rise to a 100% input VAT deductibility entitlement and consequently High Hopes Limited claims back all of the input VAT which the builder charges. High Hopes Limited makes up its accounts to 31 December.

The building is completed as defined on 1 January 2011. However, High Hopes Limited subsequently finds that for a number of reasons it would be preferable to avoid surrendering the lease of its existing rented head office until 31 December 2011. Consequently, it does not move into its new head office premises until early in January 2012. The initial interval nonetheless commences on 1 January 2011, as the building is completed on that date. A review is required under the CGS at the end of the initial interval, i.e. on 31 December 2011. Although the building has not been used in the initial interval, Section 12E(4)(c) provides that the initial interval proportion of deductible use is the proportion of the total input tax incurred that is deductible by the capital goods owner in accordance with Section 12, i.e. in this case the initial interval proportion of deductible use is still 100%.

As a result the total reviewed deductible amount as defined is equal to the total tax incurred as defined. The reference deduction amount as defined is the same as the "base tax" amount, as defined. No adjustment is required under the capital goods scheme.

What happens if the gap period is in a subsequent interval? Section 12E (5)(b) states that: [3-36]

"Where for the second or any subsequent interval, a capital good is not used during that interval, the proportion of deductible use in respect of that capital good for that interval shall be the proportion of deductible use for the previous interval."

Example – period of disuse in a subsequent interval

Peter purchases a commercial property on 1 May 2011, claims back the input VAT and grants a five-year lease to Maggie. He accounts for VAT on rents for the term of Maggie's lease. Maggie's lease ends on 30 April 2016 and she vacates the property. Peter is unable to find a new tenant until 1 September 2017. He opts to tax this lease also. When Peter reviews the VAT position towards the end of 2016, he does not have to make an adjustment even though the property is vacant at that date. Instead Section 12E(5)(b) provides that *"the proportion of deductible use ... is ... the proportion of deductible use for the previous interval"*, i.e. 100%.

Destruction of the capital good

[3–37]   Section 12E(11) provides that:

> *"If a capital good is destroyed during the adjustment period in relation to that capital good, then no further adjustment under this section shall be made by the capital goods owner in respect of any remaining intervals in the adjustment period in relation to that capital good."*

This provision confirms that destruction of a capital good is not an adjusting event. For example, there would be no requirement to repay input VAT reclaimed on the basis that the property would no longer be put to a VAT-able use. Some practical difficulties might be envisaged based on how the term "destroyed" is defined in practice.

Disposing of immovable property

Sales to which VAT applies

[3–38]   If a capital good is sold during the adjustment period and it is still "new" under the two- or five-year rules, then the vendor is required to charge the purchaser VAT on the sales consideration. Assuming that the purchaser was fully entitled to recover input VAT arising upon the acquisition of the property, this approach is reasonably equitable and seems as VAT-neutral as possible.

[3–39]   However, a vendor who was **not** entitled to recover 100% input VAT in respect of the capital good is still required to account for output VAT in respect of the full sales consideration. Section 12E(7)(a) allows such a vendor to reclaim a proportion of deductible VAT upon the disposal of the property.

> *Example – VAT-able sale of a property where the vendor was not entitled to recover 100% input VAT*
>
> MediQuack purchased a building for its practice on 1 March 2009. 50% of the building was to be used for VAT-able alternative medicine services, whereas the other half was occupied by general medical practitioners. The building cost €5,000,000 plus VAT at 13.5% (€675,000). MediQuack makes up its accounts to 31 December.
>
> MediQuack soon needed a bigger premises, and agreed to dispose of the existing building to a GP practice for €6,000,000 plus VAT. The sale closed on 1 March 2011, i.e. during the 3rd interval. As MediQuack's sale consideration will be fully subject to VAT,

Section 12E(7)(a) entitles it to use the following formula to calculate an additional input VAT credit on the occasion of the sale:

$$\frac{E \times N}{T}$$

E = the non-deductible VAT (in this case €337,500, i.e. 50% of €675,000).

N = the number of full intervals remaining in the adjustment period plus one (in this case 18).

T = the total number of intervals in the adjustment period (20).

MediQuack is therefore allowed to claim a credit of €303,750 in its March–April 2011 VAT return (€337,500 × 18/20). It is also required to account for additional output VAT of €810,000 (€6,000,000 × 13.5%).

Effectively, MediQuack is treated as if the property is passing to a fully VAT-able use at the date of sale. This makes sense on the basis that the sale is fully VAT-able.

Its total VAT recovery is €641,250 (€337,500 plus €303,750). This corresponds to 50% of 2/20 of the total tax incurred (€675,000 × 2/20 × 50% = €33,750) plus 100% of 18/20 of the total tax incurred (€675,000 × 18/20 × 100% = €607,500). €607,500 plus €33,750 = €641,250, i.e. the total VAT recovery.

Exempt sales

Sales of capital goods within the adjustment period but outside of the "new" period are *prima facie* exempt. If the vendor recovered some or all of the input VAT upon acquiring the property and if the vendor and purchaser do not opt to tax the sale (see paragraph **2–66**), then the vendor will suffer a clawback of input VAT under Section 12E(7)(b) of the VAT Act.

[3–40]

Example – Exempt sale where the vendor was entitled to recover all or some input VAT

Let us say that MediQuack in the above example does not sell the building until 1 March 2018, i.e. the 10th interval. All other circumstances are the same. Because the purchasers would not be entitled to recover input VAT, MediQuack agrees that the option to tax will not apply to the sale. Consequently, the sale is exempt. Where does this leave MediQuack? It is not required to account for any VAT on the sale of the building. However, it recovered 50% of the total tax incurred when it acquired the building in 2009. Under Section 12E(7)(b), in these circumstances, MediQuack is required to use the following formula to calculate an additional amount of VAT which it would account for in its March–April 2018 VAT return:

$$\frac{B \times N}{T}$$

B = the total reviewed deductible amount (in this case €337,500).
N = the number of full intervals remaining plus one (in this case 11).
T = the total number of intervals (20).

Applying the formula, MediQuack repays €185,625 (€337,500 × 11/20). Effectively, it has recovered net input VAT of €151,875 (the original €337,500 minus the €185,625 clawed back on the occasion of the exempt sale). The total tax incurred originally was €675,000. MediQuack is treated as if it has used the building for 50% VAT-able activities for a nine-year period, i.e. it is entitled to recover €675,000 × 9/20 × 50% = €151,875.

Tenant refurbishments

[3-41]   Under Section 12E(3), refurbishment means development on a previously completed building, structure or engineering work. (See Chapter 4 below for more detail on the concept of development). Refurbishment only arises when:

1. the work carried out constitutes development, as defined; and

2. the property being developed has already been completed, as defined.

Example – tenant refurbishment

The general rule set out in Section 12E(8)(a) provides that if a lease is assigned or surrendered and the tenant has undertaken refurbishment work and the assignment or surrender takes place before the 10-year adjustment period in respect of the refurbishment has ended, then the tenant is required to calculate a VAT lump sum in accordance with the formula set out in Section 12E(7)(b).

Let us say that John grants a VAT-able 25-year lease to DIY Limited on 1 May 2007. On 1 March 2010, DIY Limited completes development work on the property. This refurbishment work costs €250,000 plus VAT at 13.5% (€33,750). DIY Limited is entitled to recover 100% of the input VAT. DIY Limited makes up its accounts to 31 December. On 31 May 2012 (i.e. during the third interval in relation to the refurbishment) DIY Limited surrenders the lease to John. For VAT purposes, it is effectively surrendering two capital goods, i.e. the original property subject to the lease and also the refurbishment work.

To look at the surrender of the refurbishment first:

The formula set out in Section 12E(7)(b) is:

$$\frac{B \times N}{T}$$

B = the total reviewed deductible amount, i.e. in this case €33,750.
N = the number of full intervals remaining in the adjustment period in relation to the refurbishment at the time of surrender plus one. In this case therefore, N = 8.
T = the total number of intervals (10).

The VAT lump sum is therefore €33,750 × 8/10 = €27,000. The general rule set out in Section 12E(8)(a) provides that upon surrendering the lease to John, DIY Limited is required to repay this amount of VAT via its May-June 2012 VAT 3.

However, Section 12E(8)(b) provides that DIY Limited can avoid the clawback in the above example if:

(i) it was entitled to recover all of the VAT initially suffered in respect of the refurbishment **and**

(ii) it enters into a written agreement with John confirming that he will take over DIY Limited's responsibilities under the CGS **and**

(iii) DIY Limited provides John with a copy of its capital good record.

In these circumstances, John effectively steps into the shoes of DIY Limited in respect of the refurbishment as John had originally undertaken the refurbishment himself.

Refurbishment constitutes a capital good that is separate to the underlying property. Under Section 12E(3)(a), the adjustment period for refurbishment is 10 years, rather than the standard 20 years. [3-42]

Section 12E(8) contains particular provisions to address the CGS position when a tenant, rather than the lessor, has carried out refurbishment and then surrenders or assigns the lease. The tenant in this case would be a capital goods owner in respect of the refurbishment. [3-43]

Section 12E(8)(d) specifies that the above provisions do not arise if the refurbishment is destroyed. Destruction might arise for example if DIY Limited were able to dismantle or remove all of its refurbishment before the surrender. [3-44]

Similar provisions would arise if DIY Limited were to assign the lease instead of surrendering it.

[3–45]   In the above example, not only does a VAT issue arise in relation to the refurbishment, the tenant also surrenders a legacy lease, i.e. a long lease which was granted to it before 1 July 2008. As seen previously, the legacy lease is also a capital good. (See Chapter 5 in relation to the surrender of legacy leases.)

[3–46]   Finally, Revenue has confirmed in its e-brief 37/2008 (reproduced in Appendix 2) that if a lease simply expires under the lease terms (as opposed to being assigned or surrendered), then there would be no obligation on the tenant to apply adjustment provisions in relation to any refurbishment, assuming that the adjustment period in respect of the refurbishment is ongoing on the lease expiration date. Revenue has also pointed out that it would "examine cases" where a tenant seeks input credit in respect of refurbishment close to the date when a lease is due to expire.

Disposal of a capital good as part of a transfer of a business

[3–47]   Section 12E contains detailed provisions for the VAT treatment of capital goods that form part of the assets in a Section 3(5)(b)(iii) transfer of business.

Section 3(5)(b)(iii) provides that the transfer of ownership of goods being the *"totality of assets, or part thereof, of a business even if that business or part thereof had ceased trading, where those transferred assets constitute an undertaking or part of an undertaking capable of being operated on an independent basis shall be deemed … not to be a supply of the goods"*.

[3–48]   From a VAT perspective, two types of building can transfer in a Section 3(5)(b)(iii) transfer of trade:

1. a building the transfer of which would have been subject to VAT *except for* the application of Section 3(5)(b)(iii); and

2. a building in relation to the transfer of which the vendor would not have been required to charge VAT due to the operation of Section 4B(2), i.e. the building was no longer "new" under the two- or five-year rule.

[3–49]   Section 12E(7)(c) contains limited guidance as to how to address the VAT position when only **part** of a capital good transfers under Section 3(5)(b)(iii) and the remainder is retained.

Transfer subject to VAT but for Section 3(5)(b)(iii)

Under normal circumstances, when VAT arises on the sale of a capital [3-50]
good, it arises on the full sales consideration. This is a fair provision if
the vendor has been entitled to recover full input VAT. In those circumstances, disposing of the capital good under Section 3(5)(b)(iii) has no
negative implication for the vendor. S/he has already recovered all the
input VAT in respect of the capital good.

A vendor who has *not* been entitled to recover full input VAT would [3-51]
also be required to charge VAT in respect of the full sales consideration
if the property is "new" as defined, if it were not for Section 3(5)(b)(iii).
Section 12E(7)(a) provides that upon disposal, such a vendor would be
treated as if using the property for fully VAT-able purposes for the
remainder of the adjustment period, i.e. the vendor would be entitled to
recover additional input VAT under a formula set out as follows:

Example – vendor disposing of VAT-able capital good

Consultus Limited is engaged in management consultancy and
training. It purchases a new premises on 1 March 2009 for €4,000,000
plus VAT at 13.5% (€540,000). 30% of its turnover is from exempt
training activities and consequently it recovers 70% of the input
VAT, i.e. €378,000. Its non-deductible VAT is therefore €162,000.
On 30 September 2010, Consultus Limited sells the business to
Cerebellum Limited. The transfer falls under Section 3(5)(b)(iii) of
the VAT Act. Consequently, the transfer is deemed not to be a
supply for VAT purposes and Consultus Limited does not charge
VAT on the sale of its assets, including the premises.

In its VAT return for September-October 2010, Consultus Limited
is entitled to recover an amount of deductible VAT as if it were
putting the property to a fully VAT-able use for the remainder of
the adjustment period. This amount is calculated as follows:

€162,000 (the non-deductible VAT) × 19/20 = €153,900.

In total, Consultus therefore recovers input VAT of €531,900,
i.e. €378,000 initially plus €153,900 via the adjustment upon disposal. It is effectively treated as if it had used the property for a
fully VAT-able purpose for 19 years out of the 20 years in the
adjustment period (€540,000 × 19/20 = €513,000) and had 70%
deductibility for one interval (€540,000 × 1/20 × 70% = €18,900)
(€513,000 + €18,900 = €531,900).

Example – transferee acquiring VAT-able capital good

Arising from the above example, what is Cerebellum's VAT position in relation to the transfer of the property?

Under Section 12E(1)(b), it acquires a capital good. Under Section 12E(3)(b)(ii)(II), the *"total tax incurred"* is the amount of VAT which **would** have been chargeable but for the application of Section 3(5)(b)(iii).

Consequently, if the consideration for the premises alone is, say, €4,500,000 when Cerebellum acquires the building, Cerebellum will be deemed to have paid €4,500,000 plus VAT at 13.5% (€607,500). For the purpose of the CGS, Cerebellum will be treated as if it had recovered €607,500 of input VAT.

The position would be somewhat different if the nature of Cerebellum's business is such that it is only entitled to partial recovery under Section 12 of the VAT Act. This situation is dealt with under Section 12E(7)(d) of the VAT Act. For example, let us say that Cerebellum is engaged in 40% exempt training activities and 60% VAT-able management consultancy.

Under Section 12E(7)(d), on its acquisition of the building, Cerebellum would be required to account for 40% of the VAT it **would** have suffered on the purchase of the building if Section 3(5)(b)(iii) had **not** applied. The logic behind the provision is to prevent Section 3(5)(b)(iii) from effectively removing the premises from the VAT "net" altogether. As it acquires the building on 30 September 2010, then under Section 12E(7)(d), Cerebellum would be required to account for the following amount of VAT via its September-October 2009 VAT return:

$$F - G$$

Where F is the amount of VAT that **would** have been charged on the capital good but for the operation of Section 3(5)(b)(iii) (in this case €607,500) and

G is the amount of VAT which Cerebellum would have been entitled to deduct under Section 12 of the VAT Act (in this case €364,500, or 60% of €607,500).

$F - G$ (€607,500 − €364,500) = €243,000.

Consequently, Cerebellum has to account for €243,000 of purchase VAT in respect of its acquisition of the building, notwithstanding that Section 3(5)(b)(iii) applied to the transfer. This is its "total tax incurred" for the purposes of the CGS.

Had Section 3(5)(b)(iii) not applied to this transfer, Cerebellum would have paid VAT on the sale consideration for the premises amounting to €607,500. It would only have been entitled to recover 60% of same under Section 12 of the VAT Act. Consequently, it would not have been entitled to recover the remaining 40% of the input VAT, i.e. €243,000.

$$\frac{E \times N}{T}$$

E = the non-deductible VAT incurred at acquisition/development.
N = the number of full intervals remaining in the adjustment period plus one.
T = the total number of intervals in the adjustment period.

These provisions are an important element in preserving VAT neutrality in the CGS. Section 12E(7)(d) is comparable to Section 12D(4), which applied to similar transfers until 30 June 2008. **[3–52]**

Transfer would have been exempt under Section 4B(2) even without Section 3(5)(b)(iii)

If a capital good is "old" under the five- and two-year criteria in Section 4B(2), and is disposed of during its adjustment period, then the vendor does not charge VAT on the sale, even if s/he has recovered input VAT when acquiring/developing the property. However, in these circumstances, unless the vendor opts to tax the sale, it is liable for a proportionate clawback of the input VAT which was originally reclaimed in respect of that capital good. **[3–53]**

If an "old" property transfers under Section 3(5)(b)(iii), the transfer is deemed not to be a supply for VAT purposes. Consequently, the option to tax cannot be exercised, even if the vendor wishes to avoid a potential clawback of input VAT. **[3–54]**

Section 12E(10) of the VAT Act provides measures for dealing with the transfer of capital goods under these circumstances. The vendor is required to give the purchaser a copy of the capital goods record under Section 12E(10)(a) and the purchaser effectively replaces the vendor in respect of the CGS. The net result is that the transferor does not suffer any clawback of input VAT and the transferee operates the CGS in respect of the capital good transferred for the remainder of the existing adjustment period. **[3–55]**

[3–56]   In these circumstances, the transferor is required under the legislation to provide the transferee with a copy of the transferor's capital good record (some commentary on the capital good record is made later in this chapter).

Example – transfer of "exempt" capital good under Section 3(5)(b)(iii)

Ken buys a premises on 1 June 2012 at a cost of €1,000,000 plus VAT at 13.5% (€135,000). Ken makes up his annual accounts to 31 December. He runs his fully VAT-able auto repair shop from the premises until 30 September 2018, i.e. the seventh interval, at which point he sells the business to PistonsRUs Limited under Section 3(5)(b)(iii) of the VAT Act. The total consideration paid by PistonsRUs is €2,000,000, of which €1,500,000 is for the premises. The premises is no longer new, i.e. disposal of it would *prima facie* be exempt under Section 4B(2) of the VAT Act, even if Section 3(5)(b)(iii) did not apply. However, under Section 12E(10), the transfer is dealt with as follows:

Ken is required to provide PistonsRUs with a copy of the capital good record, PistonsRUs takes over all of the obligations under the capital goods scheme, as if it had acquired the property itself on 1 June 2012 and as if Ken had carried out any adjustments under the CGS which he was required to make. Under Section 12(3)(b)(ii)(I), the total tax incurred for PistonsRUs is that which is required to be included in the copy of the capital good record provided to PistonsRUs by Ken, i.e. the total tax incurred by Ken originally. In other words, the total tax incurred is the VAT on Ken's purchase price of €1,000,000 as opposed to VAT on the €1,500,000 which the parties agreed was the part of the consideration attaching to the capital good.

It may be that PistonsRUs would have a different accounting year from Ken (see paragraphs **3–15** to **3–18** in relation to changes of accounting year, at paragraph **3–16)**. Regulation 21A (2) of the Value-Added Tax (Amendment) Regulations 2008 makes specific reference to Section 12E(10) transfers. When the transferee's accounting year does not match that of the transferor, the general rule is that the subsequent interval for the transferee will have a duration of 12 months from the date on which the transfer takes place. However, Regulation 21A(2)(b) also allows the interval to be extended, as outlined at paragraph **3–17**.

Transfers of trade when the vendor retains part of the capital good

[3–57]   Section 12E(7)(c) provides that when such a transfer takes place, the vendor adjusts the total tax incurred, the total reviewed deductible amount and all other definition amounts *"on a fair and reasonable basis"*.

While the provision is not specific as to what this might mean, it seems logical to assume that some sort of value-based apportionment might be carried out.

In the case of Ken, above, Ken might decide to retain a room in part **[3–58]** of the premises where he would renovate classic cars. The original parts business and most of the original premises would still be sold to PistonsRUs under Section 3(5)(b)(iii), but a decision would have to be made as to the value of that part of the capital good to be retained by Ken. In the above case, if €150,000 of the original €1,000,000 consideration is deemed to correspond to the room to be retained, then logically the capital good record to be passed to PistonsRUs would be amended to show that the "total tax incurred" from its perspective would be based on a purchase consideration of €850,000 instead of €1,000,000. Ken would also have to retain a copy of the original capital good record and amend it to show his own "total tax incurred" based on his original purchase price of €150,000.

Disposals between connected persons

Section 12E(9) deals with transfers of capital goods between connected **[3–59]** persons, as defined. It applies to **all** taxable transfers of capital goods between connected persons, whether or not the provisions of Section 3(5)(b)(iii) apply.

The section contains two formulae. The first is used to calculate an **[3–60]** "adjustment amount", which consists of the total tax incurred to which the vendor was entitled upon acquisition of the capital good, adjusted to reflect the number of intervals for which it has been used. The second formula compares this adjustment amount with the amount of output VAT to which the consideration agreed between the connected parties will give rise. If the output VAT is less than the adjustment amount, then the vendor is required to repay additional VAT corresponding to the difference upon disposing of the property.

Example – disposal of capital good between connected persons

Mr Brown builds a commercial unit at a total cost of €3,500,000 plus VAT at 13.5% (€472,500). The unit is completed on 1 July 2009. Mr Brown intends to use the unit for the purpose of fully VAT-able supplies and consequently he recovers all of the input VAT. He commences to carry on a fully taxable trade on the premises. Mr Brown makes up accounts to 31 December.

On 1 July 2013, i.e. in the fifth interval, Mr Brown decides to sell the unit to his daughter, Tess. The building is no longer "new" as defined and they opt to tax the sale. The disposal consideration agreed is €2,000,000 plus VAT. Tess will continue to use the unit for fully VAT-able supplies.

Mr Brown and his daughter are connected, as defined under Section 7A(3) of the VAT Act. Consequently, under Section 12E(9), Mr Brown is initially required to calculate an "adjustment amount" as follows:

$$\frac{H \times N}{T}$$

where –

H is the total tax incurred in relation to that capital good for the capital goods owner making the supply or transfer (in this case €472,500).
N is the number of full intervals remaining in the adjustment period in relation to that capital good plus one (in this case 16).
T is the total number of intervals in the adjustment period in relation to that capital good (20).

The adjustment amount in this case is therefore €472,500 × 16/20 = €378,000.

The VAT arising on the proposed sale consideration is €270,000 (€2,000,000 × 13.5%).

Mr Brown is then required to apply the second formula:

$$I - J$$

I = the adjustment amount (€378,000 in this case).
J = the VAT on the proposed sale consideration (€270,000 in this case).

I − J = €108,000 in this case (€378,000 − €270,000). Under Section 12E(9), Mr Brown is required to pay additional VAT of €108,000 via his July–August 2013 VAT return. Interestingly, the legislation does not state whether this additional VAT is to be treated as a repayment of input VAT or an additional amount of output VAT.

Ultimately in this case Mr Brown accounts for €378,000 of VAT when he disposes of the capital good to Tess (€270,000 plus €108,000 = €378,000). This corresponds to 16/20 of the original €472,500 input VAT which he reclaimed.

[3–61]   The operation and application of Section 12E(9) is an anti-avoidance mea-sure similar in operation to the economic value test which existed under Section 4(3A) of the VAT Act, which no longer has application after

30 June 2008. In the same manner as the economic value test, Section 12E(9) prevents VAT "leakage". Section 12D(9) applies to the transfer of a capital good, i.e. it has no application to lettings. The economic value test applied to the creation and transfer of long leases, as these were treated as supplies of goods under the VAT regime in place until 30 June 2008.

The capital goods record

Section 12E(12) provides that a capital goods owner *"shall create and* **[3–62]** *maintain a record (in this section referred to as a 'capital good record') in respect of each capital good and that record shall contain sufficient information to determine any adjustments in respect of that capital good required in accordance with this section".*

Section 12E(13) provides that: **[3–63]**

> *"The Revenue Commissioners may make regulations necessary for the purposes of the operation of this section, in particular in relation to the duration of a subsequent interval where the accounting year of a capital goods owner changes."*

Details are provided in Regulation 3 of the Value-Added Tax (Amend-   **[3–64]** ment) Regulations 2008. Regulation 3 replaces the existing paragraph (u) of the Value-Added Tax Regulations 2006 (S.I. No. 548 of 2006).

Under the new provision, the capital goods record is required to show the following information:

"(i)   *the total tax incurred,*

(ii)   *the amount of the total tax incurred which is deductible in accordance with section 12 of the Act,*

(iii) *the date on which the adjustment period begins,*

(iv)   *the number of intervals in the adjustment period,*

(v)   *the initial interval proportion of deductible use,*

(vi)   *the total reviewed deductible amount,*

(vii) *the proportion of deductible use for each interval,*

(viii) *details of any adjustments required to be made in accordance with section 12E and*

(ix)   *details of any sale or transfer of the capital good or details of any assignment or surrender of a lease where section 12E(8)(b) applies in relation to that capital good."*

[3–65]   Capital goods owners will need to ensure that they observe the requirement to keep the capital good record and are familiar with the information required. Under the legislation, the responsibility for maintaining the capital good record remains with the capital goods owner. However, in many cases it may make practical sense for an external accountant to be designated to deal with same on behalf of the capital goods owner, particularly given that it is unlikely to be possible to finalise a client's accounts unless it can be established that the capital goods record is in order. It will also be necessary to have the appropriate systems in place to ensure that the maintenance of the capital goods record and the necessary adjustments are dealt with efficiently.

[3–66]   As indicated previously, a separate record is to be kept for each capital good, including refurbishment. According to Revenue's Notes for Guidance, the capital good record will be checked by Revenue in audit situations.

[3–67]   Certain sections of the legislation provide that the purchaser of a capital good would step into the shoes of the vendor. This can apply for example in relation to transfers of capital goods which take place under Section 12E(10) of the VAT Act as part of transfers of business. In relation to Section 12E(10) transfers, the transferor is **required** under the legislation to supply a copy of the capital good record to the transferee. Provision of the capital good record may, therefore, need to be considered when certain capital goods are being transferred.

Chapter 4

The Supply of Non-Transitional Property

Introduction

Section 4B sets out the new general rules in relation to supplies of freehold interests and "freehold equivalent interests" (as defined) in immovable goods (see below). [4–01]

Before the changes introduced in the first Finance Act 2008, the general rules for supplies of property were contained to a large extent in Section 4 of the VAT Act. However, with effect from 1 July 2008, the new Section 4(11) confines the application of Section 4 to a small number of specified situations relating to disposals of transitional property (see Chapter 5). The new general rules for supplies of property are now contained in Section 4B. Some exceptions/variations for transitional properties are set out in Section 4C.

While there is interaction between the new Section 4B and the rules for the operation of the CGS set down in Section 12E, it is helpful to remember that the function of Sections 4B and 4C is to determine whether a supply is subject to VAT, whereas generally speaking the function of Section 12E is to determine how much of the VAT is chargeable or recoverable. [4–02]

Freehold equivalent interests

Section 4B applies not only to supplies of freehold interests but also to *"freehold equivalent interests"*. [4–03]

The concept of the freehold equivalent interest (FEI) was introduced under the Finance Act 2008 via a new Section 1C in Section 3 of the VAT Act. The definition was simplified in the Finance (No. 2) Act 2008.

[4-04]   In Section 3(1C) a supply of immovable goods is defined as including:

> *"the transfer in substance of the right to dispose of immovable goods as owner or the transfer in substance of the right to dispose of immovable goods."*

[4-05]   Revenue points out at paragraph 2.7 of its *VAT on Property Guide* from April 2008 (see Appendix 1) that *"the transfer of the right to dispose of property as owner is usually regarded as taking place when the contract for sale of the property is completed. It is not necessary that the legal title to the property has been transferred to the purchaser. It is sufficient that the purchaser has acquired, in substance, the right to dispose of the property"*.

[4-06]   Deposits are often paid in connection with the supply of immovable goods. In the ECJ Case C-277/05 *Société Thermale d'Eugénie-les-Bains v. Ministère de l'Economie des Finances et de l'Industrie*, the Court held that deposits are not subject to VAT if retained due to purchaser default. The Court saw the retention of the deposit as compensation for the loss suffered by the would-be supplier. The deposit was not considered to be subject to VAT because it had no direct connection with any supply. Following the judgment, Revenue issued a notice outlining its approach to the VAT treatment of forfeited deposits and cancellation charges. Revenue regards the payment of a deposit as a prepayment and therefore prima facie subject to VAT if the underlying supply is subject to VAT. However, it confirms that if the purchaser subsequently fails to proceed and the deposit is not refunded, then the supplier may reclaim the VAT previously accounted for in relation to the deposit.

In any event, if a deposit is held by a solicitor or similar and the vendor has no access to it, then no VAT liability would arise until such time as it is transferred to the vendor.

[4-07]   Prior to the enactment of the Finance (No. 2) Act 2008 on 24 December 2008, the new definition of a supply of immovable goods also contained a second paragraph dealing with cases where the holder of an interest in immovable property contracted to transfer certain rights in exchange for consideration amounting to 50% or more of the open market value of the immovable goods payable before or at the making of the agreement or within five years of same, i.e. the definition also contained a part (b), which read:

"… transactions where the holder of an estate or interest in immovable goods enters into a contract or agreement with another person in relation to the creation, establishment, alteration, surrender, relinquishment or termination of rights in respect of those immovable goods, apart from mortgages, and consideration or payments which amount to 50% or more of the open market value of the immovable goods at the time the contract or agreement is concluded are payable pursuant to or associated with the contract or agreement or otherwise either before the making of the contract or agreement or within 5 years of the commencement of such contract or agreement."

Part (b) was removed with effect from the date of the passing of the Finance (No. 2) Act 2008. However, both paragraphs were in the legislation between 1 July and 24 December 2008 and this may give rise to some confusion in a limited number of cases.

The legislation as it now stands deals with the supply of a freehold **[4–08]** property much as it was understood under the old regime. It includes the supply of very long ownership-type leasehold interests. From a VAT perspective, the grant of shorter non-ownership-type leases constitutes the supply of a service rather than the supply of an immovable good. Lettings of property are dealt with in Sections 7A and 7B of the VAT Act (see Chapter 6).

Revenue has repeated at paragraph 2.5 of its *VAT on Property Guide* that: **[4–09]**

"…a person who engages in a single property transaction on a once-off basis may be acting in the course of business. For example, a person who constructs or arranges for the construction of a residence on the site of an existing dwelling for subsequent sale would be regarded as acting in the course of business, even if the site was part of the grounds of that person's private residence."

Option to buy immovable property

Following an Appeal Commissioners case in 2003, Revenue accepts **[4–10]** that payment for granting an option in relation to buy immovable property should be accorded the same VAT treatment as the underlying property. In other words, if the supply of the underlying property is not subject to VAT, then a payment received in relation to the grant of the option to buy the property would not be subject to VAT.

This reasoning is likely to affect the VAT treatment of the "rent-to-buy"-type schemes which property developers have begun to make available to would-be property purchasers. (See Chapter 6 in this connection.)

Sales via compulsory purchase order or seizure

[4-11] Section 3(1)(d) of the VAT Act provides that a supply of goods includes:

> *"the transfer of ownership of the goods pursuant to –*
>
> *(i) their acquisition, otherwise than by agreement, by or on behalf of the State or a local authority, or*
>
> *(ii) their seizure by any person acting under statutory authority."*

Consequently, if immovable goods transfer under a C.P.O. or seizure as outlined, then a supply takes place for VAT purposes. VAT would arise in relation to the supply in the normal manner.

Whether the vendor is required to charge VAT on a disposal

[4-12] Once it is determined that there is a supply of immovable goods, the next issue is whether that supply will be subject to VAT.

Section 4B(2) sets out the circumstances in which the vendor would **not** be required to charge VAT on the sale of immovable property, i.e. it presents five sets of circumstances in which the sale would be exempt. In the writer's view, if the supply meets the requirements for exemption under an earlier paragraph of Section 4B(2), then there would be no need to continue to consider later paragraphs. In other words, if a supply meets the criteria for exemption in paragraph (a), then there would be no need to consider the position under paragraph (b) and so on. This view is borne out by the use of the word *"or"* prior to paragraph (e).

[4-13] The exempt treatment provided for in Section 4B(2) is subject to subsections 4B(3)(5) and (7) and to subsection 4C(6)(a). Even if the exemption criteria in Section 4B(2) are satisfied, the provisions of 4B(3)(5)(7) or 4C(6)(a) can still render a disposal subject to VAT. These exceptions to the exempt treatment are considered in this chapter following the analysis of the Section 4B(2) provisions.

[4-14] Immovable goods that are still within the five- and two-year periods set out in Section 4B(2) (see below) are commonly referred to as "new" property. Once the five- or two- year periods have elapsed, the properties are commonly referred to as "old". If a property is "new", then the vendor is required to charge VAT in relation to the sale. If a property is "old", then the vendor is not required to charge VAT in relation to the sale.

However, immovable goods that are in the VAT "net" do not pass out of **[4–15]**
the VAT "net" merely by meeting the criteria for an exempt sale under
Section 4B(2), i.e. merely because they are "old". If a disposal of VAT-able
property takes place during the adjustment period for that property and
the disposal meets the criteria for exemption set out in Section 4B(2), then
the vendor in an exempt-sale scenario would suffer a proportional clawback of input VAT upon the exempt sale. (The term "adjustment period"
is defined in Section 12E(2) of the VAT Act (see Chapter 3)). It is similar to
a VAT life for immovable goods and is generally approximately 20 years
in duration. Alternatively, vendor and purchaser would, in certain circumstances, be entitled to jointly opt to tax the sale, as provided for in
Section 4B(5) (see below, paragraphs **4–38** to **4–43**). If a sale is subject to
the option to tax, then no clawback arises for the vendor and the responsibility for accounting for the VAT on the sale passes to the purchaser. If
the purchaser is entitled to full input VAT recovery, then the purchaser
would be entitled to claim a simultaneous input VAT credit, i.e. it would
suffer no net VAT cost.

The following analysis of the five paragraphs in Section 4B(2) and the
accompanying examples should clarify these points.

Exemption 1 – the property is undeveloped

Section 4B(2)(a) provides that VAT is not chargeable on the supply of **[4–16]**
immovable goods that have not been developed within 20 years prior to
that supply. The definition of development did not change in the 2008
Finance Acts and is set out in Section 1 of the VAT Act as:

"(a)   the construction, demolition, extension, alteration or reconstruction
of any building on the land, or

(b)   the carrying out of any engineering or other operation in, on over
or under the land to adapt it for materially altered use."

At paragraph 2.3 of its *VAT on Property Guide* (April 2008), Revenue **[4–17]**
takes the view that:

"A property is regarded as developed when –

- A new building is constructed or

- An existing building is extended, altered or reconstructed, or

- An existing building is demolished, or

- Some engineering or other operation is carried out or work which
adapts the building for materially altered use is carried out (work
which is not designed to make a material alteration in the use to
which a building is put is not development. Thus no account is taken
of fencing, land drainage, laying of roads for agricultural purposes
and so on)."

Work on maintenance and repairs does not constitute development. The fact that planning permission has been obtained for development does not, of itself, constitute development for VAT purposes.

[4-18]   Development can be a thorny issue from a VAT perspective. The following points are also relevant.

- The provisions of Section 4B can apply to disposals of immovable goods whether the development took place before or after 1 July 2008.

- If the disposal takes place on or after 1 July 2008, then the old "10%" rule is not relevant when considering whether the property is developed, even if the development work was completed before 1 July 2008.

- Section 4B contains a new *de minimis* provision for what is commonly referred to as *"minor development"* (see Section 4B(2)(d) below, paragraphs **4-28** to **4-31**).

- Development carried out on a property which is already completed is categorised as refurbishment. Refurbishment is still development and is a capital good in its own right. Refurbishment is dealt with in Section 12E of the VAT Act (see Chapter 3).

Example – supply of undeveloped land

Anne Farmer owns a four-acre undeveloped field where she grows hemp. In 2010, she spends €100,000 draining and fencing the land and putting in a new access road. The field remains in agricultural use. In 2015, Anne Farmer sells the field to Mr Bigfarmer. Although Anne Farmer has incurred considerable expenditure and has carried out engineering works on the land, the works did not materially alter the land, since it remained in agricultural use. Consequently, Anne Farmer's disposal is exempt as the field is not developed.

Example – supply of undeveloped land

Mr Farmer sells undeveloped agricultural land for €5 million to Developer Limited. Developer Ltd engages Contractor & Son to build 70 houses. Developer Limited sells the houses to individuals and charges VAT at 13.5%. Mr Farmer disposed of his land before it was developed and there was no connection between his disposal and the development by Contractor & Son. Consequently, Mr Farmer's disposal is not subject to VAT.

It is important when examining the latter type of scenario in particular to consider whether the anti-avoidance provisions contained in Section 4B(3) (formerly Section 4(5)) might apply (see below).

Exemption 2 – the "five-year rule"

Section 4B(2)(b) provides that a vendor of developed property will not charge VAT on the sale if the property constitutes *"completed immovable goods, the most recent development of which occurred more than 5 years prior to that supply, and those goods have not been developed within that 5 year period"*.   [4–19]

The term *"completed"* is defined in Section 4B(1) and means *"that the development of those goods has reached the state, apart from only such finishing or fitting work that would normally be carried out by or on behalf of the person who will use them, where those goods can effectively be used for the purposes for which those goods were designed, and the utility services required for those purposes are connected to those goods"*.   [4–20]

In other words, the term *"completed"* means that the development of the property has reached the state where it can effectively be used for the purposes for which it was designed. Revenue has clarified at paragraph 2.11 of its *VAT on Property Guide* (April 2008 – see Appendix 1) that finishing and fitting work which is normally carried out by the person who will use the property, whether as owner or tenant, does not have to be carried out in order for the property to be "completed". However, the utility services which would enable the property to be used for the purposes for which it was designed *would* have to be connected. Revenue also indicates in paragraph 2.11 that: [4–21]

> *"the physical state that the property is in when completed – the degree of finishing and fitting that will have been carried out – will depend on its intended use and may vary from one type of building to another."*

This view suggests that the matter of the completion date is not necessarily cut and dried and may be open to interpretation. See also paragraph **2–92** in relation to Tax Briefing, Issue 69, September 2008 (see Appendix 3). Revenue has confirmed that it is prepared to accept that, in certain specified cases, a property may be regarded as not having been completed until it has been rented. This view of the term "completed" is further considered in paragraphs **5–30** to **5–35**.

Example - "completed"

Malanu Limited constructed a new head office, which was ready for use on 15 February 2009 except for fitout and connection of electricity. The electricity was connected on 1 March 2009. At that stage the fitout works were still being carried out. The completion date for VAT purposes was 1 March rather than 15 February 2009.

Example - "five-year rule"

Tiger Limited acquires a new manufacturing facility in Ballinasloe on 1 September 2008. It intends to use the property for manufacturing a new product line. Tiger Limited makes up its accounts to 31 December. A severe slump in the market causes Tiger Limited to reconsider its plans and the property lies idle until 2014, when Tiger succeeds in selling it on the open market.

The property is now in its 7th interval. The five-year rule in Section 4B(2)(b) applies and Tiger does not charge the purchaser VAT. However, Section 12E provides that the adjustment period is 20 intervals, i.e. the property is being disposed of during the adjustment period.

Unless Tiger and the purchaser jointly opt to tax the sale, as provided for in Section 4B(5), then Tiger will suffer a clawback of input VAT under a formula set out in Section 12E(7)(b) of the VAT Act (i.e. under the CGS). Let us say that Tiger recovered €270,000 of input VAT when it acquired the property. The clawback formula is as follows:

$$\frac{B \times N}{T}$$

B = €270,000 (the total reviewed deductible amount, as defined in Section 12E).

N = 14 (the number of full intervals remaining in the adjustment period plus one).

T = 20 (the number of intervals in the adjustment period).

The clawback would therefore be €270,000 × 14/20 = €189,000. Tiger would effectively be given credit for six full intervals, even though the property was not in use.

The clawback could be avoided if Tiger and and the purchaser jointly opted to tax the sale, as provided for in Section 4B(5) (see below, paragraphs **[4-38]** to **[4-43]**).

[4-22]   As indicated above, if a disposal meets the criteria for exemption under Section 4B(2)(b), then it would be exempt in the writer's view even if it would not appear to meet the criteria for exemption in subsequent paragraphs.

Exemption 3 – the "two-year rule"

Section 4B(2)(c) provides that a vendor of developed immovable prop-   **[4–23]**
erty does not charge VAT on the disposal of:

"completed immovable goods, that have not been developed since the most recent completion of those goods, where that supply –

(i) *occurs after the immovable goods have been occupied for an aggregate of at least 24 months following the most recent completion of those goods, and*

(ii) *takes place after a previous supply of those goods on which tax was chargeable and that previous supply –*

(I) *took place after the most recent completion of those goods, and*

(II) *was a transaction between persons who were not connected within the meaning of Section 7A."*

The term *"occupied"* is defined in Section 4B(1) as meaning: **[4–24]**

"(a) occupied and fully in use following completion, where that use is one for which planning permission for the development of those goods was granted, and

(b) where those goods are let, occupied and fully in such use by the tenant."

Revenue confirms at paragraph 2.12 of its *VAT on Property Guide* that: **[4–25]**

"a property is 'occupied' when it is fully in use – use being one for which planning permission for the development of the goods had been granted. It is essential to note that this use is a physical, practical use and not purely economic or legal occupation. The two-year rule for second and subsequent supplies of a property begins on the date of occupation following occupation."

Example – "occupied"

Carmusco buys a four-storey office building on 1 May 2011 and fits out the first two floors to its own requirements. On 1 November 2011, it transfers its staff into the first two floors. The date of occupancy for these two floors is 1 November 2011.

> On 1 March 2012, Carmusco grants a lease in relation to the remaining two floors to Limey Limited. Limey Limited takes two months to fit out the leased space and on 1 May 2012 its staff commences operations from the new premises. The two floors are not let, occupied and fully in use by Limey Limited until 1 May 2012. The date of occupancy for the second two floors is therefore 1 May 2012.

[4-26]　The following points are relevant:

- The term "aggregate" means that the period of occupancy can be satisfied by more than one occupant. This might occur, for example, if the property had been rented out.

- If the vendor acquired the property originally from a taxable person with whom the vendor is connected, then the two-year rule would not apply.

> *Example – "Two-year rule"*
>
> ALC acquires a new factory for the purpose of its fully VAT-able manufacturing activities in Drogheda. A year after acquiring the factory, ALC disposes of its business to BLC. ALC and BLC are both wholly owned subsidiaries of CLC, i.e. they are connected parties as defined under Section 7A of the VAT Act. ALC does not charge BLC VAT because Section 3(5)(b)(iii) of the VAT Act applies to the transfer. Two years after acquiring the factory, BLC sells it. Although no development has taken place since the property was completed initially and it has been occupied as defined for more than 24 months in aggregate, BLC must charge VAT on the sale because it acquired the property from a connected person.

Exemption 4 – "minor" development

[4-27]　Under Section 4B(2)(d) VAT is not chargeable on the supply of immovable goods:

> *"being a building that was completed more than 5 years prior to that supply and on which development was carried out in the 5 years prior to that supply where –*
>
> *(i)　such development did not and was not intended to adapt the building for a materially altered use, and*
>
> *(ii)　the cost of such development did not exceed 25 per cent of the consideration for that supply."*

If development is to be considered "minor" it must meet both the mate-   **[4-28]**
rial alteration test and the 25% test.

Although the criteria for minor development are set out in the legisla-   **[4-29]**
tion, the term "minor development" is not used. However, Revenue
uses the term in its *VAT on Property Guide* (April 2008 – see Appendix 1).
At paragraph 2.4 it takes the following view:

> *"Minor development is a level of development that does not make a
> property 'new'. It can be described as development that does not (and is
> not intended to) adapt the property for a materially altered use, provided
> that the cost of such development does not exceed 25% of the consideration
> for the supply of the property."*

If the property is materially altered, then it is developed for VAT
purposes and the 25% threshold is not relevant.

It is important to note that repairs and renewals constitute neither   **[4-30]**
development nor minor development, i.e. in order to be regarded as any
kind of development, the works carried must in any event meet the
definition of development given in Section 1 of the VAT Act.

Revenue acknowledges, for example, at point 17 of its e-brief 37/2008   **[4-31]**
that example No. 3 on page 13 of its *VAT on Property Guide* does not
describe minor development but simply repairs.

Example – minor development

Eniela Limited acquires a new building in December 2008 and uses
it as offices for its architectural practice. It incurs VAT and reclaims
100% of same. In December 2010, Eniela carries out various works
on the property to include an extension. The works cost €100,000.
Subsequent to the works, it continues to use the building as offices,
i.e. there is no material alteration in use. In 2014, i.e. more than five
years after "completion", Eniela sells its building for €2 million. It
does not charge VAT on the disposal because the development met
both of the criteria to be considered "minor". Eniela would nonetheless suffer a clawback of input VAT as indicated previously unless a
joint option to tax the sale is agreed with the purchaser.

---

*Example – disposal of property completed more than five years
previously which has undergone "minor" development in the five-
year period before the disposal date*

Quick Fix Limited built a new commercial unit for €1 million plus
VAT. The new unit was completed as defined on 1 August 2008 and

Quick Fix commenced its retail pharmacy business. In 2012, Quick Fix extended the rear of the property to provide additional secure storage space for pharmacy stock. The extension cost €400,000. In 2015, Quick Fix disposed of its premises to the Department of Education, which intended to demolish it for the purpose of extending the adjacent school. The Department is prepared to pay Quick Fix €3 million for the property.

The building was completed more than five years before the proposed sale. The work carried out in 2012 constitutes development (it was an extension to the property). It took place in 2012, i.e. three years before the proposed sale date. However, the development can be regarded as *"minor"* because it did not and was not intended to adapt the building for a materially altered use and the cost of the works was only approximately 13% of the proposed sale consideration.

Quick Fix is still disposing of the property during the 20-year adjustment period. It is not entitled to opt to tax the sale to the Department, since the Department is not a taxable person (see Section 4B(5) below). Consequently, Quick Fix would suffer a clawback of a proportion of input VAT recovered in relation both to its acquisition and subsequent development of the building.

If the circumstances were the same as above but Quick Fix had extended the unit for the purpose of accommodating new premises for medical and paramedical practitioners, then it would be obliged to charge VAT on the sale consideration because the development work would have adapted the building for a materially altered use. The development would not be minor, even though the 25% threshold was not breached.

Exemption 5 – "minor" development

[4-32]   Section 4B(2)(e) provides that VAT would not be chargeable on the supply of immovable goods:

> *"being a building that was completed within the five years prior to that supply where*
>
> (i)   *the building had been occupied for an aggregate of at least 24 months following that completion,*
>
> (ii)   *that supply takes place after a previous supply of the building on which tax was chargeable and that previous supply –*
>
>> (I)   *took place after that completion of the building, and*
>>
>> (II)   *was a transaction between persons who were not connected within the meaning of section 7A,*

and

(iii)   *if any development of that building occurred after that completion –*

    (I)   *such development did not and was not intended to adapt the building for a materially altered use, and*

    (II)   *the cost of such development did not exceed 25 per cent of the consideration for that supply."*

Section 4B(2)(e) is the final exemption test and deals with the disposal of   **[4-33]** properties that cannot be exempted under Section 4B(2)(d) (above) because they were completed as defined less than five years before being disposed of. However, if they pass the same "two-year rule" set out in Section 4B(2)(c) **and** any development that took place since the date of completion can be categorised as *"minor"*, then the sale is not chargeable to VAT.

Example – disposal of property completed less than five years before disposal which is exempted from the charge to VAT because both the two-year rule is passed and any development since completion is "minor"

Old Hat Limited bought a new factory on 1 October 2009. It used the property for its fully taxable hat-manufacturing business for approximately 18 months, at which time it closed down and sold the building to Straw Hat, which is also in the business of hat manufacturing. Old Hat and Straw Hat are not connected. Straw Hat paid VAT on its purchase of the building, which it recovered, as the manufacture of hats is fully VAT-able. It then demolished part of the building to improve the straw intake bay. It rebuilt the factory perimeter with much larger doors some distance back from the site of the original perimeter wall. The works cost €100,000 plus VAT. Straw Hat used the factory for the manufacture and supply of hats.

Straw Hat relocated its business to Greece in October 2012 and disposed of the building to StoreAll Limited, which intends to use it for the purpose of its storage-space rental business. StoreAll Limited is registered for VAT and the storage-space rental business entitles it to 100% input VAT credit.

The sale took place less than five years after the original completion date. However, the property had been in occupation for more than 24 months in aggregate by the date of sale. Old Hat and Straw Hat were not connected as defined. The works carried out by Straw Hat involved demolition, i.e. they constituted development as defined in Section 1 of the VAT Act. However, they did not and were not intended to adapt the building for a materially altered use, in that it was a factory both before and after the works.

> Furthermore when Straw Hat sold the factory to StoreAll, the cost of the development works was only 20% of the sale consideration. Consequently, Straw Hat was not required to charge StoreAll VAT on the sale. However, unless it jointly opts to tax the sale, Straw Hat will suffer a clawback of input VAT.

[4-34]   The exemptions provided for in Section 4B(2) are subject to three subsections in Section 4B, i.e. subsections (3)(5) and (7) and also to Section 4C(6)(a) of the VAT Act.

If any one of these subsections applies, then even if a supply meets the criteria for exemption set out in Section 4B(2), the supply will still be subject to VAT. Commentary on sections 4B(3)(5) and (7) is set out below. Section 4C(6)(a) is dealt with in Chapter 5.

Section 4B(3) – Supplies in connection with an agreement to develop property

[4-35]   The supply of a property that would otherwise be exempt under Section 4B(2) would nonetheless remain subject to VAT in the circumstances provided for in Section 4B(3). Section 4B(3) is an anti-avoidance provision which more or less replaces the old Section 4(5), which ceased to have effect in relation to disposals taking place on or after 1 July 2008.

[4-36]   Section 4B(3) provides that:

> *"where a person supplies immovable goods to another person and in connection with that supply, a taxable person enters into an agreement with that other person or with a person connected with that other person to carry out a development in relation to those immovable goods, then –*
>
> (a)   *the person who supplies the goods shall, in relation to that supply, be deemed to be a taxable person,*
>
> (b)   *the supply of the said immovable goods shall be deemed to be a supply of those goods to which section 2 applies, and*
>
> (c)   *subsection (2) does not apply to that supply."*

[4-37]   Supplies of property made in connection with an agreement to develop the property are **deemed** to be taxable, whether or not the person making the supply does so in the course of business. For this provision to apply, the purchaser of the property or a person connected with the purchaser must enter into an agreement with a taxable person (e.g. a builder) to develop the property. This is an area that can give rise to difficulties in relation to property sub-sales and building licence agreements.

> ### Example – sale of property in connection with an agreement to develop the property
>
> Anne Farmer owns a field which she has not developed. Dun Limited is a property developer. Jack and Jill sign a contract to buy the field from Mrs Farmer and a building agreement with Dun Limited to build a house for them. Jack and Jill's contract with Mrs Farmer is contingent on performance of the contract with Dun Limited.
>
> The sale of the field by Mrs Farmer to Jack and Jill is subject to VAT as it is connected with an agreement to develop it.

> ### Example – sale of property which is not connected with an agreement to develop the property
>
> Anne Farmer owns a field which she has not developed. Jack and Jill buy a site from Mrs Farmer subject to planning permission for a new bungalow. They receive planning permission in due course and the sale closes. Mrs Farmer does not charge Jack and Jill VAT in relation to the site as it has not been developed and she is not disposing of it in connection with an agreement to develop the property. Jack and Jill sign a building agreement with Dun Limited for construction of the bungalow. Dun Limited builds the house and charges Jack and Jill VAT at 13.5% on its consideration for construction services.

Sections 4B(5) and (6) – Opting to tax a sale of immovable goods

Section 4B(5) deals with the option to tax the sale of immovable goods and provides that: **[4–38]**

> *"Where a taxable person supplies immovable goods to another taxable person in circumstances where that supply would otherwise be exempt in accordance with subsection (2), subsection (2) or (6)(b) of section 4C, then tax shall, notwithstanding subsection (2), subsection 2 or 6(b) of section 4C, be chargeable on that supply, where the supplier and the taxable person to whom the supply is made enter an agreement in writing no later than the fifteenth day of the month following the month in which that supply occurs to opt to have tax chargeable on that supply (in this Act referred to as a 'joint option for taxation')."*

The exemptions in Section 4B(2) have been considered above. The exemptions in subsections 4C(2) and (6)(b) relate to the supply of transitional property in cases where the person making the disposal was not entitled   **[4–39]** to recover input VAT in relation to acquisition or development of the property. (These provisions are considered in greater detail in Chapter 5.)

[4-40]   The option can be exercised in writing up to 15 days following the supply of the property. However, it would make sense that the agreement would in reality be one of the closing documents. In any case, once the 15-day period has expired, it would not be possible to revert and make a supply subject to the option to tax retrospectively.

[4-41]   Both parties to an "opted" sale must be **taxable** persons. A taxable person is defined in Section 1 of the VAT Act as "a person who independently carries out any business in the State". It can include persons carrying on an exempt business, such as an insurance company. Not all purchasers of immovable property will be taxable persons. If the purchaser is not a taxable person as defined, then the option to tax is not available. In the Quick Fix example above, the purchaser was a government department, which would not be a taxable person. The option to tax was not therefore available and consequently the vendor could not avoid a VAT clawback on the sale of the property.

[4-42]   There is a distinction between a taxable person and an accountable person. Under Section 8 of the VAT Act, an accountable person is a person who supplies taxable goods or services within the State and is accountable for the VAT arising on those supplies. If a property is sold to an exempt business, e.g. a bank or insurance company, the sale is still to a taxable person as defined under the legislation (as opposed to an accountable person). Consequently, the option to tax could apply under Section 4B(5) **provided that** both parties agree to it. However, an exempt or partly exempt purchaser is likely to resist an option to tax because it would suffer an irrecoverable VAT cost. Depending on market conditions, a vendor may still decide to proceed with a disposal which is not opted and to suffer the VAT clawback.

[4-43]   The joint agreement to opt must be in writing, and it is likely that in relevant cases, execution of this agreement will be one of the documents needed to close the sale.

Section 4B(6) provides that:

> "*where a joint option for taxation is exercised in accordance with subsection (5) then –*
>
> (a)   *the person to whom the supply is made shall, in relation to that supply, be an accountable person and shall be liable to pay the tax chargeable on that supply as if that person supplied those goods, and*
>
> (b)   *the person who made the supply shall not be accountable for or liable to pay the said tax.*"

This section provides that when the parties opt to tax a sale as provided for in Section 4B(5), then it is the purchaser who is required to account for the VAT, i.e. a reverse-charge mechanism applies. The purchaser would be entitled to claim a corresponding input VAT credit under Section 12 of the VAT Act to the extent that s/he intends to put the property to a taxable use. Section 12(1)(c)(iiic) of the VAT Act provides for a deduction for the purchaser *"for the tax chargeable during the period, being tax for which the accountable person is liable by virtue of section 4B(6) (a) ..."*. Revenue has confirmed that in order to claim its Section 12 deduction, the purchaser would rely on the joint option to tax in writing (the vendor would not be required to issue a VAT invoice or other document). The option to tax clause is not to be confused with a standard VAT clause and both may be required. **[4–44]**

> *Example – option to tax*
>
> UCo, a taxable person, agrees to dispose of a warehouse which it has been using for the past seven years for its taxable business to Day Limited, which is also a taxable person. UCo has not developed the warehouse since acquisition. Section 4B(2)(b) provides that UCo is not required to charge VAT on the sale. However, UCo does not wish to suffer a VAT clawback and Day Limited would be fully entitled to recover input VAT in relation to its purchase. Consequently, the parties opt to tax the sale. UCo does not charge Day Limited VAT. Instead, under Section 4B(6), Day Limited is required to account for the VAT on the reverse-charge basis. Day Limited has no net VAT cost. Day Limited becomes a capital goods owner on its acquisition of the property. A new 20-year adjustment period commences and Day Limited is required to maintain a capital goods record (see Chapter 3).

A variety of scenarios can arise in association with the joint option to tax. Two examples may help to illustrate the position. **[4–45]**

> *Example – joint option to tax – vendor suffered irrecoverable input VAT*
>
> Evadco purchases a new building for its insurance business in 2011. It was charged VAT when it acquired the building but was not entitled to recover it because of the exempt nature of its business. In 2021, it sells the building to Estev Limited, which is entitled to 100% input VAT credit. Evadco would in this case be better off if Estev would agree to the option to tax. When Estev Limited accounts for the VAT

on the consideration on the reverse-charge basis, as provided, it would suffer no net input VAT cost because it has 100% input VAT recovery entitlement. In addition, from Evadco's perspective, jointly opting to tax the sale would entitle it to recover part of the input VAT it originally suffered in relation to the building. This credit is provided for in Section 12E(7)(a) of the VAT Act. In the above case Evadco's building would have had an adjustment period of 20 intervals. Evadco would therefore be entitled to reclaim approximately $^{10}/_{20}$ of the input VAT in the event of an "opted" sale.

Example – joint option to tax - purchaser not entitled to recover input VAT

Same circumstances as above but, in this example, Estev Limited (fully taxable) is selling the building to Evadco (exempt). Evadco is not keen on an opted sale because as the reverse-charge mechanism applies, it would suffer an irrecoverable input VAT cost. However, if Estev simply accepts Evadco's position and agrees not to jointly opt to tax the sale, then under Section 12E(7)(b) of the VAT Act, Evadco would suffer a clawback of $^{10}/_{20}$ of the input VAT it recovered in 2011.

Instead of opting to tax the sale, the parties might find a middle ground whereby Evadco would pay a higher consideration to Estev, which might compensate it in full or in part for the VAT clawback. Any such decision would have implications for Evadco in relation to financing the transaction. Estev would have to consider direct tax implications in relation to stamp duty and capital gains tax.

Section 4B(7) – Supply of residential property by a property developer

[4–46]   Section 4B(7) states that:

"(a)   *Where a taxable person supplies immovable goods to another person in circumstances where that supply would otherwise be exempt in accordance with subsection (2), tax shall, notwithstanding subsection (2) be chargeable on that supply where –*

(i)   *the immovable goods are buildings designed or capable of being used as a dwelling,*

(ii)   *the person who makes that supply is a person who developed the immovable goods in the course of a business of developing immovable goods or a person connected with that person, within the meaning of Section 7A, and*

> (iii) *the person who developed those immovable goods was entitled to a deduction under Section 12 for tax chargeable to that person in respect of that person's acquisition or development of those immovable goods."*

Consequently, the supply of property which otherwise appears to meet the exemption criteria set out in Section 4B(2) would nonetheless be subject to VAT (regardless of the two- and five- year rules) **if:** **[4-47]**

- it is residential property; **and**

- it is sold in the adjustment period by a developer or someone connected with a developer (see the definition of "connected" as set out in Section 7A); **and**

- the vendor was entitled to recover input VAT under Section 12 of the VAT Act.

If the above criteria are met, then Section 4B(7) applies whether the property was completed before or after 1 July 2008, i.e. it also has application in relation to disposals of "transitional" property (see Chapter 5). **[4-48]**

Example – disposal of residential property by a property developer

O Limited, a property development company, buys an undeveloped site for €350,000. It acquires full planning permission and in 2009 builds a substantial dwelling at a cost of €2.5 million plus VAT of €337,500. O Limited, anticipating a VAT-able sale of the property, claims back the input VAT on costs. However, it is unable to sell the property immediately and in fact it lies idle for approximately six years.

Notwithstanding the five-year rule, Section 4B(7) provides that the sale in 2015 is subject to VAT in the normal manner, i.e. O Limited is required to charge the purchaser VAT at 13.5%.

Example – exempt letting of residential property by a property developer, followed by a disposal of the property

In the O Limited example above, in reality it would be highly unlikely that a developer could keep a completed property on the books for that length of time without generating some kind of income from it. In the circumstances outlined above, one might expect O Limited to find a tenant for the house pending sale.

> Under Section 7A, the letting of residential property could only be exempt, as there is no option to tax it. Consequently, O Limited has claimed back 100% input VAT and now proposes to put the house to a completely exempt use, albeit perhaps only for a few years.
>
> Section 4B(7)(b) deals with this scenario and states that:
>
> *"In the case of a building to which this subsection would apply if the building were supplied by the taxable person at any time during the capital goods scheme adjustment period for that building –*
>
> *(i) Section 12E(6) shall not apply, and*
>
> *(ii) Notwithstanding Section 12E(4) the proportion of total tax incurred that is deductible by that person shall be treated as the initial interval proportion of deductible use."*

[4-49] Paragraph (b) has the effect that the developer will pay back $\frac{1}{20}$ of the input VAT recovered at the end of the second interval and each subsequent interval. It does this by providing that Section 12E(6) will not apply in this case. Section 12E(6) would otherwise give rise to a clawback of all of the VAT when the developer makes an exempt letting. In addition, subparagraph (ii) provides that the proportion of the *"total tax incurred"* deductible by the developer (i.e. VAT deducted on the acquisition or development of the property) is treated as the *"initial interval proportion of deductible use"*. The full adjustment that would otherwise be required in accordance with Section 12E(4) as the use for the initial interval is effectively deemed to be 100% taxable.

[4-50] In summary, where this type of property is let prior to the first supply, the adjustment under the capital goods scheme is the annual adjustment as provided in Section 12E(4), i.e. usually $\frac{1}{20}$ of the input VAT claimed. The letting is effectively treated as a temporary arrangement and it does not take the first supply out of the VAT "net". A $\frac{1}{20}$ repayment would occur each year that property is let.

The reference to Section 12E(6) is to that part of the CGS provisions which deal with "big swings" in taxable use. The "big swing" provisions do not apply in this scenario, i.e. the lump sum input VAT clawback that would be expected in these circumstances due to the significant change from taxable to exempt use does not arise (see Chapter 3 in relation to the CGS).

Example – letting of residential property by developer prior to sale

In the previous example, if O Limited lets the house for a period of two years, it would have to make the following adjustments of input VAT:

End of 1st interval: No adjustment.

End of 2nd interval: $\frac{1}{20}$ €337,500 = €16,875.

During third year – sells the house for €4 million. O Limited is required to charge VAT on the full sale consideration.

If, in the above example, O Limited completed development of the same property prior to 1 July 2008, then it would be a transitional property. The strict position in relation to transitional property in the circumstances set out above is that an exempt letting would give rise to a clawback of a lump sum of input VAT rather than the interval-based adjustments set out above. However, in September 2008 (see Appendix 3), Revenue issued Tax Briefing, Issue 69, which appears to allow lettings of transitional **residential** property to benefit from the interval-based adjustment also. For more detail, see Chapter 5 in relation to Section 4C of the VAT Act.   **[4–51]**

Rent-to-buy schemes

The exempt letting of property pending sale of property is not to be confused with rent-to-buy schemes, which in recent times have been set up by various property developers. The idea is that persons wishing to buy property but unsure whether they can make the long-term commitment to a particular location, property, mortgage, etc., initially rent the property from the developer. At the time of writing, Revenue has not confirmed its position in relation to the VAT treatment of rents paid in relation to such schemes. However, the rents would appear of necessity to be linked to an option to buy the property. Following a 2003 Appeal Commissioners case, the rents in such schemes would be accorded the same VAT treatment as the underlying property, i.e. they would be subject to VAT at 13.5% rather than the standard rate. Alternatively, the rent could be regarded as prepayments in relation to the property purchase, in which case they would still be subject to VAT at 13.5%.   **[4–52]**

The VAT registration threshold does not apply in relation to disposals of immovable property

[4–53]   Finally, Section 4B(1) is similar to the old Section 4(7) of the VAT Act in that it provides that the registration thresholds do not apply to property transactions.

[4–54]   Various case law has confirmed that the supply of goods takes place when the purchaser receives the right to dispose of tangible property as owner, even if there is no transfer of legal ownership of the property (see, for example, ECJ Case C-320/99 (the 'Safe' case), the Irish Supreme Court case *Tempany v. Hynes* [1976] I.R. 101 and the Irish High Court case *Fitz-pack Cartons Ltd v. Companies Acts* [2008] IEHC 41). Ultimately the supply has been held to take place when the payment for the property transfers, as this is when the purchaser acquires the right to transfer of the property as owner. Usually, the funds do not transfer until completion of the contract and consequently the supply will usually take place upon completion. Nonetheless, under Section 19(2) of the VAT Act, payments made prior to completion, e.g. deposit, stage payments, etc., would be regarded as prepayments and would also be subject to VAT if the underlying supply would be subject to VAT. If a deposit is paid and is subsequently retained because a purchaser has failed to proceed, then the vendor is entitled to seek a refund of VAT on the deposit (see the *Eugénie-les-Bains* case at paragraph **4–06**).

Chapter 5

The Supply of Transitional Property

Introduction – "transitional property"

This chapter examines Section 4C of the VAT Act, which applies to: [5–01]

> "(a) immovable goods which are acquired or developed by a taxable person prior to 1 July 2008, being completed immovable goods before 1 July 2008, and have not been disposed of by that taxable person prior to that date, until such time as those goods have been disposed of by that taxable person on or after that date, and
>
> (b) an interest in immovable goods within the meaning of Section 4, other than a freehold interest or a freehold equivalent interest, created by a taxable person prior to 1 July 2008 and held by a taxable person on 1 July 2008 and the reversionary interest, within the meaning of section 4(9), on that interest until that interest is surrendered after 1 July 2008."

In other words, Section 4C provides for certain measures in relation to VAT arising on disposals of certain interests in property, i.e.:   [5–02]

- Interests in property acquired or developed by a taxable person **before** the new legislation was introduced and still held by that person **after** the new legislation was introduced **and also**

- Long leases granted by a taxable person under the **old** regime and still in existence under the **new** regime. These are referred to as "legacy leases" in Revenue's *VAT on Property Guide* from April 2008 (see Appendix 1). (The transitional measures for what were **short** leases under the old rules are contained in Section 7B.)

To the extent that long leases granted pre-1 July 2008 simply continue in place after that date and the relevant property is not further developed, then the leases are not affected by the new rules. This is because any VAT on legacy leases would have been dealt with under the old regime,   [5–03] i.e. when the leases were granted initially. However, specific measures were needed to deal in particular with the assignment and surrender of legacy leases from 1 July 2008 onwards.

[5-04] When considering the provisions contained in Section 4C, it is important to be aware that the **general** rules in relation to the supply of immovable goods are contained in Section 4B (see Chapter 4). Unless Section 4C makes a specific provision in relation to transitional property, then Section 4B would generally apply.

[5-05] Certain provisions of Section 4C refer to the "old" Section 4 of the VAT Act. Section 4(11) provides that

> *"subject to Section 4C, the other provisions of this section ... [Section 4] ... shall not apply as regards –*
>
> *(a)   a disposal of an interest in immovable goods, or*
>
> *(b)   a surrender of possession of immovable goods,*
>
> *which occurs after 1 July 2008."*

The words *"subject to 4C"* indicate that although Section 4 is, for the most part, no longer relevant in relation to disposals of property arising on or after 1 July 2008, certain Section 4 provisions can still be relied upon **if** specific reference is made to them in the provisions contained in Section 4C.

Transitional property is a capital good

General application of the CGS to transitional property

[5-06] Section 4C(11)(a) and (b) confirm that the CGS applies to transitional property and the owner of such property is a capital goods owner.

[5-07] Section 4C(10) confirms the CGS *"only applies to supplies of such properties"*, i.e. the interval-based adjustments provided for in Sections 12E(4)(5) and (6) of the VAT Act would not apply. However, Section 4C(10) also provides that if the capital goods are refurbished as defined and the refurbishment is completed on or after 1 July 2008, then the normal CGS interval-based adjustments would apply in respect of the refurbishment.

> *Example – application of the CGS to transitional property*
>
> Ms X purchased a building, claimed back the relevant input VAT and began using the building for her fully taxable supplies on 1 December 2006.

Six years later, i.e. on 1 December 2012, Ms X sold her interest in the building. It had been fully in use by her business until that date. The building was not developed during her period of ownership.

The building is transitional property and Section 4C(11)(a) confirms that it is a capital good. The disposal takes place following more than 24 months occupancy, as defined, but within the adjustment period. As it is no longer "new", the sale of the building is subject to output VAT. However, unless Ms X and the purchaser jointly opt to tax the sale, then Ms X will suffer a proportional clawback of input VAT under the CGS.

Length of the adjustment period for transitional property

Section 4C(11)(c) confirms the adjustment period for transitional prop-   [5–08]
erty. It provides that:

"…the period to be treated as the adjustment period in respect of immovable goods or interests in immovable goods to which this section applies is –

(i)   *in the case of the acquisition of the freehold interest or freehold equivalent interest in those immovable goods, 20 years from the date of that acquisition,*

(ii)   *in the case of the creation of an interest in those immovable goods, 20 years, or, if the interest when it was created was for a period of less than 20 years, the number of full years in that interest when created, whichever is the shorter,*

(iii) *in the case of the assignment or surrender of an interest in immovable goods prior to 1 July 2008, the period remaining in that interest at the time of the assignment or surrender of that interest or 20 years, whichever is the shorter, or*

(iv)   *in the case of –*

   (I)   *the surrender or first assignment of an interest in immovable goods on or after 1 July 2008, the number of full years remaining in the adjustment period as determined in accordance with subparagraphs (ii) and (iii) plus one, or*

   (II)   *the second or subsequent assignment of an interest in immovable goods after 1 July 2008, the number of full intervals remaining in the adjustment period as determined in accordance with clause (I), plus one,*

> *And this number shall thereafter be the number of intervals remaining in the adjustment period,*
>
> *but where the immovable goods have been developed since the acquisition of those immovable goods or the creation of that interest, 20 years from the date of the most recent development of those goods..."*

[5-09]   Paragraph (i) provides that the adjustment period for transitional freehold or freehold equivalent interests is 20 years from acquisition date.

[5-10]   Paragraph (ii) provides that, when the interest consists of a legacy lease, then the adjustment period will be 20 years or a shorter period if the legacy lease had a term of less than 20 years. Even if a legacy lease had a term of 25 years at grant, it would have a maximum adjustment period of 20 years.

[5-11]   Paragraph (iii) provides that, in the case of leases surrendered or assigned prior to 1 July 2008, the adjustment period would be the period remaining in the lease term at assignment or surrender, or 20 years, whichever is shorter.

[5-12]   Paragraph (iv)(I) provides that the adjustment period in relation to a leasehold interest which is subject to surrender or a first assignment on or after 1 July 2008 is determined in accordance with (ii) or (iii) above, as appropriate, plus one.

[5-13]   Paragraph (iv)(II) provides that the adjustment period in relation to a leasehold interest subject to a second assignment or surrender on or after 1 July 2008 is determined in accordance with (iv)(I) above, plus one.

[5-14]   If the immovable goods have been developed, the last paragraph of Section 4C(11) provides that the adjustment period will be 20 years from the most recent development of the property. Revenue has confirmed that this last paragraph is interpreted as meaning developed to completion. In other words, if I purchase an undeveloped site in 1995 and develop a building on it to completion in 2000, then the adjustment period for the capital good is 20 years from 2000. If I carry out a further development in 2006 (completed in that year) it is a refurbishment and has its own adjustment period of 10 years.

[5-15]   However, if I buy a completed building in 1985 and VAT is charged on the acquisition, the adjustment period for the building is 20 years from 1985. Any subsequent development is treated as a separate capital good (refurbishment) and has an adjustment period of 10 years.

> **Example – duration of adjustment period**
>
> The capital goods owner granted a 25-year lease on 15 April 2006. The adjustment period would be 20 years from 15 April 2006 and not 25 years from 15 April 2006.

> **Example – duration of adjustment period**
>
> The capital goods owner was assigned a lease on 1 October 2007. The original duration of the lease was 20 years. There were 17 full years remaining on the date of assignment. The adjustment period is 17 years and not 20 years.

Although "per interval"- type adjustments do not arise in relation to transitional property, in the event of a disposal of the transitional property during the adjustment period it may nonetheless be necessary to establish how much input VAT is attributable to each interval. This calculation would be required for example if a clawback of input VAT were to arise on the basis that an exempt sale arises within the adjustment period.   [5–16]

Section 4C(2) – No right to recover – no VAT on disposal

Section 4C(2) states that: [5–17]

> *"…in the case of a supply of immovable goods to which subsection 1(a) applies [a freehold interest which was acquired or developed pre 1 July 2009], being completed immovable goods within the meaning of Section 4B –*
>
> (a) *Where the person supplying those goods had no right to deduct under Section 12 in relation to the tax chargeable on the acquisition or development of those goods prior to 1 July 2008 and,*
>
> (b) *if any subsequent development of those immovable goods occurs on or after 1 July 2008 –*
>
>   (i) *that development does not and is not intended to adapt the immovable goods for a materially altered use, and*
>
>   (ii) *the cost of that development does not exceed 25% of the consideration for that supply,*

then, subject to Section 4B(3), that supply is not chargeable to tax but a joint option for taxation may be exercised in respect of that supply in accordance with section 4B(5) and that tax is payable in accordance with Section 4B(6)."

[5-18] This provision means that if a person who was not **entitled** to recover input VAT on the acquisition or development of a freehold interest in immovable goods before 1 July 2008 disposes of the property on or after that date **and** the property was not developed on or after 1 July 2008 (or if it was, the development fell into the category of "minor" development – see Section 4B and Chapter 4), **then** no VAT will be chargeable in relation to a disposal on or after 1 July **unless** Section 4B(3) applies or the sale is subject to the option to tax provided for in Section 4B(5).

[5-19] Section 4B(3) is an anti-avoidance measure which deems supplies of otherwise exempt property to be subject to VAT when made in connection with an agreement to develop the property. Both Section 4B(3) and the option to tax disposals of property contained in Section 4B(6) are examined in some detail in Chapter 4. If neither Section 4B(3) nor 4B(6) applies **and** the person disposing of the transitional property had no entitlement under Section 12 of the VAT Act to recover input VAT in relation to the acquisition/development of the property, then the disposal is exempt.

[5-20] Clearly in this context the matter of **entitlement** to recover input VAT would be critical. Entitlement arises when the person who acquired/ developed the property **intended** to put it to a taxable use.

[5-21] In the High Court case *Crawford v. Centime Limited* ([2005] IEHC 328), it was also held that "the true test is the genuine economic intention of the party". This is sometimes referred to as the "Eircom Park" case. The circumstances were that the Football Association of Ireland planned to build a soccer stadium which was to be called Eircom Park. Centime Limited, the development company incorporated for this purpose, spent about €4 million, including VAT, on legal fees, architects' fees, planning consultancy fees, etc. It was decided in March 2001 for commercial reasons that the project would be abandoned. Revenue initially took the view that Centime had no entitlement to recover input VAT on the basis that the project had not gone ahead. Centime Limited did not have taxable status. However, the Appeal Commissioners and the High Court held in favour of the appellant. If there is any doubt about a taxpayer's intention, Revenue would be entitled to seek objective evidence of it (see, for example, ECJ case C-400/98 *Finanzamt Goslar* and *Brigitte Breitsohl*).

Example – no entitlement to recover input VAT

Mr P has built up a portfolio of rental residential properties over a number of years. He never registered for VAT or waived his short-term letting exemption. Mr P bought a further second-hand house for his portfolio in 2006. The house had a large garden. He put the house into residential lettings, obtained planning permission and engaged a builder to build another house in the garden. This house was completed in September 2007. Mr P fitted out the house for letting and engaged a letting agent, with whom he signed a contract. He also made some enquiries with the Private Residential Tenancies Board (PRTB) in relation to letting the house and received a response from the board in writing.

Around this time, interest rates went up, residential property values decreased sharply and Mr P's bankers became concerned at his level of borrowings. Although Mr P had intended to put the new house into residential lettings, his bank manager put pressure on him to sell it instead and reduce his loans. Mr P did not wish to sell but ultimately felt the bank was leaving him with no choice. The house was put on the market on 20 July 2008 and the sale closed in September of that year. Mr P can prove that his intention was to put the property to an exempt use and consequently was not entitled to recover input VAT on the costs of developing same. He relies on the provisions of Section 4C(2) and does not account for VAT on the sale of the house.

Example – entitlement to recover input VAT

Yo Ireland develops a new office premises for use in its fully taxable business. It announces its relocation to new premises in the relevant media and engages a public relations consultant to maximise the publicity associated with the opening. Yo incurs significant VAT in relation to development work but delays reclaiming this until it gets settled in the new premises. The building is completed in early 2009 but in March of that year Yo Worldwide suddenly announces it is closing down the Irish operation. Under the circumstances, Yo Ireland is forced to sell the property late in 2009. It is still "new" as defined for VAT. Yo would be required to charge VAT on the full sale consideration even if it had not yet reclaimed the input VAT on the development work. Omitting claiming back input VAT does not cancel out an underlying entitlement to do so. VAT still arises in relation to the sale. Delaying a claim to recover input VAT when there is an entitlement to do so is unwise. If the sale in this case is postponed until, say, the fifth interval, Yo Limited would still be required to charge VAT on the sale but could find itself prevented from recovering the corresponding input VAT on the basis of the four-year "cap".

See also the example of Mr Q, at paragraph **5-29**, which also deals with the matter of entitlement.

[5-22]   Section 4B(5) is the provision entitling two taxable persons to jointly opt to tax a sale. This was also considered in Chapter 4 and again it is important to bear in mind that:

- the option to tax is only available by joint vendor-purchaser written agreement; and
- the option is only available in cases where **both** parties are taxable persons, i.e. persons independently carrying out a business in the State.

[5-23]   If the option to tax is exercised, then not only is the sale subject to VAT but the vendor would be entitled to reclaim an input VAT credit under Section 12E(7)(a) of the VAT Act.

> *Example – disposal of freehold transitional property on or after 1 July 2008 – vendor not entitled to recover input VAT at acquisition*
>
> Surefire, an insurance company, purchases a new building for its insurance business on 1 January 2006. Surefire makes up its accounts to 31 December each year. It was charged VAT of €540,000 on its acquisition but had no entitlement to recover it because of the exempt nature of its business. On 1 January 2011 it sells the building to Rich Cover, another insurance company. Surefire did not develop the property. It is not required to charge Rich Cover VAT. Although both parties are taxable persons as defined, neither is entitled to recover input VAT. They would be entitled to opt to tax the sale (see below) but it would be unlikely that Rich Cover would agree to same as Rich Cover would then suffer an irrecoverable VAT charge in relation to its acquisition.

Section 4C(5) – Nil or restricted right to recover – sale is opted to tax

[5-24]   Section 4C(5) provides that:

> "...if a person makes a supply of immovable goods to which this section applies and tax is chargeable on that supply and that person was not entitled to deduct all the tax charged to that person on the acquisition or development of those immovable goods, that person shall be entitled to make the appropriate adjustment that would apply under section 12E(7) (a) as if the capital goods scheme applied to that transaction."

This means that if transitional property is sold during its adjustment period and the vendor suffers all or some of the input VAT at acquisition/development of the property and the circumstances are such that the sale is subject to VAT, then the vendor would be entitled to recover a proportion of the input VAT initially suffered.

This type of recovery would arise, for example, in the case of Surefire in **[5–25]** the above example if it had jointly opted to tax the sale with the purchaser. An opted sale would more likely be agreed if the purchaser was entitled to recover full input VAT credit.

Under Section 4B(6), the responsibility for accounting for the VAT **[5–26]** would pass to the purchaser. The purchaser would apply the reverse-charge procedure. If the disposal is to a taxable person who is entitled to 100% input VAT recovery, then the purchaser would suffer no net input VAT cost, but it should still reflect the transaction in its VAT 3 return.

Example

If Surefire were to jointly opt to tax the sale in the example above, then its VAT refund would be calculated using a formula set out in Section 12E(7)(a), which provides that it would be entitled to claim input VAT under Section 12 of the VAT Act for the taxable period in which the supply occurs by an amount calculated in accordance with the following formula:

$$\frac{E \times N}{T}$$

where –

- E is the non-deductible amount in relation to that capital good, i.e. in this case €540,000.
- N is the number of full intervals remaining in the adjustment period at the time of supply plus one, i.e. 15.
- T is the total number of intervals in the adjustment period in relation to the capital good, i.e. 20.

Surefire would therefore be entitled to reclaim input VAT of €540,000 × 15/20 = €405,000.

Surefire would need to be registered for VAT in order to submit the appropriate VAT 3. The purchaser would self-account for the VAT. The extent of the purchaser's entitlement to claim a simultaneous input VAT credit would depend on the purchaser's general input VAT entitlement position. A purchaser with restricted input VAT recovery entitlement may suffer a net VAT cost. Revenue has confirmed that a purchaser reclaiming input VAT credit would rely on the written option to tax document to do so.

4C(3) Right to recover – owner puts transitional property into exempt lettings

[5-27]   Section 4C(3) provides that:

> *"Where a person referred to in subsection (1) –*
>
> (a)   *acquired, developed or has an interest in immovable goods to which this section applies,*
>
> (b)   *was entitled to deduct tax, in accordance with section 12 on that person's acquisition or development of those goods, and*
>
> (c)   *makes a letting of those immovable goods to which paragraph (iv) of the First Schedule applies,*
>
> *then, that person shall calculate an amount in accordance with the formula in section 4(3)(ab), and that amount shall be payable as if it were tax due by that person in accordance with section 19 for the taxable period in which that letting takes place."*

[5-28]   Under Section 4C(3), when a taxable person who has an interest in transitional property was entitled to deduct the relevant input VAT and then puts the property into exempt lettings, then that person is required to repay the relevant input VAT under the "old" Section 4(3)(ab). The adjustment made under Section 4(3)(ab) is referred to as a deductibility adjustment. It was introduced with effect from 1 May 2005, i.e. more than three years before the new VAT and property regime took effect. There are strong arguments to say that Section 4(3)(ab) never had legal effect because it was in conflict with the EU VAT Directives. Nonetheless, the deductibility adjustment follows the logic of the CGS, as it provides that the amount of input VAT to be repaid in these circumstances is to be calculated using the following formula:

$$\frac{T \times (Y-N)}{Y}$$

T = input VAT.
Y = 20, unless the interest held by the person in question is shorter than 20 years.
N = the number of **full** years since the person acquired his/her interest before granting an exempt lease.

[5-29]   Repaying the input VAT in this manner, even if the repayment amounts to all of the input VAT, does not mean that there was no entitlement to recover input VAT in the first place. In other words, it would not generally speaking be correct to assert that the disposal of a transitional property which had been subject to a clawback of input VAT under Section 4(3)(ab) is exempt under Section 4C(2).

Example – exempt letting and subsequent disposal of transitional property

Mr Q has built up a portfolio of mixed property over a number of years. He is registered for VAT. Mr Q bought the freehold interest in a site in 2006 and had two warehouses constructed on it. He claimed back input VAT on development costs. This amounted to approximately €270,000 per warehouse. The properties were completed as defined in December 2007. Mr Q granted a long lease in relation to Warehouse A in January 2008 and output VAT was accounted for as required under the "old" VAT and property provisions. In August 2008, having made various attempts to sell Warehouse B, Mr Q allowed his own company, Q Qabs Limited, to use it as a temporary base for its exempt taxi services. Mr Q repaid the input VAT he had claimed in respect of developing Warehouse B. He calculated this VAT liability using the Section 4(3)(ab) formula, i.e.

$$\frac{T \times (Y - N)}{Y}$$

T = €270,000.

Y = 20 (this is the maximum and would apply even in the case of freehold interests).

N = 0 (N = the number of **full** years since Mr Q acquired his interest before granting an exempt lease. Warehouse B was completed in December 2007 and the exempt letting was granted in August 2008. Consequently the number of full years in this case is nil).

Mr Q is not entitled to opt to tax the lease to Q Qabs Limited because Q Qabs Limited is not entitled to recover input VAT and it is connected with Mr Q as defined in Section 7A(3) of the VAT Act (see Chapter 6). Consequently, the deductibility adjustment in this case is €270,000 x 20/20 = €270,000. Mr Q duly repays all of the input VAT.

In August 2009, Mr Q finally secures a buyer for Warehouse B. The property has been occupied as defined for less than two years and consequently is still "new" as defined (see Chapter 4). The buyer is another taxi company, which would not be entitled to recover input VAT if VAT arises on the sale.

Mr Q may think that Section 4C(2) should put the sale outside of the VAT "net", i.e. he asserts that having repaid all of the input VAT, he "had no right to deduction" under Section 12.

This would be an **incorrect interpretation**, however. The sale is subject to VAT on the full market consideration. Where does this leave Mr Q? In principle the property cannot, on the one hand, have been subject to a clawback of all of the input VAT and, on the other hand, still be subject to output VAT on the full sale consideration.

Pre 1 July 2008, Section 12(5) of the VAT Act provided that a person who disposed of a property on which they had suffered a Section 4(3)(ab) deductibility adjustment would be entitled to a proportional input VAT credit in the taxable period in which the taxable sale took place. However, Section 12(5) was deleted with effect from 1 July 2008.

There seems to be a slight difficulty with applying Section 4C(5) in this case in that it specifically applies where the vendor *"was not entitled to deduct all the tax charged"*. Mr Q was initially entitled to deduct his input VAT and then he repaid it under Section 4(3)(ab). It would seem correct in this case to allow a proportionate credit in respect of the original VAT clawback. To deny the credit would be to create double taxation. Section 4C(5) appears to be the only mechanism available to Mr Q.

In any event, no actual formula for the credit is provided in Section 4C(5) itself. Instead the section refers to the formula contained in Section 12E(7)(a). Section 12E(7)(a) applies in cases where a capital goods owner is making a disposal under Section 3(5)(b)(iii) (transfer of business). Revenue has confirmed that the taxpayer may rely on Section 12E(7)(a) in such circumstances. If the CGS owner was not entitled to full input VAT credit in respect of his/her acquisition/development of the property which is subject to a Section 3(5)(b)(iii) disposal, then Section 12E(7)(a) provides for a proportionate credit of input VAT when the property is disposed of. (This section is examined in more detail in Chapter 3, which deals with the CGS.)

In relation to Mr Q's disposal, the formula is as follows:

$$\frac{E \times N}{T}$$

E = non-deductible input VAT, i.e. in this case €270,000.

N = the number of full intervals remaining in the adjustment period at the time of supply plus one. The property was completed at the end of December 2007. It was put into exempt lettings in August 2008. It was sold in August 2009. The number of full intervals in the adjustment period in August 2009 was 18, plus one = 19.

T = the total number of intervals in the adjustment period in relation to that capital good, i.e. 20.

Consequently, the formula gives rise to the following input VAT credit on the occasion of Mr Q's sale of Warehouse B in August 2009:

$$€270,000 \times 19/20 = €256,500$$

Exempt lettings of transitional residential property by property developers prior to sale

It may be recalled that Section 4B(7)(b) provides for an interval-based adjustment in cases where property developers put non-transitional residential property into exempt lettings. There is a clawback of input VAT in relation to the exempt use, but it arises at the end of each interval and amounts to approximately $\frac{1}{20}$ of the input VAT for each interval in which the property is in exempt lettings (see Chapter 4). **[5–30]**

The provisions of Section 4C(3) as set out above are quite harsh in relation to non-transitional property which is put into exempt lettings. The clawback is not $\frac{1}{20}$, but amounts to a lump sum arising when the exempt letting commences. **[5–31]**

Tax Briefing, Issue 69 (September 2008) outlines a concessional alternative treatment that would allow a property developer renting out transitional **residential** property to avail of the treatment arising in Section 4B(7)(b) instead of suffering the lump sum clawback provided for in Section 4C(3). (Tax Briefing, Issue 69 is reproduced in Appendix 3.) **[5–32]**

It is important to be aware that the concessional treatment only applies to situations involving property developers and residential property. Other types of transitional property and non-developer owners could not avail of it and exempt lettings in such scenarios would be dealt with under Section 4B(3) as outlined above. **[5–33]**

Under Tax Briefing, Issue 69 the concessional treatment available hinges on Revenue's view of the term "completed", i.e. "Revenue is prepared to accept, in cases to which this article applies, that a property may be regarded as not having been completed until it has been rented". This seems quite a liberal approach to the definition of "completed", which is defined in Section 4B as meaning *"that the development of those goods has reached the state, apart from only such finishing or fitting work that would normally be carried out by or on behalf of the person who will use them, where those goods can effectively be used for the purposes for which those goods were designed, **and the utility services required for those purposes are connected to those goods**".* **[5–34]**

Revenue takes the view in Tax Briefing, Issue 69 that **"the fact that the utility services are connected does not in itself mean that a property is completed."** **[5–35]**

Perhaps this view of utility services might be presented in other cases where a tax payer wishes to argue a later completion date than might otherwise be acceptable.

[5–36]   The exempt letting of property pending sale of property is not to be confused with rent-to-buy schemes, which in recent times have been set up by various property developers. The idea is that persons wishing to buy property but unsure whether they can make the long term commitment to a particular location, property, mortgage, etc. initially rent the property from the developer. At the time of writing, Revenue has not confirmed its position in relation to the VAT treatment of rents paid in relation to such schemes. However, the rents would appear of necessity to be linked to an option to buy the property. Following a 2003 Appeal Commissioners case, the rents in such schemes would be accorded the same VAT treatment as the underlying property, i.e. they would be subject to VAT at 13.5% rather than the standard rate. Alternatively the rent could be regarded as prepayments in relation to the property purchase, in which case they would still be subject to VAT at 13.5%.

> *Example – VAT treatment of transitional residential property put into exempt residential lettings after 1 July 2008.*
>
> MacDev Homes Limited finished a new housing development in Longford on 1 December 2007. It recovered input VAT in the region of €20,000 in relation to each house. The market for new houses in this area declined in 2008 and MacDev found itself unable to sell the houses. As it was under pressure to repay financing in relation to the development, it began renting out houses to tenants from 1 October 2008. MacDev's accounting period ends on 31 December.
>
> If the provisions of Section 4C(3) were to apply, then for each house rented out, MacDev would be obliged to repay €20,000 to Revenue. However, under Tax Briefing, Issue 69, notwithstanding that by 1 December 2007 the houses had reached the state where they could effectively be used for the purposes for which they were designed and notwithstanding that MacDev would probably have had the utilities connected by that date, Revenue would be prepared to regard any house put into exempt lettings as not being "completed" until the letting commenced.
>
> Instead of repaying a lump sum VAT clawback with the September-October 2008 VAT return, MacDev would be in the following position:
>
> • Rental house is deemed "completed" on 1 October 2008 on the commencement of letting. No lump sum clawback would arise.
>
> • The initial CGS interval in respect of the property would commence on that date and would end on 30 September 2009. No clawback arises on 30 September 2009 because Revenue is relying

on Section 12(E)(5) of the VAT Act, which does not provide for an adjustment at the end of the initial interval.

- The second interval would end on 31 December 2009 (the deemed completion date means that the property is not regarded as "transitional" and consequently the non-transitional provisions in relation to the definition of intervals applies). Under the provisions of Section 12(E)(5) of the VAT Act, an adjustment would arise at this point as follows:

$$C - D$$

C = reference deduction amount (in this case €20,000/20) = €1,000.
D = interval deductible amount (in this case 0, because the letting is exempt).

C − D = €1,000. MacDev is required to pay €1,000 as VAT payable per house that is exempt let with its November-December VAT return.

- The same amount would be due in the same taxable period each year of the adjustment period for as long as the property remains in exempt lettings.

If MacDev is able to sell the rental house on, say, 1 January 2016, the provisions of Section 4B(7)(a) would require it to charge the purchaser VAT in the normal way (i.e. the property would not be regarded as "old" under the five-year rule). VAT would be calculated on the full consideration receiveable. No Section 4C(5) - type input VAT credit would be available. This is because, under the CGS adjustments already made, MacDev would only have repaid that proportion of input VAT corresponding to intervals when the property is in exempt use.

Legacy Leases - Assignments, surrenders and reversionary interests

The tenant was not entitled to recover input VAT

Section 4C(2) provides that no VAT arises on a disposal of **freehold** [5–37]
transitional property where the vendor had no entitlement to recover input VAT in relation to purchase/development.

Section 4C(6)(b) specifies this treatment also in relation to assignments/ [5–38]
surrenders, i.e. it states that *"tax shall not be chargeable where the person who makes the assignment or surrender had no right to deduction under Section 12 on the acquisition or the development of those immovable goods, but a joint option for taxation of that assignment or surrender may be exercised".*

Example – assignment of legacy lease by tenant who was not entitled to recover input VAT

BlingBank acquired a 25-year lease from HoldCo on 1 January 2005. HoldCo charged BlingBank VAT of €500,000. BlingBank was not entitled to recover same because it was engaged in solely exempt supplies.

On 1 January 2009, BlingBank assigns its lease to CompuTech Inc, which is engaged in fully taxable supplies. BlingBank has already suffered the VAT on the lease and is not obliged to charge output VAT on the assignment. However, it could jointly opt with Compu Tech to tax the assignment. If BlingBank were to do this, it would be entitled under Section 4C(5) to recover approximately 16/20 of the input VAT suffered when it was granted the lease, calculated as using the formula set out in Section 12E(7)(a) of the VAT Act, i.e.:

$$E \times N/T$$

E = the non-deductible amount, i.e. €500,000.
N = the number of full intervals plus one in the adjustment period, i.e. 16.
T = the total number of intervals in the adjustment period, i.e. 20.

Consequently the VAT recovery claim would be €500,000 x 16/20 = €400,000.

The tenant was entitled to recover input VAT

[5–39] Section 4C(6)(a) provides that output VAT arises in respect of the surrender or assignment of a leasehold interest of transitional property if the person assigning or surrendering the lease was entitled to input VAT credit in respect of the acquisition of the leasehold interest or its development.

Example

Mr Tee acquired a 25-year leasehold interest in a commercial property on 1 March 2003. VAT of €300,000 arose on the capitalised value under the "old" rules. The lessor obtained a VAT 4B and passed responsibility for accounting for the VAT on the lease to Mr Tee as tenant. Mr Tee accounted for the VAT on the reverse-charge basis. Mr Tee intended to use the property for the purpose of his fully taxable supplies. Consequently he was entitled to claim an input credit which matched the VAT on the lease and did not suffer any net VAT cost. Nonetheless he was still **entitled** to input VAT credit on his acquisition. As a result, output VAT would arise if he assigns the lease during the adjustment period.

Section 4C(7)(a) provides that the amount on which VAT is charge-able on a taxable assignment or surrender of transitional property is calculated using a formula set out in paragraph 4C(7)(b), divided by the reduced VAT rate referred to in Section 11(1)(d) of the VAT Act, as expressed in decimal form. At the time of writing, this is 13.5%. Section 10 of the VAT Act, which deals with the amount of which VAT is chargeable, does not apply under these circum-stances.

The formula set out in Section 4C(7)(b) is:

$$\frac{T \times N}{Y}$$

T = the total tax incurred.

N = the number of full intervals plus one remaining in the adjust-ment period at the time of the assignment or surrender.

Y is the total number of intervals in the adjustment period, i.e. generally 20.

Example

Following on from the Mr Tee example above, if Mr Tee assigns the lease on, say, 1 August 2009, the formula would apply as follows:

T = €300,000.

N = 14 (the total number of intervals in the adjustment period is 20, not 25. The lease was granted initially on 1 March 2003. Six years and four months later, on 1 August 2009, Mr Tee assigns the lease. There are 13 years and 8 months left in the lease term. N = the number of full intervals remaining plus one, i.e. 14).

Y = 20 (not 25. Although the original lease term was 25, the total number of intervals in the adjustment period cannot exceed 20).

Applying these figures to the formula would give the following outcome:

$$€300,000 \times 14/20 = €210,000.$$

This gives the amount of VAT payable in respect of the assignment. The amount on which VAT is chargeable as referred to in Section 4C(7)(a) is this VAT figured divided by 0.135 = €1,555,555 approx.

Finally, Section 4C(7)(b) provides that the VAT arising is to be accounted   **[5–40]**
for under Section 4(8) of the VAT Act. Section 4(8) is one of the provi-sions of the old Section 4 which may apply under Section 4(11) subject to Section 4C.

[5–41] Section 4(8) provides that if a taxable leasehold interest is surrendered or assigned to:

"*(i) an accountable person,*

(ii) a Department of State or a local authority, or

(iiii) a person who supplies immovable goods of a kind referred to in paragraph (a) of the definition of 'exempted activity' in section 1 or services of a kind referred to in paragraphs (i), (iv), (xi), (xia), (xiii) and (xiv) of the First Schedule, in the course or furtherance of business",

then the VAT arising is accounted for on the reverse charge basis, i.e. by the recipient. Section 4(8) also provides that the person surrendering or assigning the leasehold interest in these circumstances would issue a document to the recipient of the supply.

It will be recalled that an accountable person is a taxable person who is required to be registered for VAT. The term "accountable person" does not include persons engaged in exempt activity. However, paragraph (iii) provides that, if a taxable leasehold interest is surrendered or assigned to persons engaged in the exempt supplies set out in the First Schedule paragraphs specified, then these recipients would also be required to register and account for VAT in relation to the surrender/assignment. Finally, under paragraph (ii), Departments of State and local authorities, which are not taxable persons, would also be required to register and account for VAT if a taxable leasehold interest is surrendered or assigned to them.

[5–42] An accountable person would be entitled to claim a simultaneous input VAT credit to the extent that they intended to put the surrendered/ assigned property to a taxable use. Consequently, an accountable person might not suffer any net VAT cost in relation to a taxable assignment/ surrender of a leasehold interest in immovable goods. However, a local authority/government department would suffer an irrecoverable VAT cost given that it would not be entitled to recover input VAT. In general, a landlord or an assignee engaged in the exempt activities outlined in paragraph (iii) would not be entitled to recover input VAT in relation to the surrender or assignment of a taxable lease either. However, their position is different from that of the local authority/government department. Depending on circumstances, if a person engaged in exempt supplies did not intend to use the property for their own exempt activities, they would be entitled to register for VAT and opt to tax the lease of the property to a new tenant. This is because an exempt entity such as an insurance company is a taxable person, whereas a local authority/government department is not. Under Section 4B(5), taxable persons are entitled to opt to tax lettings. While this would require them to register for VAT, the VAT registration and option to tax would extend to the specific letting and would not make otherwise exempt activities subject to VAT.

Section 4C(8) reiterates the requirement to include the amount of VAT due and payable in the "document". It also contains an additional requirement, which is to state on the "document" the number of intervals remaining in the adjustment period. In the above case this would be 14. **[5–43]**

The document is required to indicate the **value** of the interest being surrendered or assigned (i.e. €1,555,555 in the above example) and the amount of VAT arising (€210,000 in the example). The recipient would be entitled to recover a corresponding input VAT credit under Section 12 to the extent that they intended to put the property to a taxable use.

Section 4C(8)(b) provides that the recipient of the interest is a capital goods owner. The adjustment period and total tax incurred in respect of the leasehold interest received is as provided for in Section 4C(11) and *"as correctly specified on the document"* (see above). **[5–44]**

Section 4C(8)(b) also clarifies that the initial interval for the new capital goods owner would be a 12-month period commencing on the date on which the assignment or surrender took place. In the above example, the assignment took place on 1 August 2009. This is the start date of the new owner's initial 12-month interval. The adjustment period for the leasehold interest would be 14 intervals from this date.

Finally, on the topic of the surrender of "legacy leases", Revenue has clarified that if the tenant pays a **reverse** premium to a landlord, it does not consider it to be within the scope of VAT. However, if the landlord pays the tenant a premium on surrender, then this would be subject to VAT at the standard rate, being regarded as a payment to the tenant in consideration of his relinquishing a legal right. **[5–45]**

In relation to reversionary interests in transitional property, Section 4C(11)(b) provides that the owner of the reversionary interest of a legacy lease is not regarded as a capital goods owner provided that the property has not been *"developed by, on behalf of, or to the benefit of that person"*. This phrase recalls the "old" Section 4(9) of the VAT Act and indeed the new Section 4(11), which confirmed that most of the "old" Section 4 would no longer apply from 1 July 2008 onwards, provided that the "old" Section 4(9) would continue to apply *"as respects a reversionary interest created prior to 1 July 2008"*. **[5–46]**

Example – disposal of reversionary interest

Jane granted a 25-year lease in a commercial property on 1 May 2005. She disposed of the property with the tenant *in situ* on 1 May 2009. The property had not been developed in the intervening years. Under Section 4C(11)(b), the disposal of Jane's reversionary interest is not subject to VAT.

Holiday homes

[5-47]   Section 4C(9) provides as follows:

"Where a person cancels an election to be an accountable person in accordance with Section 8(5A) then, in respect of the immovable goods which were used in supplying the services for which that person made that election, Section 12E does not apply if those immovable goods are held by that person on 1 July 2008 and are not further developed after that date."

[5-48]   Section 8(5A) provided that a person who had elected to register for VAT in respect of the letting of holiday accommodation could de-register subject to repaying a cancellation amount which is calculated using a formula set out in Section 8(5A) of the VAT Act. Section 4C(9) allows the Section 8(5A) formula to be used in the event that a person cancels such an election on or after 1 July 2008 and provides that in this case the provisions of the CGS would **not** apply. (See detailed example in Chapter 2, at paragraph **2-12**.) This also deals with the cancellation of the election to register when the property was acquired pre 1 July 2008 and developed after that date.

Post-Letting expenses

[5-49]   Section 4(11) provides that Section 4(10) of the VAT Act continues to apply in relation to lessors who grant long leasehold interests prior to 1 July 2008. Section 4(10) of the VAT Act deals with post-letting expenses and provides that the lessor is allowed to deduct certain input VAT incurred in:

- Carrying out services which the lessor was required to provide under the lease and the value of which was reflected in the rent on which the capitalised value was based

- Rent collection and any rent review and

- Exercising an option to extend or end the lease.

Revenue expands on this topic in its *VAT on Property Guide* (April 2008), which is reproduced in Appendix 1.

Service charges

The treatment of service charges incurred by landlords and charged on to tenants is a different matter, i.e. it is not dealt with under Section 4(10) of the VAT Act.   [5–50]

A Revenue concession applies in relation to one category of service charge, i.e. situations where the landlord buys in services, allocates the costs and shares them between the tenants. The landlord's own resources are not used, i.e. there is no management charge per se but a mere passing on of costs. The landlord in such a case is not in the business of property management. Previously, Revenue took the view that this was not a supply for VAT purposes. This approach resulted in trapped VAT. The invoices were made out to the landlord, who had no recoverability. The tenant had no recoverability either because the invoices were not in the tenant's name. Revenue now allows landlords to pass on the input VAT to tenants thereby allowing tenants to reclaim the VAT, subject to the tenant having an entitlement to recover input VAT in the first place.

For this category of service charge only, the landlord issues one invoice per year and the tenant can reclaim the VAT charged on the annual invoice. This has the following implications: [5–51]

- Neither landlord nor tenant accounts for VAT in respect of payments on account.

- If the landlord has no other VAT-able activities, s/he will file five "Nil" VAT returns each year. At the end of the landlord's accounting year, s/he issues an annual invoice. Both parties account for VAT in respect of this invoice. The landlord's corresponding VAT return will indicate purchase VAT = sales VAT, i.e. his/her net VAT position in relation to service charges is "Nil".

Landlords who are already registered for VAT may avail of the concession once they obtain the agreement of their Inspector of Taxes.

If the landlords are applying the "landlord's concession" they will merely be conduits for the expenses. Their own resources will not be used and there will be no separate management charge per se. Expenses are charged on to tenants at the VAT rate at which they are incurred, e.g. electricity will be charged on at the 13.5% incurred, insurance will be passed on on an exempt basis, etc. There is no provision for any "profit" to be taken by the landlord. As stated above, the landlord's VAT inputs in respect of the costs are equal to his/her VAT outputs.

[5–52]   A **second category** of service charge relates to situations where the landlord supplies the various services to the tenants using the landlord's own staff. No concessional treatment applies in such cases. The landlord would in principle be carrying on a taxable activity – property management. Assuming the obligatory VAT registration threshold is reached in relation to services, the landlord would be required to account for VAT. The standard VAT rate would apply where the landlord makes one charge for a composite supply of the various services, e.g. security, maintenance, cleaning, etc. If the one invoice is used and each service is charged for separately, then the VAT rate appropriate to each service would apply. There is no provision in such cases for the "once a year" VAT invoice. VAT invoices would be raised in the normal way.

Chapter 6

Lettings of Immovable Goods

Lettings

Under Article 135(l) of the recast Sixth Directive, EU Member States are **required** to exempt *"the leasing or letting of immovable property"*.

[6–01]

The term "letting" is not defined in the VAT Act or the Sixth Directive. However, lettings have been considered on many occasions by the ECJ and what has been gleaned from ECJ case law is that *"the letting of immovable property for the purposes of Article 13B(b) of the Sixth Directive essentially involves the landlord of property assigning to the tenant, in return for rent and for an agreed period, the right to occupy his property and to exclude other persons from it"* (C–275/01 *Sinclair Collis*). (Article 13B(b) is now Article 135(l) of the recast Sixth Directive.)

Over time, some guidelines have emerged which are commonly used as indicators that there is a letting (as opposed, for example, to a mere licence to use the property). The indicators are:

[6–02]

1. The owner gives the user a right to occupy the property.

2. The user has the right to exclude others from the property.

3. The user pays for its use.

4. The agreement is for a defined period.

5. The area occupied is precisely delineated.

6. What the user has is the passive provision of a particular area.

In principle, under the Directive, all supplies are subject to the charge to VAT. Treating lettings of property as exempt supplies is therefore an exception to the general rule. The ECJ has held on many occasions that as exceptions, lettings are to be narrowly interpreted. Despite this narrow interpretation, there can still be a letting for VAT

[6–03]

purposes even if only some of the six indicators set out above are present.

In the ECJ case C 281/03 *Temco*, it was, however, held that the strict interpretation does not mean that the exemptions should be construed in such a way as to deprive them of their meaning.

When easements are to be granted or conacre/agistment arrangements put in place they are likely to have the characteristics of either a licence or a lease and the potential VAT issues may need to be considered on that basis.

[6–04]   Under the VAT and property rules in place in this country until 30 June 2008, only **short** lettings were *prima facie* VAT-exempt (i.e. lettings of less than 10 years in duration). Under Section 7 of the VAT Act, lessors seeking an entitlement to recover input VAT were entitled to waive their short-term letting exemption, thereby making the otherwise exempt short letting taxable. Once the waiver was in place, it extended to all short-term lettings by the same taxable person, with some exceptions in relation to short lettings of residential property following changes introduced in the Finance Act 2007 (see paragraphs **[6–52]** to **[6–86]** below on Section 7 and 7B).

[6–05]   The changes introduced under the Finance Act 2008 provided that no new waivers of exemption would commence on or after 1 July 2008 and that in general waivers existing at that date would not extend to lettings of property acquired or developed on or after 1 July 2008.

[6–06]   In certain circumstances, waivers of exemption already in place at 1 July 2008 were allowed to remain in place. The provisions dealing with the continuation of pre-existing waivers are set out in Section 7B.

[6–07]   In relation to new lettings of property not covered by pre-existing waivers, an alternative to the waiver of exemption, the option to tax, is set out in the new Section 7A.

[6–08]   If a letting is subject to VAT by virtue of a pre-existing waiver of exemption, then it is not an "opted" letting.

Section 7A – the option to tax lettings – introduction

[6–09]   Under the new system, all new lettings of property (i.e. all lettings commencing on or after 1 July 2008) are *prima facie* exempt, **regardless of duration**. There is no longer a requirement to calculate capitalised values or to pass the economic value test.

This general exemption would not apply to the following:

- New lettings which are still covered by pre-existing waivers of exemption (see Section 7B below).
- Long leases which were put in place prior to 1 July 2008 – these are dealt under the new Section 4C (see Chapter 5).
- Leases of a duration such that they would be regarded as freehold equivalents (see above, Chapter 4).

Section 7A provides for an option to tax lettings and sets out the circumstances in which the option is available. Taxing a letting makes the rents subject to VAT at the standard rate. The lessor is required to issue VAT invoices to the tenant and to account for output VAT in the normal manner. [6–10]

Once the option to tax is exercised, a letting is no longer exempt but constitutes a VAT-able supply of services. Putting the property to a VAT-able use gives the lessor an entitlement in principle to recover input VAT in relation to costs associated with acquisition/development of the relevant property. [6–11]

A significant difference between the old "waiver" system and the new "option" system is that the option to tax is exercised on a "per letting" basis. The previous broad application associated with the waiver does not apply under the new system. [6–12]

In addition, the option to tax a letting is unilateral, i.e. under the legislation, a lessor does not need the tenant's acquiescence in order to tax a letting. This is different from opting to tax a sale, which has to be done jointly. However, the legislation does require the lessor to notify the tenant in writing that a letting will be opted (see below). Clearly, from a commercial perspective, a tenant with restricted entitlement to recover input VAT may not agree to an "opted" lease. The option to tax clause is not to be confused with a standard VAT clause and both may be required. [6–13]

The option to tax lettings – general rules

Under Section 7A, when a taxable person reclaims input VAT incurred on the acquisition/development of a property to be used for a letting, then s/he is regarded as having opted to tax the letting, even though it may not be known for certain at the acquisition/development stage that the letting will ultimately qualify for the option to tax. [6–14]

[6–15] This initial assumption stands until such time as the letting is actually granted. At that stage, one of the following situations will arise:

1. The letting qualifies for the option to tax under the legislation and the option is formally exercised, as prescribed.

2. The letting qualifies for the option to tax but the option to tax is not exercised for commercial reasons or simply because the written formalities are omitted. In these circumstances the option to tax is automatically terminated. The lessor would suffer a clawback of input VAT under Section 12E(6) of the CGS.

3. The letting does not qualify for the option to tax. Again, the option to tax would be automatically terminated. The lessor would suffer a clawback of input VAT under Section 12E(6) of the CGS.

If the option to tax is exercised, then the lessor is required to account for VAT on rents at the standard rate and is required to issue VAT invoices to the tenant.

[6–16] Subsequent to the formal exercise of the option to tax, the option can also be terminated if:

- The landlord terminates the option expressly using one of the formal mechanisms set out in Section 7A(d)(ii).

- The letting ceases to qualify for the option to tax.

Again, if the option to tax is terminated during the adjustment period for the underlying capital good, then the lessor would suffer a lump sum clawback of input VAT under Section 12E(c) of the VAT Act.

[6–17] Certain other points are also relevant, e.g. premia, rent holidays and accounting for VAT on rents. These points are examined in more detail below – see paragraphs **6–40**, **6–48** and **6–49**.

Formally exercising the option to tax

[6–18] Under Section 7A(1)(c) the lessor is required to exercise the option formally via:

> "(i) ... a provision in writing in a letting agreement between the landlord and the person to whom the letting is made (in this section referred to as a 'tenant') that tax is chargeable on the rent, or
>
> (ii) the issuing by the landlord of a document to the tenant giving notification that tax is chargeable on the letting."

The option to tax may therefore be exercised either by including a clause in the lease or via a separate document, such as a letter.

As indicated above, when a taxable person reclaims the input VAT incurred on the acquisition/development of a property to be used for a letting, then s/he is regarded as having opted to tax the letting. [6–19]

Under Section 7A(1)(b)(ii), this initial "deemed" option terminates automatically if the written notice is not given as prescribed. This would result in a lump sum clawback of the lessor's input VAT under the CGS. [6–20]

The legislation does not require the lessor to notify Revenue that s/he is opting to tax a letting. Observing the prescribed procedures at the appropriate time is the lessor's responsibility. An unplanned clawback due to the lessor's failure to have the relevant written notification in place could be extremely disadvantageous. There is no provision in the legislation for the retrospective application of the option to tax, i.e. an omission in relation to documentation cannot be rectified later on. [6–21]

If the option to tax is being exercised at the commencement of a lease, it would seem to be preferable to include the option clause in the lease document. This would be clearer for all parties – including Revenue, in the event of an audit – and only a single document would need to be retained as evidence of both the lease and the option to tax it. [6–22]

Example – clawback of input VAT due to failure to formally opt to tax a letting

Care, Less & Co buys a shop unit on 1 September 2009, incurs purchase VAT of €200,000 and reclaims same on the basis that it expects to grant a VAT-able lease. For the purpose of the CGS, the adjustment period for the new property is 20 intervals. Pending securing of a tenant, Care, Less & Co. is treated as having opted to tax the letting.

Care, Less & Co. signs a lease with Cash and Hand Retailers on 1 November 2009. However, there is no "option" clause in the lease document and no separate written document is issued to advise Cash and Hand Retailers of the position. In the absence of the prescribed "option" documentation, the lease with Cash and Hand Retailers is an exempt letting and under Section 7A(1)(d)(i), the "deemed" option to tax is automatically terminated on the date the exempt letting commences.

Under Section 12E(6)(c) of the VAT Act, Care, Less & Co is deemed to sell the shop unit in an exempt sale on 1 November 2009 and to immediately reacquire it on the same date. A clawback of input VAT would therefore arise as follows:

$$\frac{B \times N}{T}$$

B in this case = the total VAT reclaimed by Care, Less & Co. (€200,000).

N = the number of full intervals plus one remaining in the adjustment period (20).

T = the total number of intervals in the adjustment period (20).

Care, Less & Co. would suffer a clawback of input VAT of €200,000. This would be repaid in accordance with Section 19 of the VAT Act, i.e. via the November-December 2009 VAT return.

Deciding not to opt to tax a letting

[6-23]   As indicated above, when a taxable person reclaims input VAT incurred on the acquisition/development of a property to be used for a letting, then s/he is regarded as having opted to tax the letting, even though it may not be known for certain at the acquisition/development stage that the letting will ultimately qualify for the option to tax. If, ultimately, the lessor **decides** not to opt to tax a letting, the presumed option to tax is terminated when the exempt letting is granted.

[6-24]   A lessor might agree not to opt to tax a letting if, for example s/he acquires an attractive tenant but the tenant's activities are such that it would not be entitled to recover input VAT on rents, e.g. a medical practice, a bank, government offices or similar. The lessor might be willing to suffer the clawback of input VAT for the sake of having a stable tenant. The tenant might be persuaded to pay a higher rent to reflect the higher cost incurred by the lessor due to the VAT clawback.

The clawback would be calculated as per the example above.

[6-25]   Provided that the lessor repays the input VAT in accordance with Section 19 of the VAT Act, interest on the VAT clawback would not apply.

If it is the lessor's intention from the time of acquisition/development to grant an exempt letting, then there would be no initial entitlement to recover input VAT and clearly no clawback could arise.

Lettings which do not qualify for the option to tax

Regardless of what the lessor or tenant might want, some lettings will not in any event qualify for the option to tax.   **[6–26]**

Fundamentally, these are lettings which fail the "connected persons" provisions and lettings of residential property.

The "connected persons" provisions and opting to tax a letting

If the landlord and the tenant/occupant are connected, as defined in Section 7A(3), then the option to tax may only be exercised at the start of a new letting if the tenant or occupant is entitled to recover at least 90% input VAT. In relation to ongoing "opted" lettings, if the landlord and the tenant/occupant become connected (due, for example, to a change in circumstances) then the existing option to tax would cease unless the tenant/occupant is entitled to recover at least 90% of the input VAT in respect of that letting.   **[6–27]**

In relation to *existing* lettings, Section 7A(1)(d) provides as follows: **[6–28]**

> "A landlord's option to tax in respect of a letting is terminated –
>
> (iii)   *when the landlord and tenant become connected persons,*
>
> (iv)   *when the landlord or a person connected with the landlord occupies the immovable goods that are subject to that letting whether that person occupies those goods by way of a letting or otherwise ...*"

Section 7A(1)(d)(iii) and (iv) deal with termination of an existing option to tax when either the tenant or the occupant become connected with the landlord. The input VAT deduction entitlement position of the tenant/occupant are not mentioned at this point (but see Section 7A(2)).   **[6–29]**

Section 7A(2) essentially deals with the option to tax and **new** lettings i.e. lettings granted after 1 July 2008. It provides that: **[6–30]**

> "(a)   *Subject to paragraphs (b) and (c), a landlord may not opt to tax a letting-*
>
> (i)   *Where that landlord and the tenant in respect of that letting are connected persons, or*
>
> (ii)   *Where the landlord, whether or not connected to the tenant, or a person connected to the landlord, occupies the immovable goods that is subject to that letting whether that landlord or that person occupies those goods by way of letting or otherwise.*

>   (b)   *Paragraph (a)(i) and subsection (1)(d)(iii) shall not apply where the immovable goods which are the subject of the letting are used for the purposes of supplies or activities which entitle the tenant to deduct at least 90 per cent of the tax chargeable on the letting in accordance with section 12. However, where a landlord has exercised a landlord's option to tax in respect of a letting to which paragraph (a)(i) would have applied but for this paragraph, paragraph (a)(i) shall apply from the end of the first accounting year in which the goods are used for the purposes of supplies or activities which entitle the tenant to deduct less than 90 per cent of the said tax chargeable.*

>   (c)   *Paragraph (a)(ii) and subsection (1)(d)(iv) shall not apply where the occupant (being any person including the landlord referred to in that paragraph or that subsection) uses the immovable goods which are the subject of a letting for the purpose of making supplies which entitle that occupant to deduct, in accordance with section 12, at least 90% of all tax chargeable in respect of goods or services used by that occupant for the purpose of making those supplies. However, where a landlord has exercised a landlord's option to tax in respect of a letting to which paragraph (a)(ii) would have applied but for this paragraph, paragraph (a)(ii) shall apply from the end of the first accounting year in which the immovable goods are used for the purpose of making supplies which entitle that occupant to deduct less than 90% of the said tax chargeable."*

[6–31]   Paragraph (a) provides that the option to tax may not be exercised where either the tenant or the occupant are connected as defined with the landlord. However, paragraph (a) is subject to paragraphs (b) and (c).

[6–32]   Paragraph (b) provides that an option to tax a lease can still be exercised when landlord and tenant are connected as defined, provided that the tenant is entitled to at least 90% input VAT recovery in respect of the letting.

It also provides that an existing option to tax a lease may remain in place (see Section 7A(1)(d)(iii)) when landlord and tenant become connected, provided that the tenant is entitled to at least 90% input VAT recovery in respect of the letting.

[6–33]   Paragraph (c) deals with connected occupants (as opposed to connected tenants). It provides that the option to tax can still be exercised when the occupant is connected with the landlord at the commencement of a lease.

It also provides that an existing option to tax a lease may remain in place (see Section 7(a)(d)(iv)) when landlord and occupant become connected, provided that the occupant is entitled to at least 90% input VAT recovery in respect of that letting.

Connected persons

Section 7A(3) sets out detailed definitions in relation to the term **[6–34]** "connected persons". The legislative provisions are set out in Chapter 2. Page 29 of Revenue's *VAT on Property Guide* (April 2008) (see Appendix 1) gives a useful general summary of what it calls "connectivity", describing it as follows:

"Individuals are connected with:

- *their spouses,*

- *their relatives (brothers, sisters, ancestors or lineal descendants) or relatives of their spouses,*

- *individuals or spouses of individuals with whom they or their spouses are in partnership,*

- *the settlor or beneficiary of a trust where the individual is a trustee of that trust and vice versa.*

Companies or other bodies of persons are connected with:

- *Persons who control that company,*

- *Other companies that act in pursuit of a common purpose with the company, or*

- *A person or persons with a reasonable commonality of interests who have the power to determine the activities of two companies."*

Example – connected tenant with at least 90% input VAT recovery

Mr Tee, a taxable person, acquires a new property and claims back input VAT. He grants a lease to Tee Limited. Mr Tee is the 99% shareholder and managing director of T Limited. T Limited will use the property for the purpose of its fully taxable trade. Although Mr Tee is connected with T Limited, he is entitled to rely on the 90% rule and may opt to tax the lease.

Example – connected tenant with less than 90% input VAT recovery

Same circumstances as above, but T Limited's trade is partly VAT exempt, e.g. its input VAT recovery rate is only 85%. Mr Tee will not be entitled to rely on the 90% rule and consequently would not be entitled to opt to tax the lease with T Limited. Assuming that Mr Tee had initially recovered the input VAT associated with developing/acquiring the property, Mr Tee would suffer a clawback under the CGS (see example above, at paragraph **6–22** as to the calculation).

Example – tenant becomes connected with lessor during lease and tenant does not satisfy the 90% rule

DevCo acquires a commercial property, claims back input VAT on costs and grants a lease to TenantCo. TenantCo and DevCo are not connected. TenantCo's services are completely exempt. However, because the parties are not connected, DevCo may opt to tax the lease. A number of years into the lease, DevCo buys out the share capital in TenantCo. DevCo's option to tax terminates immediately, because DevCo is now connected with TenantCo and the 90% rule is not satisfied. DevCo suffers a clawback of input VAT under the CGS (see clawback calculation earlier in the chapter).

Example – lessor and tenant are connected from the outset and tenant's input VAT recovery percentage falls below 90% during the course of the lease

BigCo acquires a commercial property, claims back input VAT on costs and grants a lease to SmallCo. SmallCo and BigCo are connected but SmallCo is entitled to recover 95% input VAT. Consequently the 90% rule applies and BigCo may opt to tax the lease. After four years, SmallCo acquires a new exempt income stream. Its overall input VAT recovery percentage falls to 85%. Consequently the 90% rule is no longer satisfied.

Under Section 7A(2)(b), when a connected tenant's recovery rate falls below 90%, then the option to tax is terminated *"from the end of the first accounting year in which the goods are used for the purposes of supplies or activities which entitle the tenant to deduct less than 90%"* … of its input VAT. The term "accounting year" is defined in Section 1 of the VAT Act. An accounting year would normally end on 31 December but alternatively can end on the date to which a set of 12-month accounts is made up.

Insofar as a connected tenant's rate of VAT recovery may affect the option to tax, it would be prudent for a lessor to include a clause in the lease requiring the tenant to notify the lessor of a change in its input

VAT recovery rate as soon as this arises. A clause might also be included terminating the lease within a certain period of time if the connected tenant's recovery rate falls below 90%. If the lease is terminated before the end of the relevant accounting year (i.e. before the option to tax is terminated) then, provided that the lessor intends to grant a new VAT-able lease, it would not suffer a clawback of input VAT.

In reality, for commercial reasons, the lessor would rarely be completely at liberty to dictate the terms of the lease and a termination clause might not be acceptable to the tenant.

Termination of the option to tax in the above example would result in a clawback of part of BigCo's input VAT under the CGS (see example showing clawback calculation earlier in the chapter).

Example – existing option to tax – occupant becomes a connected person during the course of the letting

MultiCo develops new premises and grants a lease to one of its 100% subsidiaries, SubCo. SubCo is entitled to 100% input VAT recovery. MultiCo opts to tax the lease and SubCo commences to trade from the premises.

Some time later, SubCo sublets the premises to SubCo2, a 100% subsidiary of MultiCo. SubCo2 has 95% input VAT recovery. The legislation provides that, if the occupant satisfies the 90% rule, then the lessor's option to tax will **not** be terminated.

Lettings of residential property

Section 7A(1)(d)(v) provides that an existing option to tax would [6–35] be terminated *"when the immovable goods that are subject to the letting are used or to be used for residential purposes within the meaning of subsection 4"*.

Example – residential letting

Retro Limited buys an old building consisting of shop units downstairs and semi-derelict upper floors. It renovates the building, converts the shop unit into a restaurant and the upper floors into two residential apartments. The work constitutes development for VAT purposes. Retro Limited claims back all input VAT in relation to the development work, expecting that it will put the entire property to a taxable use. The plan is to sell the apartments and either to sell or rent out the restaurant.

It grants a lease of the restaurant to a 24-hour restaurant operator, Sweat Kitchen, and opts to tax the lease. Rather than selling the apartments, it leases them to Sweat Kitchen also, as Sweat Kitchen wishes to provide accommodation for its staff. Retro Limited is prepared to opt to tax the apartment leases and Sweat Kitchen has no objection to paying VAT on the rents. However, even if the prescribed documentary formalities are observed, the apartment leases do not qualify for the option to tax because the property is to be used for residential purposes.

Retro Limited is required to repay a clawback of VAT in respect of the apartment development, as per the provision of Section 12E(6) (see above).

Termination of the option to tax

[6-36]   Section 7A(1)(d) provides for a number of ways in which an existing option to tax can be terminated.

Termination as a result of the failure to formalise the lease in writing has already been considered earlier in this chapter. As set out earlier, such an omission can either be accidental, in which case it is likely to result in an unanticipated lump sum VAT clawback, or deliberate, in that a lessor might make a commercial decision not to opt to tax a lease which would otherwise qualify for the option to tax.

[6-37]   An option to tax can also be terminated by choice even if it meets all the criteria for remaining in place. A tenant might, for example, negotiate such a termination due to a change in the tenant's circumstances. If the lessor wishes to terminate an option which s/he has already exercised using the documentary provisions set out in Section 7A(1)(c), then under Section 7A(1)(d) (ii), termination is done via:

> "(I)   an agreement in writing between the landlord and tenant that the option is terminated and specifying the date of termination, which shall not be earlier than the date of that agreement, or
>
> (II)   the delivery to the tenant of a document giving notification that the option has been terminated and specifying the date of termination, which shall not be earlier than the date that notification is received by the tenant."

[6-38]   If the formal documentary provisions for termination are not observed, an option to tax which otherwise qualifies and which was originally exercised as prescribed would **not** be terminated and the lessor would

remain liable to account for VAT on rents. The documentary requirements around deliberate termination of the option to tax are therefore
as important as those associated with the formal exercise of the option
to tax.

If the option to tax a letting is terminated during the adjustment period   **[6–39]**
applying to the underlying property, then the lessor will suffer a
clawback of input VAT under the CGS (see earlier example in relation
to the clawback calculation).

Premia

A premium is usually a sum payable in connection with the granting of a   **[6–40]**
lease, the surrender of a lease or the assignment of a lease. The following
paragraphs apply in cases where the lease is **not** a freehold equivalent
interest, as referred to in Section 3(1C) of the VAT Act (see Chapter 4).

Payment by tenant to lessor

The following scenarios are not uncommon: **[6–41]**

- Tenant pays a lump sum to the lessor at the commencement of a
  letting (key money).

- Tenant pays a lump sum to the lessor upon the surrender of a letting
  as consideration for the lessor's agreement to the surrender.

Since the new VAT and property rules took effect on 1 July 2008, it is   **[6–42]**
also becoming more common to have a tenant pay a lump sum to the
lessor in consideration for the lessor's foregoing the exercise of his/her
option to tax.

The VAT treatment in this case will depend on whether the lease is   **[6–43]**
subject to the option to tax. If it is, then the premium is subject to VAT
at the standard rate. If the option to tax has not been exercised, then
the premium is VAT-exempt. In both cases the lessor has of course to
consider the direct tax position also.

Payment by lessor to tenant

This is a type of reverse premium which is sometimes referred to as   **[6–44]**
"key" money. The lessor pays the tenant to take up the lease. At times
the payment is described as a contribution to the cost of the tenant's
fit out.

Revenue takes the view that in merely agreeing to take a lease, a tenant   **[6–45]**
is not providing any service to the lessor. In this case, there would be

no supply for VAT purposes and the receipt of payment would not give rise to a VAT liability for the tenant. The tenant may be making a supply, however, if s/he does anything else in addition to agreeing to taking up the lease. There is a suggestion in Revenue's *VAT on Property Guide* from April 2008 (see Appendix 1) that agreement by a well-known brand proprietor to take a lease in a shopping centre may involve provision of advertising services by the tenant. In such scenarios, the payment would be liable to VAT.

Payment by an assignee to an existing tenant (the assignor)

[6–46]   The assignee effectively pays the sitting tenant for being allowed to take over the sitting tenant's lease. Revenue takes the view that the assignor in this case would be providing a service to the assignee, i.e. the assignor would transfer its rights under the tenancy to the assignee and the assignee would pay for same. The assignor would be viewed as providing a taxable service, which would be subject to VAT at the standard rate. The VAT position is not dependent on whether or not the option to tax applies.

Payment by an existing tenant (an assignor) to an assignee

[6–47]   This is a type of reverse premium in that the existing tenant, wishing to extricate itself from a lease, pays an inducement to the assignee in consideration for the assignee's taking over the sitting tenant's obligations under the lease. Again, Revenue takes the view that the assignee is providing a service in this case, i.e. s/he agrees to take over the sitting tenant's obligations. Such a service would be subject to VAT at the standard rate. The VAT position is not dependent on whether or not the option to tax applies.

Rent "holidays"

[6–48]   Revenue has confirmed that a rent-free period allowed for *bona fide* commercial reasons does not require special VAT treatment provided that the option to tax is not terminated while the lease granting the rent "holiday" remains in effect.

Accounting for VAT on rents

[6–49]   When the option to tax is exercised, the relevant letting becomes taxable and rents from that letting are subject to VAT at the standard rate. VAT on the rents should be included in the VAT return for the period in which the rents become due, unless the lessor has been authorised to account for VAT on the cash receipts basis. If rents are paid in advance, the VAT is due in the period in which the advance payment is received. If a schedular invoice is used, then the schedule would correspond with the provisions for lease payments in the lease document (see paragraph **6–50**).

The tenant in an opted lease will need a valid VAT invoice in order to claim input VAT credit in respect of VAT-able rents. Furthermore, under Section 17 of the VAT Act, the lessor in an opted lease is obliged to issue VAT invoices to the tenant *"in such form and containing such particulars as may be specified by regulations"*. The Value-Added Tax (Amendment) Regulations 2008 amend Regulation 9 of the Value-Added Tax Regulations 2006 to allow for a schedular-type invoice in respect of taxable rents. **[6–50]**

Rent-to-buy schemes

In recent times, given the difficulties in sourcing purchasers for newly completed properties, various property developers have set up what are referred to as "rent-to-buy" schemes, usually in relation to residential property. The idea is that persons wishing to buy property but unsure whether they can make the long-term commitment to a particular location, property, mortgage, etc., initially rent the property from the developer. At the time of writing, Revenue has not confirmed its position in relation to the VAT treatment of rents paid in relation to such schemes. However, the rents would appear of necessity to be linked to an option to buy the property. Following a 2003 Appeal Commissioners case, the rents in such schemes would be accorded the same VAT treatment as the underlying property, i.e. they would be subject to VAT at 13.5% rather than the standard rate. Alternatively, the rent could be regarded as prepayments in relation to the property purchase, in which case they would still be subject to VAT at 13.5%. **[6–51]**

Sections 7 and 7B – transitional measures where waivers of exemption were in place on 1 July 2008

Waivers of exemption – Introduction

The Finance Act 2008 provided for changes to Section 7 of the VAT Act in relation to waivers of exemption. **[6–52]**

Significant changes had already been introduced to Section 7 via the Finance Act 2007. With effect from 2 April 2007, a waiver of exemption could not be exercised in respect of residential lettings and an existing waiver in place at that date did not extend to a letting of a property for residential purposes where that property was either:

- acquired on or after 2 April 2007, unless a binding written contract had been entered into before that date; or

- developed on or after 2 April 2007, unless an application for planning permission to develop the property as a house, apartment or similar establishment had been received by a planning authority before that date.

[6-53] Nonetheless as at 1 July 2008, there were many waivers of exemption still in place, both in respect of residential and non-residential lettings.

Changes to Section 7(5) and the introduction of a new Section 7B set out the provisions to apply in these cases.

The general rule

[6-54] A new Section 7(5) introduced under the Finance Act 2008 provides that:

> *"(a)   No waiver of exemption from tax in accordance with this section shall commence on or after 1 July 2008.*
>
> *(b)   Any waiver of exemption from tax which applies under this section shall not extend to any letting of immovable goods where those goods are acquired or developed on or after 1 July 2008".*
>
> *(c)   For the purpose of applying paragraph (b), a waiver of exemption, which is in place on 18 February 2008 in respect of the letting of immovable goods which are undergoing development on that day by or on behalf of the person who has that waiver, may extend to a letting of those immovable goods."*

[6-55] In brief, this means that:

- No new waivers of exemption are to commence on or after 1 July 2008 (this is **not** to say that pre-existing waivers necessarily cease on that date).

- A waiver already in existence at 1 July 2008 would not, generally speaking, extend to a letting of property if the property is acquired or developed on or after 1 July 2008. Revenue has confirmed that this is to be interpreted as meaning that if the property was developed to completion before 1 July 2008 (or where developed to completion after 1 July 2008 in cases to which Section 7(5)(c) applies), then a pre-existing waiver would continue to apply to those goods.

- If a waiver already existed at 18 February 2008 **and** a particular property was undergoing development on that date, then the pre-existing waiver of exemption would continue to apply in respect of lettings of that property, **even if** the development continues on or after 1 July 2008 and/or the letting does not commence until on or after 1 July 2008.

*Example – extension of pre-existing waiver of exemption –
development in progress as at 18 February 2008*

Mr and Mrs Manny are the joint owners of a varied portfolio of
investment properties. Some of the properties were in short-term
lettings pre-1 July 2008 and continue to be rented out on this basis
after that date. Mr and Mrs Manny waived their short-term letting
exemption in 2002. They commenced development of a new
warehouse in 2007 and work was well under way by 18 February
2008. However, the property was not finished until 31 August 2008
and consequently it was not possible to commence a new letting
until 1 October 2008. The new tenant and Mr and Mrs Manny are
not connected. Under paragraph (c) above, Mr and Mrs Manny's
pre-existing waiver could be extended to the new letting and they
would not have to opt to tax it.

Section 7B contains further qualifications which also must be satisfied if   **[6–56]**
a pre-existing waiver is to remain in place from 1 July 2008 onwards (see
below).

In general terms, then, under certain circumstances, a lessor could put a   **[6–57]**
waiver in place until 30 June 2008 and it would continue to apply. The
pre-existing waiver would apply to all new **qualifying** lettings (see
below). Pre-existing waivers can also continue to apply to **qualifying**
lettings of residential property, **but** as set out earlier, in general terms,
due to the changes in the Finance Act 2007, such waivers would have
had to have been in place by 2 April 2007.

In cases where the pre-existing waiver meets the qualifications for   **[6–58]**
continued application, simply changing tenants would not cause an
existing waiver to cease to apply, *unless* the new tenancy is not a
qualifying tenancy.

If a particular letting ceases to qualify for extension of the waiver post-   **[6–59]**
1 July, only that particular letting is affected, i.e. the waiver may
continue to apply to other qualifying lettings. This is quite different
from the position pre-1 July 2008, when the application or cessation
of a waiver usually had general effect.

A landlord remains entitled to cancel a pre-existing waiver of exemption   **[6–60]**
on or after 1 July under the "old" rules. A voluntary cancellation **would,**
however, have broad application, i.e. it would apply to all of the
landlord's short-term lettings and would require the landlord to
calculate and possibly repay a clawback of VAT under Section 7(3) of the
VAT Act.

The rules applicable to cancellation of waivers of exemption have not changed and Regulation 4 of the Value-Added Tax Regulations 2006 still applies.

[6-61] Whereas the waiver pre-1 July 2008 applied only to "short" lettings as defined at the time, i.e. lettings with a term of 10 years or less, waivers which continue in place at 1 July 2008 may be extended to qualifying lettings of any duration, provided that they are not freehold equivalent interests.

> *Example – continued application of pre-existing waiver of exemption to a letting commencing on or after 1 July 2008*
>
> Mr and Mrs Manny are the joint owners of a varied portfolio of investment properties. Some of the properties were in short-term lettings pre-1 July 2008 and continue to be rented out on this basis after that date. Mr and Mrs Manny waived their short-term letting exemption in 2002. One of the properties, which was purchased in 2003 and has not been developed since then, falls vacant on 31 July 2008. Mr and Mrs Manny obtain a new tenant (with whom they have no connection) and grant a new letting, with a term of 15 years, commencing on 1 September 2008. Because the property had been acquired before 30 June 2008, a waiver was already in place at that date and there is no question of the property having been developed on or after 1 July 2008, then the pre-existing waiver can extend to the new letting on 1 September 2008. Consequently, it is not necessary to opt to tax the new letting.

[6-62] When a pre-existing waiver would not apply

> *Example – acquisition of a new rental property on or after 1 July 2008*
>
> If a lessor has a waiver of exemption in place by 1 July 2008 and acquires a new property on or after that date, then lettings of the new property would be *prima facie* exempt, i.e. the pre-existing waiver would not apply to them. This is because the legislation provides that a pre-existing waiver of exemption *"shall not extend to any letting of immovable goods where those goods are acquired or developed on or after 1 July 2008"*.
>
> If the lessor wishes to be entitled to claim input VAT credit in respect of the new property, then s/he would have to opt to tax the lettings under Section 7A. The letting would have to meet the qualifying criteria for the option to tax, as discussed earlier in this chapter.

The letting does not satisfy the option to tax criteria in Section 7A(2) ("connected persons" criteria)

Section 7B(3) provides that if a letting would not satisfy the option to tax criteria set out in Section 7A(2) (the "connected persons" criteria), then, **subject to** relieving provisions set out in Section 7B(4) (see "minimum threshold" section, below), the waiver would in any event cease automatically **in relation to the letting in question** as at 1 July 2008. The conditions in Section 7A(2) are the connected persons criteria, as set out above.   **[6–63]**

> *Example – cessation of waiver of exemption on the "connected persons" basis*
>
> Dr C has owned the building from which his medical partnership operates for many years. He waived his short-term letting exemption when he purchased the building and has been charging the medical practice VAT at the standard rate on rents. The property has not been developed since acquisition.
>
> Although the waiver and letting have been in place for many years, Dr C's waiver will be cancelled automatically on that date because it would not satisfy the connected persons criteria in relation to the option to tax, as set out in Section 7A(2) (it is assumed that the letting does not meet the conditions for the Section 7B(4) minimum threshold relieving provision, see para below). Dr C is connected with the medical practice and the medical practice fails the "90% rule" in terms of input VAT recovery.

> *Example – landlord and tenant are not connected but the tenant fails to meet the 90% criteria – the pre-existing waiver continues to apply*
>
> Dr C has owned a building for many years which he lets to a medical practice. The property has not been developed since acquisition. Dr C waived his short-term letting exemption when he acquired the building. Dr C has no connection with the tenant.
>
> Although the tenant would not be entitled to recover any input VAT, the pre-existing waiver of exemption may remain in place at 1 July 2008.

Example – landlord has a pre-existing waiver of exemption and a number of lettings in place as at 1 July 2008 – continued application of the waiver applies on a letting-by-letting basis

Dr C has owned two buildings for many years and waived his short-term letting exemption in 2001, i.e. when he acquired the first property. As at 1 July 2008, one property is leased to his own medical partnership. The other is leased to an unconnected dental partnership.

Dr C's pre-existing waiver of exemption will continue to apply to the dental tenant because there is no "connectivity". However, the waiver of exemption would not extend to the lease with his own medical partnership because it is connected with him and also fails to satisfy the 90% criterion. It is assumed that the letting does not meet the condition for the Section 7B(4) provision, see paragraph **6-66**.

Lettings of residential property

[6-64]   As indicated above, Section 7B(3) provides that if a particular letting would not satisfy the option to tax criteria set out in Section 7A(2), then, **subject to** relieving provisions set out in Section 7B(4), the waiver would cease automatically **in relation to the letting in question** as at 1 July 2008. The conditions in Section 7A(2) are the connected persons criteria, as set out above. Section 7A(2) does not refer to residential lettings (these are referred to in Section 7A(4)), Consequently the fact that a property may be in residential lettings as at 1 July 2008 is not of itself sufficient to cause a pre-existing waiver of exemption to cease to apply on that date.

[6-65]   In other words, provided that (in general terms) the waiver was already in place as at 2 February 2007 (see above in relation to the abolition of "residential waivers" as at that date) and the property has not been developed since that date, then a pre-existing waiver of exemption can continue to apply to residential lettings, assuming of course that the residential letting is not with a connected tenant.

Example – continuation of pre-existing waiver of exemption in relation to residential lettings

Mr Landlord has had two houses in residential lettings for many years. He waived his exemption under the "old" rules. Both houses are occupied by tenants on 1 July 2008. The tenants are not connected with Mr Landlord. However, both of the leases are due to end on 31 August 2008. On 1 September 2008, one of the tenants renews his lease and remains *in situ*. The other tenant does not renew.

Consequently the house is vacated. Mr Landlord obtains a new tenant and grants a new lease on 1 October 2008. Neither property is developed on or after 1 July 2008. Neither tenant is connected with Mr Landlord.

Mr Landlord satisfies the waiver extension criteria. Consequently the pre-existing waiver continues to apply to both the renewed letting and the new letting, even though both lettings commence after 1 July 2008. It is interesting to note that neither letting would qualify for the option to tax. In any event, because the waiver can remain in place, Mr Landlord retains his entitlement to VAT input credit on the basis of the continued waiver.

Mr Landlord should be advised that:

- On or after 1 July 2008, Mr Landlord would be entitled to cancel his pre-existing waiver on the basis of Section 7(3) of the VAT Act. This would be a "global" cancellation and not a "per property" cancellation, because the cancellation would be at Mr Landlord's discretion as opposed to being a cancellation imposed due to the connected persons rule. Mr Landlord might do this, for example, if the input VAT claimed in respect of the properties to which the waiver extends equals the output VAT accounted for in respect of rents.

- Subsequent to cancelling his waiver, Mr Landlord would be entitled to sell the relevant properties without charging VAT on the sale proceeds. This is because, under Regulation 11 of the Value-Added Tax Regulations 2006, when a person cancels a waiver of exemption under Section 7(3), then *"the person shall be treated as a person who had not waived his or her right to exemption"*.

The minimum threshold exemption

Even if a pre-existing waiver would *prima facie* be liable for cancellation as at 1 July 2008 under the connected persons criteria set out in Section 7A(2), Section 7B(4) contains relieving provisions which would allow it to extend to a letting subject to: [6-66]

- Meeting a minimum VAT repayment threshold set out in Section 7B(5) **and**

- Satisfying the qualifying conditions set out in **either** Section 7B(4)(c)(i) or Section 7B(4)(c)(ii). These are two **completely** separate sets of qualifying conditions. Provided that the threshold is met, a pre-existing waiver of exemption can remain in place if the conditions in **either** paragraph (i) **or** paragraph (ii) are met.

[6-67]   To examine the qualifying conditions first, under Section 7B(4)(c)(i):

The waiver must have been in place on 18 February 2008 **and**:

- the letting which was in place on 1 July 2008 must already have been in place at 18 February 2008; **or**
- the property in question must have been owned by the lessor and been in the course of development by him/her or on his/her behalf on 18 February 2008.

> *Example – lessor with waiver in place at 18 February 2008 – same letting is in place on 18 February and on 1 July 2008*
>
> LetCo, a property holding company, acquires a premises in 2006, waives its short-term letting exemption and grants a four-year-and-nine-month lease to Loans-R-Us, which is an exempt entity. LetCo and Loans-R-Us are owned and controlled by the same people. The lease remains in place at 18 February and at 1 July 2008. Consequently the waiver of exemption would remain in place on 1 July 2008, *subject to also meeting the minimum threshold requirement,* even though the lease to Loans-R-Us would not qualify for the option to tax under the connected persons rules set out in Section 7A(2).

> *Example - lessor with waiver in place at 18 February 2008 also owns and is developing a property at 18 February 2008*
>
> Dr Foster registered for VAT, acquired a site, waived his short-term letting exemption and began to construct a new surgery on 15 January 2008. Development was ongoing as at 18 February 2008 but the new surgery was not finished until 31 December 2009. Dr Foster granted a lease to The Foster Medical Partnership, an exempt GP practice in which he is a partner, on 1 January 2010. Because Dr Foster met the 18 February 2008 deadline in respect of both the waiver and the development work, the waiver can extend to the letting to his GP practice, *subject to also meeting the minimum threshold requirement.* It does not matter in this case that he is connected with the practice, which is an exempt entity, and would not qualify for the option to tax under the general connected persons rules.

[6-68]   The alternative qualifying conditions are set out under Section 7B(4)(c)(ii) as follows:

- If the lessor's own interest is a long lease (a lease of 10 years or more in duration),

- which was granted to him/her in the period between 18 February 2008 and 30 June 2008,

- by an unconnected person,

- then the conditions for extending a pre-existing waiver of exemption are still satisfied, regardless that the waiver may not have been in place at 18 February 2008 and regardless of the connected persons criteria set out in Section 7A(2).

For the second set of qualifying conditions to apply, it would of course also be necessary that the waiver would at least be in place at 1 July 2008. If these conditions are met, development work between 18 February and 30 June 2008 would not cause any particular issue and the date of the new lease would not be relevant, i.e. it could be granted on or after 1 July 2008.   **[6–69]**

Example - lessor with waiver in place at 1 July 2008 acquires its own interest in the property between 18 February and 30 June 2008

Tom, Richard and Harry are granted a 25-year lease on 1 May 2008 by an unconnected developer. The partnership registers for VAT with effect from 1 May and waives its short-term letting exemption from that date. It reclaims the input VAT on the basis that it intends to put the property into a taxable letting. Richard and Harry are dentists and the plan is to sublet the property under a short letting to them, for use in their exempt dental practice. On 1 May the partnership grants a nine–year-and-nine-month lease to Richard and Harry.

The partnership is connected with the dentists and the dental practice would be VAT exempt. Consequently this letting would not qualify for the option to tax under Section 7A(2). The partnership does not wish to have its waiver cancelled on 1 July 2008 because it wants to retain its entitlement to claim the input VAT incurred on the lease granted by the developer.

Although the partnership does not put its waiver of exemption in place until 1 May 2008 and although its tenant is both connected and exempt, it meets the second set of qualifying conditions for extension of the waiver, i.e. it was granted a long leasehold interest by an unconnected person between 18 February and 30 June 2008.

(This is not to say it will necessarily also meet the minimum threshold – that is another matter and will be considered below.)

What is the "minimum threshold"?

Under Section 7A(5), the VAT on the rents must at least equal the permitted minimum amount provided for in the formula set out below.   **[6–70]**

The permitted minimum rent payable must be an amount which will ensure that output VAT equivalent to the input VAT deducted by the lessor in respect of the acquisition or development of the property will be accounted for within not more than 12 years. It is calculated by the formula:

$$\frac{A-B}{12-Y}$$

A = the input VAT claimed by the lessor in respect of acquisition or development of the property.

B = the VAT chargeable and paid on rents which would be taken into account if the waiver were cancelled at 1 July 2008.

Y = the lesser of:

- 11 **or**

- The number of full years since the date of the first letting of the property or the date on which the lessor waived exemption, whichever is later.

Example

Take the case of Tom, Richard and Harry, above. The partnership incurs input VAT of €540,000 in relation to the long lease on 1 May 2008. This is also the date on which it waives its exemption. The terms of the lease with the dental practice provide that it will pay rent of €120,000 per annum, plus VAT at 21% (the standard VAT rate on that date) of €25,200. Rent is to be paid monthly, i.e. €10,000 per month plus VAT of €2,100 is to be lodged to the partnership's bank account on the 15th of each month, starting from 15 May 2008.

A = €540,000.
B = €4,200 (€2,100 VAT on rents for May and June 2008).
Y = Zero. The number of full years since the date of the first letting and the date on which the waiver was exercised is Nil.

Consequently the threshold formula works out as follows:

$$\frac{€540,000 - €4,200}{12}$$

i.e. $$\frac{€535,800}{12}$$

$$= €44,650$$

The lease in place at 1 July 2008 provides for an annual repayment of VAT of €25,200, i.e. it does not satisfy the minimum threshold

---

in the formula. If no change is made to rents, then although the letting would satisfy the other qualifying conditions, the waiver would still be cancelled as at 1 July 2008.

If acceptable to the dental practice, the partnership would be entitled to vary the lease at 1 July 2008 to provide for an increase in the rent to, say, €212,619 plus VAT per annum. This minimum threshold would then be satisfied (€212,619 x 21% = €44,650).

Under Section 7B(4)(a) the VAT the partnership would account for **[6-71]** "in equal instalments" over the 12 months following 1 July 2008 would not be less than €44,800. While Revenue appears to have no difficulty with the rent being artificially inflated for VAT purposes in order to satisfy the minimum threshold rule, consideration would have to be given by the lessor to the direct tax consequences of taking such a course of action.

This does not mean that the rent can be put back to its previous non- **[6-72]** qualifying level after, say, 1 July 2009. Section 7B(4)(b) provides that *"if the conditions in paragraph (a) fail to be satisfied because of a variation in the terms of the lease or otherwise or if the tax paid at any time in respect of the letting is less than the tax payable, this subsection shall cease to apply"*.

This would suggest that, regardless of the references to a 12-month **[6-73]** period in paragraph (a), if the VAT paid in respect of a particular letting is less than the threshold minimum in any given year, then the waiver will be deemed to be cancelled, presumably as at 1 July 2008.

Anti-avoidance provision

Section 70 of the Finance (No. 2) Act 2008 introduced an additional anti- **[6-74]** avoidance provision by adding a new Section 7B(6) after Section 7B(5). This provides that:

"Where a landlord has a letting to which subsection (3) or (4) applies and that landlord becomes a person in a group within the meaning of Section 8(8) on or after 1 July 2008 and the person to whom that letting is made is a person in that group, then the person referred to in section 8(8)(a)(i)(I) in respect of that group shall be liable to pay the amount as specified in subsection (3)(a) as if it were tax due in accordance with section 19 –

(a)   in the case of a landlord who became a person in that group before the date of the passing of the Finance Act 2009, in the taxable period in which that Act is passed, or

(b)   *in the case of a landlord who became a person in that group after the*
       date of passing of the Finance Act 2009, in the taxable period during
       which that landlord became a person in that group."

[6-75]   According to the Explanatory Memorandum to the legislation, "the
              amendment ensures that the landlord cannot avoid the liability imposed
              in subsection (3) simply by being part of VAT group with the tenant".

[6-76]   No VAT would arise in relation to lettings of property granted by one
              member of a VAT group to another. This is because under the VAT
              group provision, no supply takes place between VAT group members
              and VAT would not, in any event, be charged on rents even when the
              waiver of exemption continues to apply.

[6-77]   Section 7B(6) provides that if a pre-existing waiver of exemption would
              not qualify for continued application to a particular letting under the
              connected persons provisions referred to in Section 7B(3)/(4), then a
              clawback of VAT still arises under the CGS.

[6-77A]   Revenue's e-brief 37/2009 dated 5 June 2009 refers to relevant guidance
              material which has been published in Chapter 7B.1 of the VAT Manual
              on the subject of Section 7B(6). The guidance material clarifies as
              follows:

              "Section 70 of the Finance (No. 2) Act 2008 introduced a new
              subsection (6) into section 7B of the VAT Act 1972 (as amended).
              This deals with situations where a landlord who has a letting of
              less than ten years with a waiver in place to a connected tenant
              becomes a member of a VAT group (where the tenant is a member
              of that group) on or after 1 July 2008. In such cases, the subsection
              provides for two separate scenarios –

              (1)   Where the landlord enters the group between 1 July 2008 and
                     the date of passing of the Finance (No. 2) Act 2008 (i.e.
                     24 December 2008), a waiver cancellation adjustment is trig-
                     gered and the person in the group liable to account for VAT
                     (the group remitter) is liable to pay the cancellation amount
                     as if it were tax due in the taxable period in which the Act is
                     passed (i.e. Nov/Dec 2008).

              (2)   Where the landlord enters the group after the date of passing
                     of the Finance (No. 2) Act 2008 (i.e. 24 December 2008), a
                     waiver cancellation adjustment is triggered and the person in
                     the group liable to account for VAT (the group remitter) is
                     liable to pay the cancellation amount as if it were tax due in
                     the taxable period in which the landlord enters the VAT
                     group.

This rule ensures that connected persons cannot use the grouping provisions to avoid the rules in section 7B VAT Act 1972 (as amended) for lettings between connected persons where a waiver of exemption has been exercised. This rule will not apply where the underlying use of the property is for other than exempt purposes and the property is used by the group for the purpose of making supplies that entitle that group to deduct at least 90% of the VAT incurred by it in relation to those supplies.

…

In relation to cases where (1) above applies, Revenue are willing to accept that the cancellation amount may be accounted for in the return for the taxable period following the passing of the Finance (No. 2) Act 2008, i.e. Jan/Feb 2009 return. This is to take account of the fact that there is a very short time period between the passing of the Act and the end of the taxable period (Nov/Dec).

…

Revenue are willing to accept that where a landlord applies to leave the VAT group before the end of February 2009, the landlord can keep the waiver in place by availing of the 12-year rule. In order for this to be acceptable the landlord must –

(1) Apply in writing to their local Revenue Office to leave the group and specify that the reason they wish to leave is to avail of this concessional treatment.

(2) Ensure that VAT accounted for in respect of the rents charged to the connected tenant meets the minimum amount in accordance with the formula in section 7B(5) VAT Act 1972 (as amended)."

Clawback on cancellation of waiver

As indicated above, the pre-existing waiver is deemed to be cancelled in certain circumstances. If a waiver of exemption is cancelled after 1 July 2008, then under Section 7B(3)(a) the lessor is required to calculate any VAT repayment arising using the "old" Section 7(3) provisions, i.e. input VAT reclaimed originally minus any VAT recovered in respect of rents up to the end of the taxable period immediately before that in which the waiver is deemed cancelled. **[6–78]**

If a waiver is deemed to be cancelled, for example on connected persons grounds, then the cancellation arises on a **per letting** basis. The lessor is **[6–79]** required to repay any Section 7(3) clawback in accordance with Section 19 of the VAT Act.

[6 80]   However, as mentioned previously even on or after 1 July 2008, the lessor can still rely on the provisions of Section 7(3) to deliberately cancel his/her waiver of exemption. When a pre-existing waiver of exemption is cancelled deliberately at the discretion of the lessor, then it is a global cancellation, i.e. it applies to all lettings subject to the waiver, as opposed to on a "per letting" basis.

[6–81]   In addition, regardless of the circumstances in which a waiver is cancelled on or after 1 July 2008, if a lessor has other lettings in place to which a qualifying option to tax applies, these lettings would be unaffected by a cancellation of waiver. The waiver and the option to tax are separate legislative provisions.

Example – cancellation of waiver in respect of a particular letting – pre-existing waiver continues to apply to other lettings

Dr C has owned the building from which his medical partnership operates for many years. The building originally cost €1.5 million plus input VAT at 13.5% of €202,500. He waived his short-term letting exemption when he purchased the building and has been charging the medical practice VAT at the standard rate on rents. As at 1 July 2008, Dr C also has a number of other short-term lettings with unconnected parties. Up until 30 June, all of his lettings had been taxable on the basis of his waiver of exemption.

As at 30 June 2008, Dr C has accounted for VAT of €15,000 on rents from the medical practice. The property has not been developed since acquisition.

As at 1 July 2008, on the connected persons basis, Dr C's waiver of exemption would no longer apply to the letting to the medical practice. He must calculate a clawback under Section 7(3), i.e. €202,500 input VAT minus €15,000 VAT on rents up to 30 June 2008 = €187,500. The clawback would be deemed to arise in the July-August 2008 taxable period and under Section 19 Dr C would have to repay it no later than 19 September 2008.

Dr C's other lettings are such that the waiver can continue to apply. The automatic cancellation only applies on a **per letting** basis.

Example – taxable person elects to cancel pre-existing waiver of exemption

Dr C has owned a number of investment properties for several years and has a waiver of exemption in place as at 1 July 2008 which he has not cancelled. As at 1 July, all of his lettings are such that his pre-existing waiver of exemption remains in place.

On 1 July 2009, Dr C's accountant points out that his VAT position in relation to the properties is as follows:

	Input VAT claimed	Output VAT on rents	Net position
Property A	(300,000)	300,000	Nil
Property B	(250,000)	250,000	Nil
Property C	(400,000)	20,000	(380,000)
Overall net position			(380,000)

Dr C has heard that the "global" cancellation of waiver provisions provided for in Section 7(3) no longer applies after 1 July 2008 and wonders if he might simply cancel his waiver in relation to properties A and B, while allowing it to continue to extend to Property C. He is thinking of selling some property and it may be advantageous to him to place them outside the VAT "net".

However, the per-letting waiver cancellation provision only applies in cases where the lessor suffers an automatic cancellation of waiver under the rules set out above. If Dr C elects to cancel a pre-existing waiver post 1 July 2008, then all of Section 7(3) would apply, i.e. he would have to pay a cancellation sum of €380,000.

See also Chapter 2 of this publication, which examines in detail the circumstances which in a cancellation of waiver can arise under the Finance Act 2009 amendments to the VAT Act.

Is it still possible to obtain back-dated waivers of exemption?

Notwithstanding the introduction, with effect from 1 July 2008, of Section 7(5)(a) of the VAT Act, i.e. *"no waiver of exemption from tax in accordance with this section shall commence on or after 1 July 2008"*, Revenue has confirmed that **after** that date a waiver of exemption may still be back-dated subject to certain conditions.   [6–82]

[6–83]   To consider the background to this provision, Section 7 of the VAT Act and Regulation 4 of the Value-Added Tax Regulations 2006 provide that Revenue would grant a back-dated waiver of exemption on request and upon provision of specific information.

[6–84]   The back-dated waiver has been used in certain circumstances to prevent lessors who had, perhaps unwittingly, granted an exempt short lease from suffering a clawback of input VAT. Under the Regulations, the earliest date to which it can extend is 26 March 1997.

The back-dated waiver is only available in cases where the tenant is, for the entire period for which back-dating is sought, fully entitled to an input VAT deduction under Section 12 of the VAT Act.

[6–85]   Furthermore, Revenue would only grant the back-dated waiver if the lessor already had a VAT registration number in place as at the date on which s/he seeks to have the back-dated waiver commence. In other words, these provisions allow for the back-dating of a waiver of exemption, rather than a back-dating of the VAT-registration. The legal basis for Revenue's refusal to grant a back-dated registration in these circumstances is unclear.

[6–86]   A back-dated waiver of exemption can only commence between 26 March 1997 and 30 June 2008. Under Section 7(5)(a), the "back-dating" cannot commence on or after 1 July 2008.

However, a back-dated waiver, once in place, may meet the criteria for extension beyond 1 July 2008.

> ### Example – back-dated waiver granted after 1 July 2008
>
> Mr Forgetful, who is registered for VAT, buys a commercial property on 1 June 2006 and claims back his purchase VAT. He agrees lease terms with an unconnected tenant, Frosty Limited. Frosty Limited is entitled to 100% input VAT recovery. Frosty Limited takes up occupancy and begins to pay rent. However, the lease is never formalised. Consequently it would be regarded as a short-term letting, i.e. *prima facie* exempt. Mr Forgetful's accountant discovers this situation in September 2008, i.e. after 1 July 2008.
>
> Mr Forgetful would be entitled to obtain a back-dated waiver of exemption with effect from 1 June 2006. In addition, the waiver could remain in place at 1 July 2008. He would thus be able to avoid a clawback of input VAT.
>
> The back-dated waiver of exemption should not be confused with the option to tax. There is no provision in the legislation for a back-dated option to tax.

Example – option to tax not exercised

Mrs Unfortunate, who is registered for VAT, buys a commercial unit on 1 July 2009 and reclaims input VAT of €400,000. She grants a lease to a fully taxable tenant on 1 September 2009. The rent agreed is €24,000 per annum. However, although she intends to opt to tax the lease, Mrs Unfortunate never puts the option in writing and does not account for VAT on rents. Consequently the property is put to an exempt use on 1 September 2009. Mrs Unfortunate has a Revenue audit on 1 August 2011 and Revenue seeks a refund of input VAT.

No provision exists in the legislation for the back-dating of the option to tax. Furthermore the property was acquired after 1 July 2008, so there is no question of a back-dated waiver of exemption. The best Mrs Unfortunate can do would be to opt to tax the letting as early as possible, e.g. with effect from 1 September 2011.

Under Section 7A(1)(b), Mrs Unfortunate would have been regarded as having exercised her option to tax initially when she reclaimed the input VAT. Under Section 7A(1)(d), her deemed option to tax terminates automatically on 1 September 2009, i.e. when she grants the exempt letting. Consequently on 1 September 2009, Mrs Unfortunate becomes liable for a clawback of input VAT, payable under Section 19 of the VAT Act no later than 19 November 2009 (i.e. with the September-October 2009 VAT 3).

Under Section 12E(6)(c), Mrs Unfortunate is deemed to sell the property in an exempt sale on 1 September 2009 and to immediately reacquire it. Her clawback would be calculated as follows:

$$\frac{B \times N}{T}$$

B = the total reviewed deductible amount (in this case €400,000).
N = the number of full intervals remaining in the adjustment period plus one (in this case 20).
T = the total number of intervals in the adjustment period (20).

Mrs Unfortunate must therefore repay the full €200,000 of input VAT reclaimed. Revenue would be entitled to impose an interest charge from 19 November 2009 and would also be likely to impose a penalty.

However, if Mrs Unfortunate opts to tax the lease with effect from 1 September 2011, then under Section 12E(6)(d), she would be entitled to recover a portion of input VAT, calculated as follows:

$$\frac{E \times N}{T}$$

E = the non-deductible VAT (€200,000).

N = the number of full intervals remaining in the adjustment period plus one (assuming that Mrs Unfortunate makes up accounts to 31 December, then this will be 18).

T = the total number of intervals in the adjustment period (20).

Mrs Unfortunate would therefore be entitled to reclaim 18/20 of the €200,000 purchase VAT (€180,000) with her September-October 2011 VAT 3.

While this is perhaps not such a bad outcome, clearly the VAT "leakage" would increase the longer the letting is allowed to continue without opting.

Chapter 7

The New Rules Made Simple

This chapter is intended to be an easy reference guide for readers looking for a quick steer towards solving a problem connected with VAT and property. The chapter is divided into two sections. Section 1 looks at the key VAT issues that can affect various parties to a property transaction. It focuses on participants in common transactions and examines their VAT position under the new rules. It is entitled "The Players and Their Positions". [7–01]

Section 2 is a simple-to-follow chart which attempts to guide the reader to the correct VAT answer by alerting the reader to the right questions to ask.

Section 1 – The Players and Their Positions

The "players" are the participants in a property transaction. For the vast majority of transactions, these will be either vendors, purchasers, landlords or tenants. The following sections highlight the key issues, and the relevance of those issues, for each of the players which need to be considered to determine the VAT position in any transaction. [7–02]

Vendors

Did they incur VAT on acquisition? Or is VAT deemed to have been incurred (eg. under Section 13A or Section 3(5)(b)(iii))? [7–03]

This will indicate that VAT implications will arise when they sell.

When was the last development carried out? [7–04]

If the last development was not recent, the sale may be exempt from VAT. Consider opting to tax the sale if there is a capital goods scheme clawback.

Was VAT reclaimed on acquisition and/or development? [7–05]

If so, a VAT charge or clawback is likely to arise on the sale.

[7–06]   Is the building new or old?

This can determine whether the sale is subject to VAT, or not.

If new, what was period of occupation?

The sale of a non-residential property is subject to VAT if it is less than five years since completion of the building or, if less than five years and a second supply to an unconnected person, the property has been occupied for less than 24 months, on aggregate.

[7–07]   If sale exempt, should the vendor jointly opt to tax?

Relevant if VAT reclaimed or reclaimable, otherwise clawback arises.

[7–08]   Does the purchaser have an entitlement to reclaim VAT if so charged?

Clearly the answer to this question is likely to affect the price which the purchaser will be willing to pay.

[7–09]   Will the purchaser agree to a joint option to tax?

They will probably agree readily if they can recover the VAT.

If not, can another arrangement be achieved?

Perhaps the vendor and purchaser might agree to an increase in sales price to compensate for clawback rather than the purchaser suffering a higher VAT charge on the purchase price. The parties should consider whether other tax (non-VAT) implications arise in such circumstances.

[7–10]   Contract clauses

As always, it is vital that the sales contract contains a VAT clause if the sale is taxable. Similarly, if the sale would otherwise be exempt but the parties are jointly opting to tax the sale, the contract should also contain appropriate clauses.

[7–11]   Is the purchaser a connected person? Is sales price = market value?

There are anti-avoidance rules to impose market value for VAT purposes if a sale takes place between connected persons at an artificially low price.

[7–12]   Documentation

VAT legislation provides that records must be kept for six years and, for certain transactions, longer than that. The requirement to keep records extends to the capital goods record also. VAT invoices must be issued and retained.

Purchasers

[7–13]   Is VAT being charged on sale of building?

Clearly, if the purchaser is unable to recover all of its VAT on expenditure, the purchase price of the building will be higher if VAT is charged on the sale.

If the sale of the building is exempt from VAT, but the vendor wants to jointly opt to tax, is VAT recovery possible?

If the purchaser can recover all of its input VAT, then it is unlikely to oppose option. If the option is exercised, then the purchaser acquires a capital good and will have ongoing obligations under the CGS. Clearly, if the purchaser cannot recover all of its input VAT, then opting to tax the sale represents an increased cost to it. The question of opting to tax the sale of an otherwise exempt building will invariably become part of the price negotiation between the parties. Hence, it becomes more of a commercial issue than a tax issue.

If the purchaser cannot recover input VAT, will it be more interested in older buildings? [7–14]

Or, put another way: do these VAT rules create parallel markets in property? To a certain extent, they might. The option to tax is more of an issue in the commercial property market. With industrial properties, the occupant or purchaser will invariably be carrying on taxable activity, so should always be in a position to recover VAT. There will, therefore, be less resistance to the option to tax.

For commercial properties, the position is less straightforward because there are myriad users of office buildings who cannot recover VAT (such as Departments of State, suppliers of VAT-exempt services, etc.). Clearly, if purchasers cannot recover VAT, they will be more interested in buying a building with no VAT added to the sale price than one which will be 13.5% dearer – all other things being broadly equal.

Contract clauses [7–15]

If VAT is not to apply to the sale price, the purchaser should seek to ensure that the contract does not include a VAT clause. If it does, and Revenue subsequently argues that VAT should have been charged, the vendor may be entitled to seek recovery of such VAT from the purchaser many years after the sale took place.

CGS [7–16]

Is the purchaser aware of the capital goods history of the building? Is it taking on any onerous obligations? This could happen, for example, if a partly exempt business were to take over the capital goods scheme obligations of the vendor where a building changes hands as part of the transfer of a business.

Landlords

All lettings will be exempt – no requirement to charge VAT. [7–17]

There is no statutory obligation to charge VAT on any leases, other than very long leases which have the character of freeholds, i.e. FEIs, as referred to in Chapter 4. The sale of a FEI is treated, for VAT purposes, as the sale of a freehold.

[7-18] Has the landlord reclaimed VAT on acquisition or development of property?

If so, then it will be necessary to opt to tax the lease or else suffer a capital goods scheme clawback in relation to the reclaimed VAT.

[7-19] Does the landlord have a waiver of exemption in place?

If the landlord had a waiver of exemption under the "old" VAT rules – i.e. pre-1 July 2008 – then that waiver would continue in place after 1 July 2008 in respect of pre-existing lettings provided that the property does not undergo development and the landlord does not cancel the waiver.

Will this continue to operate post-1 July 2008?

Yes, subject to the conditions set out above.

[7-20] Should an option to tax be put in place?

This should always be considered if there has been a recovery of input VAT by the landlord on the cost of acquiring/developing the property, in particular where the (proposed) tenant enjoys recovery of VAT.

[7-21] Are any of the tenants connected to the landlord?

This is critical. An option to tax a letting will not be allowed if the tenant, or occupier, of the property in question is connected to the landlord and has less than 90% input VAT recovery.

What if the tenant is a connected person and does not have 90% plus VAT recovery and there is a pre-existing waiver of exemption in place?

Check if the minimum threshold rule applies. In summary, this means that the landlord has to calculate the amount of VAT which was recovered on the acquisition or development of the property by virtue of the waiver being in place. That amount of VAT must be repaid to Revenue within no less than 12 years of the letting commencing in equal annual amounts. If that is not done, the waiver ceases to be effective and the full amount of recovered VAT, minus any VAT paid to Revenue by the landlord on rent received, is clawed back by Revenue in one sum. This rule is subject to qualifying conditions.

[7-22] Has an "option to tax" clause been included in the lease agreement?

If not, it is critical that written communication be given to the tenant that VAT will be charged on the rent before the letting commences. Otherwise, the landlord could suffer a capital goods scheme clawback.

Does a commercial decision need to be made where, for example, an [7–23] exempt tenant will not bear VAT on the rent?

The landlord may consider not opting to tax the rents and suffer a capital goods scheme clawback in relation to input VAT reclaimed if it can obtain some amount of compensation from the tenant. Care needs to be exercised as to the other, non-VAT, tax implications of any such arrangement.

Premium [7–24

Is the tenant paying a premium on the lease? If so, the VAT treatment of the premium will mirror the VAT position on the rent (i.e. exempt or opted to tax).

Concerns over sub-lettings [7–25]

The landlord should ensure that the tenant does not sub-let to a person connected to the landlord if that person has less than 90% input VAT recovery as this could give rise to a capital goods scheme clawback for the landlord.

Concerns over assignment [7–26]

The same concerns as those above with sub-lettings would apply if the tenant were to assign its interest in the lease to a person connected with the landlord.

What if the tenant surrenders? [7–27]

The surrender itself is a non-event for VAT, where the lease being surrendered is not a VATable legacy lease. If it is not the surrender of a legacy lease, then nothing turns on the surrender but the landlord will need to consider whether he should opt to tax any new lease being created if there is a pre-existing input VAT position to protect.

Invoices [7–28]

If the landlord has opted to tax the rents, he must issue a VAT invoice in respect of each rent payment to the tenant if the tenant is an accountable person for VAT in accordance with VAT Regulations. These invoices can be issued in advance in block form as long as each one is clearly identifiable as to its relevant date.

Tenants

Is VAT being charged on rent? [7–29]

This is particularly important if the tenant does not have full input VAT recovery.

Has the landlord a waiver of exemption? [7–30]

This is important if the tenant is in occupation under a lease which commenced prior to the introduction of the "new" VAT rules on 1 July 2008.

[7-31]   Does the landlord want to opt to tax?

This is unlikely to be an issue of major concern to the tenant if it has full VAT recovery. However, if it does not, then clearly VAT at the standard rate on top of the rent may represent a significant additional cost which the tenant may not be prepared to pay.

[7-32]   What is tenant's negotiating position if no VAT recovery?

The VAT can become a commercial factor in determining the price of the rent, and the tenant's negotiating position will be determined more by market conditions than anything else.

[7-33]   What if refurbishment is carried out by tenant?

If the tenant carries out refurbishment works, the refurbishment becomes a capital good in its own right and the tenant has to carry out any annual capital goods scheme adjustments that may arise. The adjustment period for refurbishments is 10 years.

[7-34]   What if letting surrendered/assigned?

Ordinarily, a surrender or assignment will create no VAT issues for the tenant. But if the tenant has carried out refurbishment works on the property and is a capital goods owner in respect of those works, there may be an adjustment at the time of surrender or assignment unless the landlord or assignee agrees to take over the tenant's capital goods scheme obligations.

What are the VAT implications of a sub-let?

If the tenant is paying VAT on the rent to his landlord, he will have to opt to tax the rent on the sub-lease if he wishes to avoid loss or clawback of input VAT.

[7-35]   Contract clauses

The tenant should not pay VAT on the rent to the landlord unless there is a clause in the letting agreement stipulating that VAT will be charged on the rent or the tenant has received some other form of written notification from the landlord advising that VAT would be charged.

Record-keeping requirements

If the tenant is reclaiming VAT on the rent, it should retain the VAT invoices which the landlord should issue. Equally, any capital goods records or written notifications to sub-tenants should also be retained.

Section 2 – Summary Chart of Standard Transactions

SALE OF FREEHOLD / FREEHOLD EQUIVALENT - TRANSITIONAL OR NON-TRANSITIONAL PROPERTY

Property / Vendor Status	Vendor Obligations	Purchaser Position	VAT based on	Other
Non-residential, "new", input VAT recovery entitlement, vacant	Issue VAT invoice if purchaser is a taxable person Charge VAT on sale	If taxable person, needs VAT invoice Commences new 20-year adjustment period and new capital good record	Entire consideration Entire consideration	
Non-residential, "old", input VAT recovery entitlement, vacant	If sold within adjustment period, do not charge purchaser VAT on sale	If taxable person, may jointly agree with vendor that the option to tax will apply to sale. If option to tax, purchaser self-accounts for the VAT	Entire consideration	If option to tax N/A, vendor may suffer CGS adjustment
Non-residential, no input VAT recovery entitlement	Supply not subject to VAT but option to tax may be available	Establish whether option to tax will apply as if it does, purchaser = accountable person	Entire consideration	Vendor may be entitled to credit re purchase VAT previously forgone
Residential, sold by property developer within 20-year adjustment period. Immaterial whether "new" or "old"	Charge VAT on sale	VAT invoice not required unless taxable person (unlikely)	Entire consideration	

ASSIGNMENT OR SURRENDER OF TRANSITIONAL LEASEHOLD INTEREST

Tenant / Property Status	Tenant Obligations	Landlord / Assignee position	VAT based on	Other
Tenant originally entitled to input VAT credit on acquisition of lease	Issue "document" under 4(8)	Landlord/assignee = accountable person Requires "document" Adjustment period = remainder of original Landlord/assignee = CG owner	T x N/Y	If tenant refurbishment, tenant clawback possible. Alternatively landlord/ takes over refurb.
Tenant not originally entitled to input VAT credit on acquisition of lease	Surrender/assignment prime facie exempt but the parties may agree to jointly tax the surrender/assignment	None if exempt. Accountable person if 'opted'	N/A if exempt	"

ASSIGNMENT OR SURRENDER OF NON-TRANSITIONAL LEASEHOLD INTEREST

Original lease constituted a supply of services from VAT perspective. From VAT perspective, nothing to assign/surrender, i.e. no consequences

GRANT OF LEASE ON OR AFTER 1 JULY 2008 (NOT A FREEHOLD EQUIVALENT INTEREST)

Lessor/Property status	Lessor Obligations	Tenant/Occupant Position	VAT based on	Other
Residential or non-residential property Lessor has valid pre-existing waiver of exemption	Account for VAT at standard rate on rents	Not connected with landlord or, if connected, has at least 90% input VAT entitlement	Rents	If pre-existing waiver n/a, potential clawback on lessor Section 7(3)
Residential property Lessor does not have valid pre-existing waiver	Exempt lease rentals	No VAT charged on rentals	N/A	In general no initial input VAT recovery entitlement Option to tax N/A
Non-residential property, lessor does not have pre-existing waiver	May opt to tax the letting, if so, must notify tenant in writing and account for VAT at standard on rents. Ensure letting qualifies for option to tax	Establish whether or not letting is to be "opted". Seek VAT invoice if input VAT credit entitlement	Rents, if option exercised	No new waivers after 1 July 2008

PROPERTY INCLUDED IN SECTION 3(5)(b)(iii) TRANSFER OF BUSINESS ON OR AFTER 1 JULY 2008

Vendor/Property Status	Vendor Obligations	Purchaser Position	VAT based on	Other
Building sale subject to VAT but for Section 3(5)(b)(iii) Vendor was fully entitled to recover input VAT	Provide copy of capital good record	If full input VAT recovery entitlement deemed to have incurred VAT	Building sale consideration	
Building sale subject to VAT but for Section 3(5)(b)(iii) Vendor **not** fully entitled to recover input VAT	Provide copy of capital good record	If full input VAT recovery entitlement deemed to have incurred VAT	Building sale consideration	Vendor may be entitled to recover portion input VAT
Building sale exempt per Section 4B(2)	Provide copy of capital good record	Deemed to incur original purchase VAT	Original building purchase consideration	

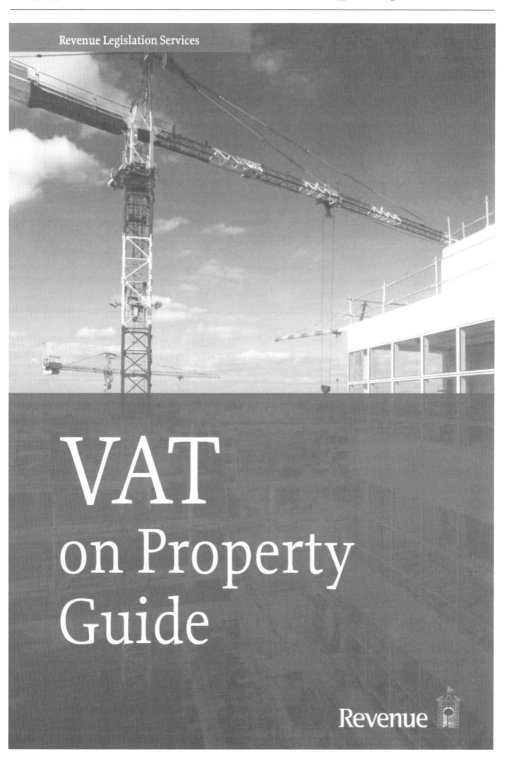

Revenue Legislation Services

VAT
on Property
Guide

Revenue

VAT
on Property
Guide

Revenue Legislation Services

This guide which sets out the current practice at the date of its issue is intended for guidance only and does not purport to be a definitive legal interpretation of the provisions of the Value-Added Tax Act 1972 (as amended).

April 2008

www.revenue.ie

Foreword

I am happy to introduce Revenue's *VAT On Property Guide*, which reflects the new system that was introduced in the Finance Act 2008.

The objective of the new system is to rationalise and simplify the VAT treatment of property transactions. The new system is a fundamental change in the way VAT is applied to property transactions and represents one of the most significant changes in the Irish VAT system since its introduction in 1972.

In 2005 Revenue announced a review of the VAT on Property system and set up a team to bring forward proposals. Following an extensive consultation with relevant stakeholders the report of the Review Group and 'pro-forma legislation' on the proposed new system was published. In his 2007 Budget statement, the Tánaiste and Minister for Finance invited a final round of consultation and in the 2008 Budget announced his intention to bring forward the new legislation in the Finance Bill 2008.

I believe the new system is a significant improvement in the application of VAT to property transactions. It represents a major long-term simplification in what had become a very complex part of the law.

The input of external stakeholders to the process of developing the new system was invaluable, was freely given and is very much appreciated. I would like to thank those in Revenue and Department of Finance who contributed to the project and a special word of appreciation goes to the VAT on Property Team – past and present – under the stewardship of John Shine, for their commitment and persistence. They should be justly proud of their work.

Josephine Feehily,
Chairman
April 2008

Contents

214

Chapter 1

Introduction

The rules for VAT on property transactions can be broadly summarised as follows.

1.1 **Sales of property (Chapter 2)**

The supply of freehold or freehold equivalent interests in "new"properties in the course of an economic activity is subject to VAT. The five and two year rules determine if a property is "new" –

- The first supply of a completed property within five years of its completion is subject to VAT.

- The second and subsequent supply of a property within five years of its completion is subject to VAT if it takes place within two years of occupation.

Generally, all sales of "old"property (those outside the period when considered "new") are exempt from VAT. The notable exception is the sale of residential properties by a developer/builder where the two and five-year rules do not apply. In such cases, the sale by the developer/builder is always taxable.

1.2 **Joint option for taxation (Chapter 2)**

Where the sale of property is exempt from VAT a joint option is provided for whereby the seller and purchaser can opt to tax the sale. Where the option is exercised, the purchaser accounts for the VAT on the sale on a reverse charge basis.

1.3 **Letting of property (Chapter 4)**

The letting of property is exempt from VAT. The landlord may opt to tax a letting and that option to tax is letting specific. In other words, the landlord has the right to opt (or not to opt) to tax each letting. However, the option to tax does not apply to –

- a letting of residential property, or

- a letting between connected parties.

1.4 **Capital Goods Scheme (Chapters 6-8)**

The new rules introduce a Capital Goods Scheme (CGS). The CGS provides for the adjustment of VAT deductibility in respect of the acquisition, development or refurbishment costs over the "VAT-life" of a property. The CGS does not have any impact in respect of properties that are used for their entire VAT-life for either fully taxable or fully exempt purposes. The purpose of the CGS is to reflect changes in the use to which the property is put over its VAT-life and to ensure fairness and proportionality in the VAT system. The VAT-life of a property is generally twenty years, but in the case of a refurbishment, the VAT-life of a property in so far as it relates to a refurbishment is ten years. (Chapter 6)

The CGS also has rules to deal with the sale of a property during its VAT-life. It is important to note that if a joint option to tax is not exercised and the person selling the property was entitled to deduct VAT on the acquisition or development costs then there is a claw-back of the residual VAT when an exempt sale occurs. Similarly, if a sale is taxable (either during the "new period" or because of an option to tax) and the seller was not entitled to deduct all of the acquisition and development VAT, a VAT credit is given for the residual VAT. (Chapter 7)

The exercising or terminating of a landlord's option to tax a letting also has CGS implications. Where the option is exercised on a letting in a property that has previously been subject to an exempt letting, an adjustment is made whereby the landlord is given a VAT credit for the residual VAT. Where an option is terminated a claw-back of the residual VAT occurs. Both of these adjustments arise at the time the option is exercised or terminated. (Chapter 7)

The CGS applies to all new properties (acquired or developed) on or after 1 July 2008 or properties refurbished on or after 1 July 2008. For all such properties, a "capital good record" must be set up and maintained. This record contains all of the information relating to the scheme including how much VAT was deducted on the acquisition or development and details of any adjustments under the scheme, etc. (Chapter 6)

1.5 **Transitional rules – freeholds and leaseholds (Chapter 3)**

Transitional rules apply to the supply of freehold properties which were taxable under the old rules in Section 4 of the VAT Act 1972 (as amended) and which are supplied on or after 1 July 2008. The rules for such properties mirror the new rules above i.e. the two and five-year rules apply.

The rules also apply to leasehold interests, which were taxable on the capitalised value as a supply of goods under the old rules and which are assigned or surrendered on or after 1 July 2008. Where an assignment or surrender of such a leasehold interest occurs on or after 1 July 2008, it is subject to VAT on the reverse charge basis. The taxable amount is calculated by reference to the number of years remaining in the CGS life of the property.

The CGS rules for dealing with changes in the use of a property during the VAT-life of the property do not apply to freehold or leasehold properties that are subject to the transitional arrangements. This means that no adjustment is required if the taxable use of a transitional property (or a transitional leasehold interest in property) changes from one year to the next[1]. However, where the sale of a transitional freehold occurs or the assignment or surrender of a transitional leasehold interest occurs, the CGS rules as outlined above apply. (Claw-back of VAT if supply exempt, VAT credit if taxable and not entitled to full deductibility.)

---

[1] The exception to this rule is if an exempt letting of a transitional property occurs on or after 1 July 2008 (Section 4C(3)).

1.6 Transitional rules – waiver of exemption (Chapter 5)

There are also rules to deal with transitional properties that were let prior to 1 July 2008 where the landlord has a waiver of exemption in place. The majority of these lettings may continue to be taxed under the old rules on or after 1 July 2008 and the waiver of exemption may also be cancelled under the claw-back rules. There are special cancellation rules that apply in respect of waivers of exemption in the case of lettings between connected parties where the waivers were in place on or before 18 February 2008 and are still in place on 1 July 2008.

Chapter 2

The Supply of Property – New System

2.1 Taxable and Exempt Supplies

This Chapter deals with supplies of properties that are completed on or after 1 July 2008 and the supply of properties that are on hand but not completed on that date. Supplies of properties that are on hand on 1 July 2008 but were completed prior to that date are dealt with in Chapter 3.

2.2 What supplies of property are subject to VAT? (Section 4B)

To come within the charge to VAT[2]

• a property must have been developed
 and

• it must be supplied for consideration in the course of business.[3]

The supply of a completed property is taxable only while the property is considered new (see paragraph 2.10). A property is considered new for a maximum period of five years from the date on which the property itself or a development of the property, other than a minor development, is completed. Where a completed property has been supplied to a person other than a connected person (see Chapter 4 for what is meant by a connected person), the period for which the property is considered new is limited to a period of two years from occupation following completion of the latest development.

Once a property is no longer new, the supply of that property is exempt from VAT. However, the person supplying such a property and the purchaser may jointly opt to have the supply subject to VAT.

---

[2] The only exception to this rule is where a property is sold and in connection with that sale there is a contract between the purchaser and another person to develop the property. This is covered more fully in paragraph 2.15

[3] See paragraph 2.5.

2.3 What is meant by developed? (Section 1)

Development in relation to land is defined as -

(a)   the construction, demolition, extension, alteration or reconstruction of any building on the land in question, or

(b)   the carrying out of any engineering or other operation in, on, over or under the land in question to adapt it for materially altered use.

Development other than minor development, essentially makes a property "new" for VAT purposes. For example, where an undeveloped property or an "old" property is developed the properties are considered "new" for VAT purposes following the completion of that development.

A property is regarded as developed when -

• A new building is constructed or

• An existing building is extended, altered or reconstructed, or

• An existing building is demolished, or

• Some engineering or other operation is carried out or work which adapts the building for materially altered use is carried out (work which is not designed to make a material alteration in the use to which a building is put is not development. Thus, no account is taken of fencing, land drainage, laying of roads for agricultural purposes and so on).

Work on maintenance and repairs does not constitute development. The fact that planning permission had been obtained for development does not, of itself, constitute development for VAT purposes.

Example 1 – Agricultural work

Farmer A owns a 2-acre undeveloped field. In 2009, she spends €50,000 (incl. VAT) on agricultural works adding an access road to get to the field, fencing the entire field and adding a drainage system. She uses the field for agricultural purposes.

In 2010 she sells the field to Farmer B. Although Farmer A has spent substantial money and has carried out engineering works on the land the work did not "materially alter" the land (since it was a farm before and still a farm after). The sale is exempt from VAT as the field is not developed.

2.4 What is minor development in relation to a property?

Minor development is a level of development that does not make a property "new". It can be described as development that does not (and is not intended to) adapt the property for a materially altered use, provided that the cost of such development does not exceed 25% of the consideration for the supply of the property.

Minor development is important in considering whether the sale of the property is taxable or not. If a sale takes place within five years of the completion of a development, and the development is considered as minor development, then the sale will be exempt from VAT. If the development is not considered minor development, the sale will be taxable, as the property has been made "new" again. Examples 2 and 3 below illustrate how this operates in practice.

Example 2 – Minor development - materially altered use

ABC Ltd owns two identical warehouses – X and Y. In 2009, work is carried out on each of them that is completed at a cost equal to less than 25% of its sale price.

Not materially altered (minor development)
During 2009 ABC carries out work on upgrading X to a standard required for modern warehouses. After the work is complete X is sold. The work has not "materially altered" the use of the building as it is still a warehouse. The sale is exempt from VAT as the work is considered "minor development".

Materially altered (developed)
During 2009 ABC carries out separate work on Y. This involves the preliminary work required for turning the warehouse into an apartment block. Y is then sold to a property developer. The work has "materially altered" the building – i.e. changed it from a commercial building to a residential building. The sale is taxable as the building is developed and had been made "new".

Example 3 – Minor development - the 25% rule

Minor development (less than 25% of the consideration & not intended to materially alter use)
Mr A purchased a shop at a cost of €500,000 plus VAT of €67,500 in January 2010. The shop had last been developed in 1995 and needed some renovation. Mr A carried out work on the shop replacing the roof and adding new fixtures. The work was completed on 1 June 2010 and cost €250,000 (excl. of VAT).

On 1 May 2013 he sold the shop for €1,250,000. Mr A must look back and examine the development as the sale takes place within five years of its completion. The work clearly did not materially alter the building, as it was still a shop after its completion. As the cost of the development did not exceed 25% of the consideration, the work done is considered minor development. The sale is exempt from VAT.

Development (Exceeds 25% of sale price)
Same scenario with Mr A above except this time the work carried out was completed on 1 June at a cost of €400,000.

Again, he sells the shop on 1 May 2013 for €1,250,000. The work did not adapt the property for a materially altered used but it did cost more than 25% of the sale price and is not therefore considered as minor development. The property is developed and had been made "new". The sale is taxable.

2.5 When is a property supplied in the course of business?

The term in the course of business is very wide. Business means any economic activity, whatever the purpose or results of that activity and whether or not the business is subject to VAT. It will generally be obvious whether a supply is made in the course of business. A transaction entered into in a private capacity is not done in the course of business. For instance, a householder who sells her/his private house does not do so in the course of business, even where that person is engaged in business. However, a landlord/investor who sells a property that was used or intended for letting is regarded as making a sale in the course of business.

It should be noted that a person who engages in a single property transaction on a once-off basis may be acting in the course of business. For example, a person who constructs or arranges for the construction of a residence on the site of an existing dwelling for subsequent sale would be regarded as acting in the course of business, even if the site was part of the grounds of that person's private residence.

2.6 What is meant by a supply of property for VAT purposes? (Section 3)

A supply of goods for VAT purposes is the transfer by agreement of ownership of the goods. In the case of property, a supply includes the transfer in substance of the right to dispose of property, whether as the owner or otherwise. It also includes any transaction where the owner of the property becomes entitled to receive 50% or more of the value of the property at any time prior to the transaction and up to five years after the date of the transaction.

The term 'in substance' is taken to mean not only the freehold of a property but also other interests in the property that amount to effective ownership. Such interests are referred to in this guide as 'freehold equivalent interests' or just 'freehold equivalent'. For instance, many apartment owners do not hold the freehold of the property. For property law reasons they generally have a very long interest in the property, for instance a 99 or 999 year lease. Such an interest would be regarded as a freehold equivalent.

A transfer of a freehold is a supply of property, as is the creation of a very long lease (a freehold equivalent), say, for a period of 99 years or more, where the consideration is a premium equal to the value of the property with a nominal rent payable annually.

2.7 When does a supply of property take place for VAT purposes?

As indicated above, a supply of property for VAT purposes involves the transfer of ownership or the transfer in substance of the right to dispose of the property, whether as owner or otherwise. The transfer of the right to dispose of property as owner is usually regarded as taking place when the contract for sale of the property is completed. It is not necessary that the legal title to the property has been transferred to the purchaser. It is sufficient that the purchaser has acquired, in substance, the right to dispose of the property.

In practice, this generally entails the payment of the full consideration due under the contract. In the more straight-forward situation of a contract for sale, with a deposit being paid and the balance being paid on completion of the contract, the supply will be regarded as taking place on completion of the contract or on payment of the full consideration, whichever is the earlier. If the supply is taxable, any advance payment, part payment or deposit received by the vendor before the supply is completed is taxable in the hands of the vendor on receipt of the payment.

However, certain transactions other than a straightforward contract for sale are also considered to be supplies of property for VAT purposes. These are transactions under which the vendor becomes entitled to 50% or more of the market value of the property at the time of the contract or agreement, where the amounts are payable either before the contract or agreement is concluded or within five years of their being concluded. As the transactions coming within this category will not be straightforward, the time of supply in such cases will need to be decided on a case-by-case basis.

2.8 When is the supply of a completed property taxable? (Section 4B(2))

A supply of a completed property in the course of business is taxable while the building is new. If development work is carried out to the property, not being minor development work, the property is again regarded as new from the date of completion of that development work.

A completed property is regarded as new for a maximum period of five years from completion. However, once the property has been disposed of to an unconnected person, the period during which the property is regarded as new is restricted to the period covering the first 24 months of occupation of the completed property. It should be noted that if part of a building has been occupied for more than 24 months and part has not, then the consideration for sale is apportioned between the part of the building that is taxable and the part of the building that is exempt.

Example 4 – Taxable supply of completed building: 5/2 year rules

D Ltd constructs a property that is completed on 1 April 2010. D sells the property to E Ltd (an unconnected company) on 23 July 2010. As the sale is made in the course of a business by D and is within the period when the property is considered "new" (first sale within five years of completion) it is taxable.

E occupies the building on 1 September 2010. It subsequently sells the property on 31 May 2011 to F. The property is still considered "new" at this time since the sale is made within five years of completion and the property has not been occupied for a period of 24 months following completion, so the supply is taxable.

F occupies the building on 1 July 2011. They then sell it on 1 November 2012. At this point there has been an aggregate of more than 24 months occupation (9 months by E and 16 months by F—the month of June 2011, between the periods of occupation, is not included) so the property is no longer considered "new". The sale is exempt.

2.9 What is the position where a property is not completed at the time of supply?

The supply of an uncompleted property that is made in the course of business is always taxable. The two and five-year rules only commence to apply once the property has been completed.

Example 5 – Sale of uncompleted building

D Ltd begins construction of a 10-storey office block in early 2011. The partially completed building is put on the market for sale. In February 2018 another builder buys the uncompleted building. The sale is taxable as the building was never completed so the five-year rule does not apply.

2.10 Are there any further exceptions to the two and five-year rules? (Section 4B(3))

Yes. Where the property is residential property, the supply by the person who developed it in the course of business (i.e. a property developer) or by a person connected with the property developer is always taxable. The two and five-year rules do not apply to supplies of residential property by a property developer/builder.

Example 6 – Sale of residential property by developer

Developer A develops 40 houses to sell. They are all completed in June 2011. She sells most of the houses but lets three of them, which she sells in 2017. The sales of all the houses are taxable since the two and five-year rules do not apply to a developer/builder selling residential property. Because the lettings are exempt she has a CGS adjustment in respect of the three houses for the duration of the letting.

2.11 When is a property completed? (Section 4B(1))

"Completion" in the context of property means that the development of the property has reached the state where the property can effectively be used for the purposes for which it was designed. The physical state that the property is in when completed—the degree of finishing and fitting that will have been carried out—will depend on its intended use and may vary from one type of building to another. Finishing and fitting work that is normally carried out by the person who will use the property, whether as owner or tenant, does not itself have to be completed for the property to have reached the point of being "completed". One essential requirement for completion in all cases is the connection of all of the utility services that will enable the property be used for the purposes for which it was designed. The five-year rule for taxable supplies of completed property begins from the date of completion.

Example 7 – Completion

> D Ltd constructed buildings side-by-side at numbers 7 and 9 Main Street. No. 7 is a small commercial building with planning permission for a shop on the ground floor and an office on the floor above; number 9 is a two-storey building with an apartment on each floor.
>
> The development of both has reached exactly the same point - outsides are painted, doors and windows fitted, the plumbing and wiring are in place and have been connected, but no internal finishing work such as plastering has been carried out.
>
> No. 7 has been completed as it has been finished to the level expected for a commercial unit. No. 9 is not completed because all finishing or fitting work on residential property is not normally carried out by the person who will occupy it.

2.12 Occupation

A property is "occupied" when it is fully in use – use being one for which planning permission for the development of the goods had been granted. It is essential to note that this use is a physical, practical use and not a purely economic or legal occupation. The two-year rule for second and subsequent supplies of a property begins on the date of occupation following completion.

Example 8 – Occupation

> D Ltd develops an office block that is completed on 15 April 2010. On 1 June D sells the property to E Ltd. E Ltd fits out the property and on 1 September transfers its staff from their previous premises to occupy the first two floors of the building. These two floors are considered occupied from this date.
>
> The third floor is not used. On 15 October E Ltd grants a 4-year-9-month lease to Mr X for the third floor. This is not considered occupation, as occupation requires that the property be occupied by and fully in use by the tenant and not merely used by the landlord in his business of letting property. On 1 February 2011 Mr X moves his staff in and thereafter operates his business from the premises. The third floor is not considered occupied until this date.

2.13 Exempt supplies

Where the supply takes place later than the date provided for under the two and five-year rules, the supply of the property is exempt from VAT. However, where the supply takes place within the VAT-life of the property, there will be CGS implications related to the supply. (see Chapter 7)

2.14 Can the supply of 'exempt properties' ever be taxable?

Yes. In the case of exempt supplies, the parties to the transaction may opt to make the supply taxable. The option may be exercised only where the person making the supply and the purchaser are taxable persons i.e. both must be engaged in business in the State. The option to tax is a joint option and must be exercised by an agreement in writing between the parties to the transaction.

Where the option to tax has been exercised, the purchaser, and not the seller, will be responsible for accounting to Revenue for the VAT payable, under the reverse charge system. The purchaser should register for VAT, if not already registered.

2.15 Supply in connection with an agreement to develop property (Section 4B(3))

Supplies of property made in connection with an agreement to develop the property are also always taxable, whether or not the person making the supply does so in the course of business. For this provision to apply the purchaser of the property or a person connected with the purchaser must enter into an agreement with a taxable person (usually a developer/builder) to develop the property. The supply of the property and the entering into an agreement to develop the property must be connected in some way. For example, a farmer who sells a site to a private individual who intends to construct a dwelling on the site would not be making a taxable supply under this provision. But where a landowner and developer jointly arrange for the development of a piece of land, on the basis that the landowner will sell plots to various people who will be required to enter into an agreement with the developer to construct a house on the plot, the sale of the plots and the agreement to develop are considered as connected and the sale of the land is subject to VAT.

Example 9 – Taxable supply – building agreement

Mr A owns a field that has not been developed.

B Ltd is a property developer. Ms C signs a contract with Mr A to buy the field and a building agreement with B Ltd for the construction of a house on that site. Ms C's contract with Mr A is contingent on her performing her contract with B Ltd.

The sale of the site by Mr A to Ms C is taxable as it is in connection with an agreement to carry out a development.

2.16 What is the taxable amount for the supply of property?

Where the supply of property is taxable, the taxable amount is the full amount of the consideration payable for the supply. Consideration can be in cash or it can also consist of the value of services to be performed by the purchaser. Generally, the consideration is the amount payable under the contract. In certain circumstances, the market value of the property may be substituted for the amount shown in the contract.

Chapter 3

Supply of Property – Transitional Measures

This Chapter deals with the supply of completed properties that are on hand on 1 July 2008 (see Chapter 2.11 for a discussion of *completion* in respect of property). Where a property is on hand at that date but is not completed, the rules described in Chapter 2 (the new rules) apply to any supply of that property on or after 1 July 2008. The properties dealt with in this Chapter can be held either under a freehold or freehold equivalent interest (see Chapter 2) or under a long lease that was treated as a supply of goods under the VAT on property rules applying prior to 1 July 2008. In this Guide these properties will be referred to as *transitional properties*. Where a property is sold in connection with a contract to develop the property, the sale is subject to VAT in any event (see Chapter 2.15).

Paragraphs 3.1 to 3.6 deal with properties held under a freehold or freehold equivalent interest at 1 July 2008.

3.1 What is the treatment of transitional properties from 1 July 2008? (Section 4C)

The treatment will depend on whether the holder was entitled to deduct any of the VAT incurred on the acquisition or development of the property.

3.2 What is the treatment when the holder was entitled to deduct any of the VAT incurred on the acquisition or development of the property?

Where the holder was entitled to deduct any of the tax incurred on the acquisition or development of the property, the VAT treatment of the supply of the property is the same as the treatment that applies to properties completed on or after 1 July 2008 (see Chapter 2). Where the property is considered new (under the two and five-year rules), the supply of the property is taxable. The taxable amount is the full consideration for the supply.

Where the property is supplied when it is no longer considered "new", the supply is exempt from VAT. However, the seller and the purchaser may jointly opt to tax the supply if they are both engaged in business. Where the option to tax is exercised the purchaser must account for the VAT on the supply on the reverse charge basis (see Chapter 2.14).

Example 10 – Transitional property – development completed pre 1 July 2008

ABC Ltd had a warehouse constructed in 2006 for €1,000,000 plus VAT €135,000. ABC deducted all of this VAT and carried on its warehouse business from the premises. The warehouse was still on hand on 1 July 2008 and no development had been carried out on it since its acquisition.

On 3 February 2009 ABC sells the warehouse for €1,500,000. As ABC was entitled to deduct the VAT on the acquisition of the property and it is the sale of a developed property within five years of completion, the sale is taxable.

3.3 What is the position where the person making the supply was not entitled to deduct any of the tax incurred on the acquisition or development of the property? (Section 4C(2))

Where the person making the supply was not entitled to deduct any of the tax incurred on the acquisition or development of the property, the supply of the property on or after 1 July 2008 is exempt from VAT. However, the seller and the purchaser may jointly opt to tax the supply, if they are both engaged in business. Where the option to tax is exercised the purchaser must account for the VAT on the supply on the reverse charge basis (see Chapter 2.14).

3.4 What is the position if further development is carried out on the property on or after 1 July 2008?

Where a development is carried out on a transitional property on or after 1 July 2008 the property is not a transitional property and is dealt with under the new rules (see Chapter 2). However, if the development work is considered a "minor development" (see Chapter 2.4) then the property is still treated as a transitional property.

3.5 Does the CGS apply to such a property? (Section 4C(10))

Yes, but only in relation to supplies of such properties. The annual adjustments under the CGS, the adjustments for big swings in the use of the property and the adjustments on exercising and terminating the landlord's option to tax a letting of the property do not apply. However, where the holder makes an exempt letting of such a property a deductibility adjustment under Section 4(3)(ab) VAT Act 1972 (as amended) is required.

Where a transitional property is supplied within the VAT-life of the property, the CGS adjustments relating to supplies apply to that transaction. If such a property is sold and the sale is exempt from VAT, the claw-back provisions of the CGS in relation to exempt supplies apply. If such a property is sold and the sale is taxable, the additional input credit provisions of the CGS in relation to taxable supplies apply. (See Chapter 7). The only exception to this is where the property was acquired after 30 June 2007. In such a case, unless the purchaser has adjusted the input credit in accordance with Section 12(4)(f) VAT Act 1972 (as amended), (apportionment following the end of the accounting period of acquisition for dual-use inputs) the ordinary CGS rules for the adjustment of the deductible amount **at the end of the initial interval** will apply to the VAT incurred in relation to the property (Section 4C(12)) VAT Act 1972 (as amended).

3.6 What is the CGS adjustment period for transitional properties?

The CGS adjustment period in relation to a freehold or freehold equivalent interest in a completed property on hands at 1 July 2008 is a period of 20 years from the acquisition of the interest. Where the property has been developed since the acquisition of the freehold or freehold equivalent interest, the CGS adjustment period is a period of 20 years from the completion of the most recent development prior to 1 July 2008. For example, where an undeveloped property was acquired in 1999 and developed in 2005, the adjustment period for CGS purposes is 20 years from 2005.

Paragraphs 3.7 to 3.18 deal with long leases (leases of ten years or more) that were created prior to 1 July 2008.

3.7 What are legacy leases? (Section 4C(1))

Legacy leases are interests in property (so called because they are a legacy from the old system of VAT on property) that were treated as a supply of goods under the old rules. The term does not include interests that constitute freehold equivalent interests (see Chapter 2). The lease must have been held by a taxable person on 1 July 2008 – it must, in other words, form part of the assets of a business at that date.

The creation of a legacy lease – and in most cases its subsequent assignment to another tenant – was chargeable to VAT @13.5% as a supply of goods (property). The capitalised value of the rent payable under the lease was added to any other amounts payable, such as a premium, to determine the consideration on which VAT was charged.

3.8 How are such leases dealt with under the new VAT on property provisions? (Section 4C(4))

The surrender or assignment of a legacy lease is regarded as a supply of goods if it occurs within a period of 20 years from the creation of the interest (the lease) or from its most recent assignment or surrender prior to 1 July 2008. This 20 year life represents the CGS life of the legacy lease.

The question of whether a liability to VAT arises on that supply of property (i. e. the surrender or assignment of a legacy lease) depends initially on whether or not the tenant was entitled to deduct any of the VAT incurred on the acquisition of the legacy lease.

3.9 What is the position where a tenant was entitled to deduct any of the tax incurred on the acquisition of the lease? (Section 4C(6))

The assignment or surrender of the lease is taxable if -

- the tenant was entitled to deduct any of the tax charged on the acquisition of that lease or on the development of the property subject to the lease, and

- the surrender or assignment occurs within 20 years of that tenant's acquisition of that leasehold interest.

When a tenant assigns such a lease, the new tenant to whom the lease is assigned and any further assignees will likewise be taxable on its surrender or assignment during that same 20 year period following that first assignor's acquisition of the interest. The treatment of a landlord following the surrender of a legacy lease is dealt with in paragraphs 3.14 and 3.17.

3.10 What is the position where the tenant was not entitled to deduct any of the tax incurred on the acquisition of the lease?

Where the tenant was not entitled to deduct any of the tax incurred on the acquisition of the lease, the assignment or surrender of the lease is exempt from VAT. However, the parties to the assignment or surrender can jointly opt to have the assignment or surrender treated as taxable.

3.11 What is the CGS adjustment period for legacy leases? (Section 4C(11))

The adjustment period for legacy leases is -

- in the case of the creation of the legacy lease, the period of 20 years from creation of the lease, or

- in the case where the person holding the interest in the legacy lease on 1 July 2008 acquired it by assignment, the period remaining in the legacy lease at the time of that assignment or 20 years, whichever is the shorter.

The first 12 months of the adjustment period is treated as the initial interval. Each subsequent interval is a period of 12 months. However, if taxpayers wish to do so, they may treat the second interval as the period from the end of the initial interval to the accounting date of the business. Subsequent intervals will then be 12 months from that date.

3.12 Who is responsible for the VAT chargeable on the assignment or surrender of a legacy lease? (Section 4(8))

The person who takes the assignment or surrender is responsible for the VAT chargeable on the assignment or surrender i.e. a reverse charge applies, where that person is a taxable person (i.e. a person who independently carries on any business in the State), a Department of State or a Local Authority. That person must account to Revenue for the VAT in the VAT return for the period in which the assignment or surrender is made.

Example 11 – Taxable assignment of lease

Business X grants Business Y a 35-year lease on 1 July 2000. VAT of €1million was charged on the capitalised value of the lease, all or part of which VAT was deducted by Business Y. Business Y is still the tenant (and so has the "interest" in the property) on 1 July 2008. The adjustment period for the legacy lease is 20 years from 1 July 2000.

On the 15 April 2012 Business Y assigns the lease to Business J. The assignment is taxable, on the reverse charge basis, as it occurs within the 20-year adjustment period. See Example 12 below for how to calculate the taxable amount.

3.13 What is the tax payable amount where the assignment or surrender of a legacy lease is taxable?

There is a formula to calculate the tax payable. The formula is –

$$\frac{T \times N}{Y}$$

T = total tax incurred on the acquisition of the lease or on the most recent development of the property,

N = the number of full intervals, plus one, that remain in the adjustment period at the time of acquisition of the interest by the person making the assignment or surrender, and

Y = the total number of intervals in the adjustment period for the person making the assignment or surrender.

The taxable amount is the tax payable re-grossed @ 13.5%.

Example 12 – Taxable amount for assignment/surrender of legacy lease

Take the same amounts and circumstances as Example 11 above. When the assignment is made by Y to J on 15 April 2012 the VAT charged on the assignment is calculated as follows -

$$\frac{T \times N}{Y}$$

$$\frac{€1,000,000 \times 9}{20}$$

Tax payable = €450,000

The taxable amount is €3,333,334 (by grossing up the tax due[4]).

The assignment is reverse charged which means that J is liable to account for VAT of €450,000 on the supply in its Mar/Apr 2012 VAT return.

3.14 What obligations does the person making the assignment or surrender have for VAT purposes?

The person making the assignment or surrender must issue a document to the person to whom the lease is assigned or surrendered. The document must contain –

- the amount of tax due on the assignment or surrender (in Example 12 above €450,000), and

- the number of intervals remaining in the adjustment period at the time of the assignment or surrender (in Example 12 above, 9 intervals).

This enables the person to whom the interest is assigned or surrendered to calculate the taxable amount for the transaction and also enables the assignee to calculate any tax payable on any future assignments or surrenders made by him or her.

Where a legacy lease is surrendered and the landlord grants a new lease, that lease is regarded as a new letting to which Chapter 4 applies: the letting will be exempt unless the landlord's option to tax is exercised (the new letting is not a legacy lease). The amount of VAT chargeable on the surrender of the legacy lease will be the basis for the landlord's calculation of CGS liability in the event that the landlord does not exercise the landlord's option to tax the new letting, or on the exempt sale of the property (see Example 13).

3.15 What is a reversion?

Where a taxable long lease was created before 1 July 2008, the landlord's interest in the property subject to that lease is regarded as the reversion on that legacy lease.

---

[4] In Example 12 the tax due is €450,000. The "taxable amount" can be calculated by grossing up this amount to 100% as follows - €450,000/.135 = €3,333,334.

3.16 What is the tax treatment of the sale of a legacy lease reversion?

Where a landlord sells a reversion on a legacy lease on or after 1 July 2008 the sale of the reversion is, in most cases, exempt from VAT. However, if the property was developed by or on behalf of or to the benefit of the landlord subsequent to the creation of the long lease, the supply of the reversion would be taxable if it occurs while the property is considered "new"[5] (see Chapter 2).

3.17 What is the treatment of a legacy lease reversion where the lease is surrendered?

Where the legacy lease that was in place on 1 July 2008 has been surrendered, the special exemption for supplies of reversions no longer applies where the property is sold during the period covered by the surrendered lease. The sale of the property during this period is a sale to which paragraph 3.2 applies. The CGS adjustment is based on the VAT charged on the surrender.

Where the parties opt to tax such a supply, the taxable amount is the consideration for the supply. The normal rules for opting to tax the supply of property apply; in particular, the purchaser will be the person responsible for accounting for the VAT on the supply on the reverse charge basis.

The adjustment period to be used in relation to that transaction is the number of intervals correctly indicated in the document that the tenant gives to the landlord on surrender of the lease.

Example 13 – Surrender of a legacy lease

Assume the transaction mentioned in examples 11 and 12 was a surrender of the lease to the landlord, Mr X and that the landlord deducted the VAT chargeable as he intended to opt to tax the next letting.

In May 2013 Mr X (the landlord) sells the freehold, without having carried out development. The sale is exempt under the normal rules because the property has not been developed within the five years prior to the sale. The CGS adjustment that Mr X would make in the event of an exempt sale would reflect that seven full and one partial intervals remain of the nine intervals applying at the time of the surrender:

$$\frac{€450,000 \times 8}{9}$$
$$= €400,000$$

Mr X would repay €400,000 as an adjustment of deductibility. The same adjustment would be required if, instead of selling the property, Mr X had cancelled his landlord's option to tax or created a new letting without exercising the option.

---

[5] The exemption under Section 4(9) VAT Act 1972 (as amended) no longer applies. The property is one in respect of which the owner was entitled to deduct VAT. Accordingly, the exemption under Section 4C(2) VAT Act 1972 (as amended) does not apply (see paragraph 3.3) and the ordinary rules regarding the taxation of a supply of the property apply (see paragraph 3.2).

3.18 What is the VAT treatment of post-letting expenses in relation to legacy leases?

A landlord who had charged VAT on the creation of a long lease or the successor to that landlord (where the landlord sold the reversion) was allowed, under the rules that applied prior to 1 July 2008, to deduct certain VAT incurred after the date of the taxable supply of the leasehold interest. The VAT in question relates to -

- carrying out services that the landlord is required to provide under the lease the value of which would be reflected in the rent on which the capitalised value was based,

- rent collection,

- any rent review, and

- the exercise of an option to extend the lease or to the exercise of an option to end the lease (break clause) provided for under the lease.

This practice is continued as regards legacy leases. If not already an accountable person, a landlord claiming input credit for such supplies may register on the basis of incurring post-letting expenses.

It should be noted that, while post-letting expenses are restricted to services provided by the landlord, the definition of services in this context is extended, by concession, to cover certain goods of the type specified in Section 3(1B) VAT Act 1972 (as amended) i.e. the supply of electricity, gas, power, heat, refrigeration and ventilation – where, if these goods were services, their supply would qualify for this treatment.

As a concession, it is also accepted that routine general overheads of the landlord may be ascribed to legacy leases, and a portion of the input VAT incurred in respect of them may therefore be deductible. Such overheads would include office expense and audit fees relating to the carrying out of the landlord's business as such – but do not include costs incurred in relation to the purchase or sale of reversions on legacy leases or costs relating to other exempt activities. Where the landlord's business includes both legacy leases and exempt lettings such inputs may be apportioned on a reasonable basis in accordance with Section 12(4) VAT Act 1972 (as amended). The landlord will be entitled to deduct VAT on such overheads in respect of taxable lettings.

The existing practice as regards 'shared services' is being continued for legacy leases. This arises where the landlord agrees under the terms of a lease to arrange for the receipt of the services on behalf of tenants (e.g. cleaning, security, etc.) on the basis of reimbursement by the tenants. The landlord passes on the VAT on such services to the individual tenants who can claim deductibility for the VAT to the extent that the property is used for their taxable activities. The landlord should issue to each tenant, once a year, an invoice showing VAT charged to the tenant on these services. The VAT deductible and payable by the landlord should be incorporated in the appropriate VAT return.

Chapter 4

Letting of Property – New System

4.1 Overview

Letting of property is exempt from VAT but the landlord may, with some exceptions, exercise an option to apply VAT to a letting. No distinction is made between leases for a period of ten years or more and shorter-term lettings, as was the case before 1 July 2008. However, certain very long leases are treated as a supply of the property; these are referred to as freehold equivalent leases and are dealt with in Chapter 2.

Letting in the context of the new VAT on Property rules includes leasing and letting.

4.2 Lettings are exempt from VAT

Lettings are exempt supplies of services for VAT purposes. A landlord who makes an exempt letting is **not** entitled to deduct VAT incurred on the acquisition or development of a property, which is subject to the letting.

A landlord may opt to tax a letting. However there are restrictions as to the circumstances where a landlord may do so (see paragraphs 4.6 and 4.7 below).

4.3 Option to tax lettings (Section 7A(1))

Where a landlord opts to tax a letting, that service becomes subject to VAT at the standard rate (currently 21%). The landlord is entitled to deduct VAT incurred on the acquisition or development of a property that is to be used for the purposes of making taxable lettings.

The option to tax applies to an individual letting of a property. Under the old waiver of exemption rules, a waiver applied to all short-term lettings (period less than 10 years) of the landlord. That is not the case with the option to tax. Indeed, it may well be that a landlord may opt to tax a letting of part of a building while making an exempt letting of the rest of the building.

4.4 How does a landlord opt to tax a new letting?

A landlord who claims a deduction for input tax incurred on the acquisition or development of a property, which is to be used for letting, is regarded as having opted to tax the lettings of that property.

When the property is let, the landlord must either agree in writing with the tenant that the letting will be taxable or issue a document to the tenant stating that the letting will be taxable. Otherwise, the option to tax that the landlord was considered to have made by claiming input credit will be regarded as terminated and the landlord will be subject to a Capital Goods Scheme adjustment on termination of the option (See Chapter 7).

Example 14 – Exercising the landlord's option to tax at development stage and at commencement of the letting

A develops a building in 2012 which is to be let to commercial tenants. He intends to opt to tax the lettings and registers for VAT on the basis that he will make taxable lettings of the property. He claims a repayment in respect of the VAT charged by the builder, architects, etc. A is regarded as having opted to tax the lettings.

When he comes to let the building, A either includes a provision in the letting agreement to the effect that the rents will be taxable or issues a document to the tenant stating that the VAT is chargeable on the rents. A then charges his tenants VAT on the rents and accounts to Revenue for that tax.

Example 15 – Terminating a development-stage landlord's option to tax

As in Example 14, A intends to exercise the landlord's option to tax the rents from the property. However, when he comes to let the property he neither concludes a written agreement with his tenant that the rents will be taxable nor issues a document to his tenant to that effect. A must make a CGS adjustment in the VAT period in which the letting is made and repay the tax deducted in relation to the property (See Chapter 7).

4.5 Can a landlord opt to tax the letting of a property where previous lettings were exempt?

Yes, the landlord can opt to tax such rents by either agreeing in writing with the tenant (either an existing or new tenant) that the rents will be taxable or by issuing a notice in writing to the tenant to this effect. With effect from the date of the agreement/ notice, rents from that property will be taxable and the landlord may be entitled to make a CGS adjustment in respect of VAT incurred in the acquisition or development of the property (See Chapter 7).

Example 16 – Opting to tax a particular letting

B incurred €250,000 VAT on the acquisition of a property in 2010 and has been letting the property for a number of years. She did not claim input credit for this VAT. In November 2014 the existing tenant leaves and in May 2015 B succeeds in getting a new tenant. The new letting agreement includes a provision that the rents will be subject to VAT. B will be required to account for VAT on the rents from the new tenant. She will be entitled to a VAT credit in respect of a CGS adjustment by reference to a proportion of the VAT incurred on the acquisition or development of the property. The input credit in this case will be €250,000 × 16/20 = €200,000 (See Chapter 7).

4.6 Can all landlords opt to tax their rents? (Section 7A(2))

No. There are restrictions on the option to tax rents. The option to tax cannot apply in the following circumstances:

- Where the property is occupied for residential purposes.

- Where the letting is between connected persons. But, if the tenant is entitled to deduct at least 90% of the tax chargeable on the rent, this restriction does not apply.

- Where the property is occupied by a person who is connected with the landlord (even if the letting agreement is between unconnected persons) (See Example 17 below).

4.7 When is a landlord regarded as connected with a tenant or a person who occupies a building owned by the landlord? (Section 7A(3))

The term 'connected persons' is defined in the legislation. The full text of the definition is reproduced in Appendix A.

Generally, connectivity can be established as outlined below.

Individuals are connected with:

- their spouses,
- their relatives (brothers, sisters, ancestors or lineal descendants) or relatives of their spouses,
- individuals or spouses of individuals with whom they or their spouses are in partnership,
- the settlor or beneficiary of a trust where the individual is a trustee of that trust and vice versa.

Companies or other bodies of persons are connected with:

- persons who control that company,
- other companies that act in pursuit of a common purpose with the company, or
- a person or persons with a reasonable commonality of interests who have the power to determine the activities of two companies.

Note: This list is indicative only. Reference should be made to Appendix A for the full definition.

4.8 Can a landlord terminate an option to tax rents?

Yes. A landlord can terminate an option to tax rents by either entering an agreement in writing with the tenant that the rents will no longer be taxable or by issuing a notice in writing to the tenant that the rents will no longer be taxable.

An option to tax rents will be terminated automatically

- if the landlord becomes connected with the tenant (see above regarding connected persons),

- if the property becomes occupied by a person connected with the landlord, or

- if the property is used for residential purposes.

4.9 What happens if an option to tax is terminated?

Where the option is terminated during the adjustment period relating to the property (see Chapter 7), a CGS adjustment will be due and the landlord must account to Revenue for the tax due as a result.

Example 17

In Example 14, A's tenant is an unconnected person but that person sublets the property to C, who is in partnership with A. Since the property is now occupied by a person connected with A, the option to tax is automatically terminated. (See diagram below.) A is obliged to make a CGS adjustment as the option has been terminated during the adjustment period (see Chapter 7).

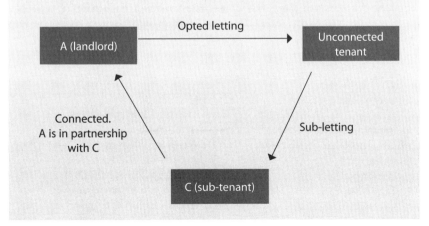

4.10 On what amount is tax chargeable when a letting is opted?

While the landlord's option may sometimes be described as "opting to tax the rent" from a particular property, the landlord is in fact opting to make the service of letting the property chargeable to VAT. All of the consideration attributable to that service while the option is in effect therefore becomes subject to VAT. Payments or other consideration received by the landlord prior to effecting the option or after terminating it—for example, a premium or balloon rent payment—are taxable as a result of the option to the extent that they relate to the service of letting supplied while the option is in effect.

A "rent holiday" – a rent-free period that is allowed for bona fide commercial reasons will not require special VAT treatment provided the option is not terminated while the lease granting the rent holiday remains in effect.

The ordinary rules apply in determining when the VAT on the rents becomes due. VAT on the rents should be included in the VAT return for the period in which the rents become due, unless the landlord has been authorised to use the cash receipts basis. Where rents are paid in advance, the VAT becomes due for the VAT period in which the payment is received.

4.11 What is the VAT treatment of premiums under the new VAT on Property rules?

A premium is a sum payable in connection with the granting of a lease, the surrender of a lease or the assignment of a lease.

Where the interest in the property that is being granted or assigned is a freehold equivalent interest (see Chapter 2.6), the premium is treated as part of the consideration for the supply of the property. The VAT treatment of such a premium will follow the general rules for VAT on supplies of property, as outlined in Chapters 2 and 3.

Where the interest in the property is not a freehold equivalent or a legacy lease (see Chapter 3.7), the VAT treatment of the premium is outlined in the following table:

Nature of payment	VAT treatment
Premium payable by tenant to landlord as consideration for landlord agreeing to grant the lease	The VAT treatment of the payment will depend on whether the landlord has opted to tax the letting in question. Where the landlord has opted to tax the letting, the premium is taxable; where the landlord has not opted to tax the letting, the premium is exempt.

Nature of payment	VAT treatment
Premium payable by tenant to landlord as consideration for the landlord agreeing to the surrender of the tenant's lease	The VAT treatment of the payment depends on whether the landlord has opted to tax the letting in question. Where the landlord has opted to tax the letting, the premium is taxable; where the landlord has not opted to tax the letting, the premium is exempt*.
Premium payable by a landlord to induce a tenant to enter into a lease; this may be in the form of a payment to assist tenant with cost of fit out	In merely agreeing to take a lease, a tenant is not providing a service to the landlord. If no other service is involved the payment is therefore not made in respect of the provision of a service by the tenant and no VAT arises. However, if by taking the lease the tenant is providing a service, that service is taxable. An example of such a service would be a well-known brand proprietor, which provides an advertising service by agreeing to be a tenant in a new shopping complex. In this case the premium is subject to VAT.
Premium payable by a tenant (the assignor) to another person (other than the landlord) as consideration for that person agreeing to accept an assignment of the lease. The person to whom the payment is made is usually referred to as the assignee.	In agreeing to take over the tenant's rights and obligations, the assignee is providing a taxable service to the assignor. The service is subject to VAT at the standard rate (currently 21%)*.
Premium payable to a tenant (the assignor) as consideration for assigning the lease to another person (the assignee)	In assigning his interest in the lease the assignor supplies a service for consideration that is subject to VAT at the standard rate (currently 21%)*.

*Independently of the tax status of the premium, a CGS adjustment may arise where the assignment or surrender occurs during the adjustment period for refurbishments carried out by the assignor. In certain circumstances, the CGS adjustment may be avoided by the assignee agreeing to be responsible for the CGS in relation to the refurbishments. (See Chapter 7.7 and 7.8.)

Chapter 5

Lettings of Property – Transitional Measures

This Chapter looks at the situation of a taxpayer that had waived exemption in respect of short-term letting of property prior to commencement of the new provisions.

5.1 What was the position prior to the introduction of the new system? (Section 7)

Prior to the introduction of the new system for VAT on Property leases were divided into short leases (those for a period of less than 10 years) and long leases (those for a period of 10 years or more).

Long leases were considered a supply of goods and tax was payable by reference to the capitalised value of the lease. The transitional measures as regards these leases are dealt with in Chapter 3.

Short leases were exempt from VAT but a landlord could waive this exemption. Where the exemption was waived, the landlord was entitled to deduct the VAT incurred on the acquisition or development of the let property. The landlord was required to charge VAT on all rents payable to her/him under short leases or lettings. The waiver of exemption applied to all properties let by the landlord under short leases or lettings. Where the landlord sold a property that was within a waiver of exemption and in respect of which the landlord was entitled to deduct VAT incurred on its development or acquisition, the supply of the property was subject to VAT.

A landlord could cancel a waiver of exemption. Where this occurred, the landlord had to make what is known as a cancellation adjustment. The cancellation adjustment is the difference between the VAT deducted by the landlord in respect of the acquisition or development of let properties or in respect of other goods or services consumed in the business of short-term letting and the VAT accounted for by the landlord in respect of rents.

Example 18 – Old rules – waiver of exemption

C acquired a property in November 2002 for €750,000. She was charged VAT of €101,250 (€750,000@13.5%) on the acquisition. She had waived her exemption before acquiring the property and was entitled to deduct this amount in 2002. The property was let with effect from 1 January 2003. By the end of 2007 she has charged VAT of €44,000 on the rent from the property. She had accounted for this in her VAT returns, but as she was entitled to deduct €5,000 of the further VAT she incurred over the years in respect of the letting, she had paid only €39,000 by the end of 2007. If C wished to cancel the waiver of exemption at the end of 2007 she would have to pay €62,250 to Revenue, i. e. the difference between the VAT deducted in respect of lettings and the VAT paid by her on rents.

With effect from 2 April 2007, a waiver of exemption could not be exercised in respect of residential lettings and an existing waiver in place at that date did not extend to a letting of a property for residential purposes where that property was either

- acquired on or after 2 April 2007 unless a binding written contract had been entered into before that date, or

- developed on or after 2 April 2007 unless an application for planning permission to develop the property as a house, apartment or similar establishment had been received by a planning authority before that date.

5.2 What changes occur from 1 July 2008 in the waiver system? (Section 7 and 7B)

- A new waiver of exemption cannot commence on or after 1 July 2008.

- An existing waiver of exemption does not extend to a property acquired or developed on or after 1 July 2008. However, development carried out after that date that completes a development that was underway on 18 February 2008, by or on behalf of the person who exercised a waiver on or before 18 February 2008, does not prevent the extension of that waiver to the property.

Example 19 – Extension of waiver to properties being developed

B has had a waiver of exemption in place for a number of years. He acquired an additional property for letting in 2007. He intended to let the property short-term, and on the basis of his waiver claimed input credit for the VAT incurred on the acquisition of the property. B carried out extensive renovations to the property. These works were on-going on 18 February 2008 and continued until the end of September 2008. The property is let on 31 October 2008. The waiver may be extended to the letting of the property, even though the property was developed on or after 1 July 2008.

Example 20 – Properties developed on or after 18 February 2008

B in Example 19 purchases an additional property in May 2008 that requires further development before it can be let. This development, too, is completed in September 2008. B's waiver does not extend to this property, as it was not undergoing development on 18 February 2008 by or on behalf of B. This would be the case even if the property were being developed on that date since it would have been undergoing development by or on behalf of someone other than B.

5.3 Are there any further restrictions on existing waivers of exemption? (Section 7B(3))

Yes. A waiver of exemption, in so far as it applies to a letting between connected persons, is cancelled with effect from 1 July 2008 – see Chapter 4 as regards when persons are regarded as connected. In such cases, the landlord will have to pay a cancellation adjustment in respect of the property. The cancellation adjustment will apply to that property only. It will be the difference between the VAT deducted in connection with that property and the VAT accounted for and paid in respect of that property. Where certain conditions are satisfied, the waiver in respect of such a letting will not be cancelled on 1 July 2008.

5.4 What will be the position as regards other properties that the landlord has and that are subject to the waiver of exemption?

The waiver will continue in place as regards these properties. In effect, the landlord will be treated as having had two waivers in place, one in respect of the property that is let to the connected person and one in respect of all the landlord's other properties.

5.5 What is the position if the connected tenant is entitled to deduct at least 90% of the VAT chargeable on the rent?

Where the tenant is entitled to deduct at least 90% of the VAT charged on the rents, then the waiver will not be cancelled with effect from 1 July 2008, but will continue as long as at least that level of deductibility applies. However, if at any point the tenant's entitlement to deduct the VAT charged on the rent falls below the 90% figure, then the waiver of exemption immediately ceases to apply to that letting. The landlord will be required to make the cancellation adjustment for the taxable period in which this occurs.

5.6 Are there other exceptions to the cancellation of a waiver where the landlord and tenant are connected?

Yes. Provided the VAT on the rents is at least the permitted minimum amount outlined in paragraph 5.7 the cancellation of a waiver is not required where a waiver was in place on 18 February 2008, where either -

• the letting that is in place on 1 July 2008 was in place since 18 February 2008, or

• the property in question was owned by the landlord and was in the course of development by or on behalf of the landlord on 18 February 2008.

The cancellation is also not required where the waiver relates to a letting of a property held by a landlord under a legacy lease acquired between 18 February 2008 and 30 June 2008 from an unconnected landlord.

Under the existing system a special purpose company ("SPC") was frequently used to spread the payment of the VAT chargeable on the creation of a legacy lease out over a period of time, generally a period of 9 years and 11 months (the maximum length of a lease that was not subject to the capitalised value rules). The ultimate user of the property was usually a company that was not entitled to deduct the full VAT charged on the creation of the legacy lease.

Example 21 – SPC waiver mechanism

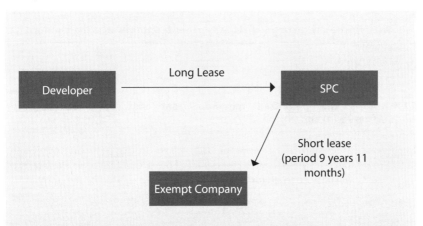

In this case, the exempt company established an SPC, which acquired a long lease of theproperty (lease for a period of 10 years or more). The SPC waived its exemption from VAT on a short lease (less than 10 years) of the property to the exempt company, claimed back the VAT on the capitalised value of the lease and charged VAT @ 21% on the rents.

In all the above cases, the cancellation can be avoided and the waiver continued where the VAT on the rents charged by the landlord is greater than the permitted minimum outlined in paragraph 5.7.

Circumstances in which waiver of exemption for letting to connected person may be retained on or after 1 July 2008 (90% deductible tenants excluded) where the VAT on rents is at least the minimum permitted amount.

Nature of landlord's interest in property	Waiver in place 18 Feb 2008	Property on hand on 18 Feb 2008	Letting in place on 18 Feb 2008	Waiver in place 1 July 2008
Freehold/Freehold Equivalent	✓	✓	✓	✓
Freehold/Freehold Equivalent under development on behalf of landlord on 18 Feb 2008	✓	✓	✗	✓
Legacy lease	✓	✓	✓	✓
Legacy lease acquired from unconnected party 18 Feb 08 to 1 July 2008	✗	✗	✗	✓

✓ = required;
✗ = not required;

5.7 What is the permitted minimum rent that must be payable? (Section 7B (4) and (5))

The permitted minimum rent is an amount that will ensure that an amount equivalent to the VAT deducted by the landlord in respect of the acquisition or development of the property will be accounted for within 12 years. It is calculated by the formula:

$$\frac{A - B}{12 - Y}$$

A = the VAT deducted by the landlord in respect of the acquisition or development of the property.

B = the VAT chargeable and paid on the rents that would be taken into account if the waiver were cancelled at that time.

Y = is the lesser of 11 or the number of full years since the date of the first letting of the property or the date on which the landlord waived exemption, whichever is later.

Example 22 – Calculation of the minimum payment

Assume that C, in Example 18, is connected with her tenant. The waiver of exemption can continue to operate from 1 July 2008 if the VAT payable in respect of the rent from the property for the following twelve months is equal to the amount calculated in accordance with the formula above.

$$\frac{A - B}{12 - Y}$$

A (VAT deducted by C on acquisition of property) = €101, 250
B (VAT chargeable and paid by C, which would form part of the cancellation amount on 1 July 2008 if the waiver were cancelled at that date): €48,000 [assuming A paid an additional €4,000 in VAT on rent in the first half of 2008, having already paid €44,000 up to the end of 2007]
Y = 5 (number of full years since the date of the first letting or the date on which A waived exemption).

$$\frac{A - B}{12 - Y} = \frac{€101,250 - €48,000}{12 - 5} = €7,607$$

If the current rent is insufficient and C wants to avoid cancelling her waiver (in respect of this property), she will have to increase the rent chargeable to her tenant to ensure that the VAT payable on that rent for the coming twelve months is at least €7,607. Provided that this amount of VAT will be paid, in equal instalments, over the following year and that she keeps her VAT payments in respect of the letting up to date, the property will remain within her waiver of exemption.

The failure, at any point from 1 July 2008 onwards, to meet these conditions will result in the immediate cancellation of the waiver and the requirement to pay the cancellation amount.

5.8 How does the Capital Goods Scheme operate in relation to properties that are subject to a waiver of exemption? (Section 7B(2))

The Capital Goods Scheme does not apply to properties that are within the waiver of exemption to the extent that the tax relating to the acquisition or development of the property is to be taken into account in calculating the cancellation amount payable if the waiver is cancelled. In general, the CGS will not apply to sales of such properties. However, a scenario in which a CGS adjustment could arise is illustrated in the next example.

Example 23 – CGS credit for waiver property

A landlord acquired property A in September 1999. He was charged VAT on acquisition of this property, which he let under an exempt short-term letting. In 2002 he purchased a second investment property B. He decided to waive his exemption, which covered his rents from both properties. He was entitled to reclaim the VAT on the acquisition of property B. In June 2009 he sells both properties and calculates the cancellation amount. The cancellation amount takes account only of the VAT on the acquisition of property B, which does not therefore fall within the CGS. He could, however, claim a CGS adjustment in relation to the VAT incurred on the acquisition of property A if its supply in 2009 is taxable. If he enters into a joint option to tax the sale of property A, then the additional deductibility is:

Non-deductible VAT on acquisition of property A $\times \dfrac{11^*}{20^{**}}$

* (number of full intervals remaining plus one)
**(total number of intervals in adjustment period)

Chapter 6

Capital Goods Scheme – Main Provisions

6.1 What is the Capital Goods Scheme?

The Capital Goods Scheme (CGS) is a mechanism for regulating deductibility over the "VAT-life" of a capital good. For VAT purposes a capital good is a developed property. The scheme operates by ensuring that the deductibility for a property reflects the use to which the property is put over the VAT-life (adjustment period) of the property. The CGS is provided for in Section 12E VAT Act 1972 (as amended). A feature of the scheme is a number of definitions, such as, initial interval, adjustment period, etc. These definitions reflect the various component parts of the scheme.

6.2 How does the scheme operate?

The VAT incurred on the acquisition or development of a property is deductible in accordance with the normal rules relating to deductibility. A person who is engaged in a fully taxable economic activity is entitled to deduct all of the VAT charged on the acquisition or development of a property to be used in the business. A person who is engaged in partly taxable and partly exempt economic activities is only entitled to deduct the percentage of VAT charged that corresponds to the percentage of taxable use.

At the end of the first twelve months following completion (or acquisition, where the property is acquired following completion), the taxpayer must review the amount of VAT deducted on the acquisition or development of the property. If the proportion of taxable use of a property during that twelve-month period differs from the proportion of the VAT deducted on the acquisition or development of that property, then an adjustment is required. If too much has been deducted, the taxpayer must pay back the excess. If too little had been deducted initially, the taxpayer is entitled to claim the deficiency as an input credit.

The first twelve months mentioned above is known as the 'initial interval'.

This adjusted amount deductible for the first twelve months is the benchmark figure for comparison purposes under the scheme for the remainder of the VAT-life of the property. The scheme requires an annual review, over the VAT-life of the property by the owner of the property, of the use to which a property is put (in terms of taxable or exempt use). Where there is a change in the proportion of use for taxable purposes for any year in comparison with the use during the initial 12 months, an adjustment of a proportion of the VAT deductibility will be required.

The annual adjustments will reflect the difference between the use in the initial twelve months and the use in the year being reviewed. Ultimately, the proportion of VAT deducted following all annual adjustments will reflect the actual use of the property over the adjustment period or VAT-life of the property. The VAT-life of a property is made up of twenty intervals. In the case of a refurbishment the VAT-life is ten intervals. Except in relation to the second CGS interval, a CGS interval is twelve months.

It is important to note that for the majority of businesses these CGS reviews will have no effect. For example, if a company deducts all of the VAT charged on acquisition or development and engages in wholly taxable activities during the adjustment period then no adjustments will arise.

Figure 1 outlines how the scheme operates. It assumes that –

• the capital good (developed property) is acquired on or after 1 July 2008 with VAT being chargeable on the acquisition,

• the person acquiring the property is engaged in an economic activity, and

• the accounting year for that person ends on 31 December each year.

The dates when each interval ends are discussed and explained below. Figure 1 can be used as a simple guide to determine whether or not an adjustment is required at the end of any interval during the *'adjustment period'*.

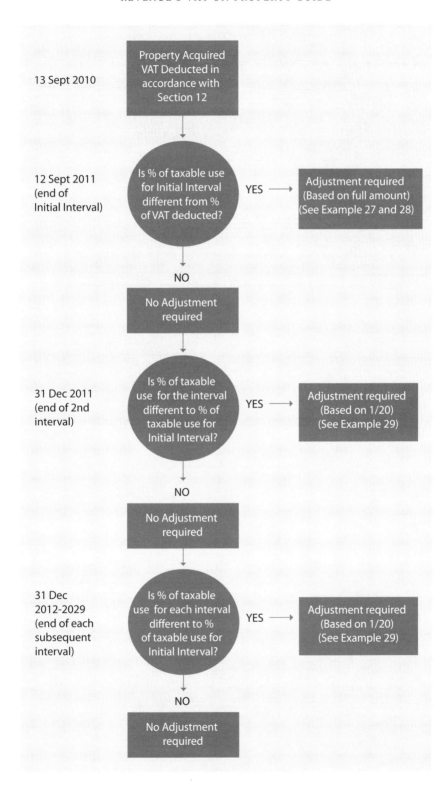

13 Sept 2010

Property Acquired VAT Deducted in accordance with Section 12

12 Sept 2011 (end of Initial Interval)

Is % of taxable use for Initial Interval different from % of VAT deducted?

YES ⟶ Adjustment required (Based on full amount) (See Example 27 and 28)

NO

No Adjustment required

31 Dec 2011 (end of 2nd interval)

Is % of taxable use for the interval different to % of taxable use for Initial Interval?

YES ⟶ Adjustment required (Based on 1/20) (See Example 29)

NO

No Adjustment required

31 Dec 2012-2029 (end of each subsequent interval)

Is % of taxable use for each interval different to % of taxable use for Initial Interval?

YES ⟶ Adjustment required (Based on 1/20) (See Example 29)

NO

No Adjustment required

6.3 When does the scheme apply? (Section 12E(1))

The scheme applies to developed immovable goods (properties) on the acquisition or development of which VAT has been charged to a "taxable person", i. e. a person that is engaging in an economic activity. In other words, to be subject to the scheme the owner of the property must have been charged VAT on the acquisition or development of the property and must be in business. Any person who acquires or develops a property in these circumstances is known as a "capital goods owner" and will be referred to, for the purpose of this guide, as the owner.

6.4 When does the scheme not apply?

The scheme does not apply to any person who acquires a property on which VAT is not chargeable. It also does not apply to persons who are not engaged in economic (business) activities or to a taxable person who acquires or develops a property in a non-business capacity. In other words, private individuals and bodies who engage in activities that are outside the scope of VAT are not subject to the scheme.

6.5 "VAT-Life" *(adjustment period)* of a capital good (Section 12E(3))

The scheme provides that in most cases each capital good will have a VAT-life or adjustment period of twenty intervals. It is during this period that adjustments are required to be made. Once the period has elapsed, there are no further obligations under the scheme.

Certain properties have an adjustment period of ten intervals. Where development work is carried out on a previously completed building a new capital good to the value of the cost of the development is "created" by this development work. This is known as a *'refurbishment'*. The adjustment period for a refurbishment is ten intervals. This means that there can, in some cases, be two or more capital goods in relation to a single property at one time.

6.6 Intervals

The adjustment period is divided up into intervals. There are twenty intervals in the case of a new capital good and ten in the case of a refurbishment. An interval, other than the *'initial interval'* and *'second interval'*, will be the owner's accounting year.

In the case of an owner who constructs a property, the initial interval begins on the date on which a property is completed[6]. In the case of an owner who purchases a property the initial interval begins on the date the property is purchased. In both cases the initial interval ends twelve months from those dates.

---

[6] For information on what constitutes 'completed' please see Chapter 2.

Example 24 – Initial Interval

ABC Ltd purchases a property on which VAT is charged[7] on 13 September 2010. The *'initial interval'* begins on that date and ends twelve months later on 12 September 2011.

The 'second interval' begins on the day after the initial interval ends and ends at the end of the owner's accounting year in which the initial interval ends. The purpose of this shorter interval is to align the adjustments that may be required under the scheme with the owner's accounting year.

Example 25 – Second Interval

Using Example 24, ABC's accounting year ends on 31 December. The *'initial interval'* ends on 12 September 2011 (in the accounting year that ends 31 December 2011). The *'second interval'* begins on 13 Sept 2011 (day following end of initial interval) and ends on 31 December 2011, i.e. at the end of the accounting year during which the initial interval ends.

'Subsequent interval' means each interval after the second interval until the end of the adjustment period. The interval immediately following the second interval begins on the day after the end of the second interval and ends at the end of the owner's accounting year.

Example 26 – Subsequent Intervals

Continuing with Example 25 above, where the 'second interval' ends on 31 December 2011, the third interval will begin on 1 January 2012 and end on 31 December 2012. Each 'subsequent interval' will run from 1 January – 31 December until the end of the twentieth interval on 31 December 2029.

Table 1 below illustrates when each interval will begin and end for a new capital good and for a refurbishment where the capital good is acquired on 13/9/2010 and a refurbishment is carried out on the property during 2023 that is completed on 31/7/2023.

---

[7] This means the property is a "capital good" for the purposes of the scheme.

Table 1 – Illustration of dates for adjustment period

20 Intervals – new capital good			10 Intervals – refurbishment		
Interval	Begins	Ends	Interval	Begins	Ends
1	13/09/2010	12/09/2011	1	31/07/2023	30/07/2024
2	13/09/2011	31/12/2011	2	31/07/2024	31/12/2024
3	01/01/2012	31/12/2012	3	01/01/2025	31/12/2025
4	01/01/2013	31/12/2013	4	01/01/2026	31/12/2026
5	01/01/2014	31/12/2014	5	01/01/2027	31/12/2027
...	...	...	6	01/01/2028	31/12/2028
...	...	...	7	01/01/2029	31/12/2029
...	...	...	8	01/01/2030	31/12/2030
17	01/01/2026	31/12/2026	9	01/01/2031	31/12/2031
18	01/01/2027	31/12/2027	10	01/01/2032	31/12/2032
19	01/01/2028	31/12/2028			
20	01/01/2029	31/12/2029			

Note – Interval 1 5 'initial interval',
       Interval 2 5 'second interval',
       Intervals 3-20 5 'subsequent intervals'.

6.7 Obligations at the end of the Initial Interval (Section 12E(4))

As illustrated above in Table 1 the initial interval for a capital good runs for a full twelve-month period. At the end of this period the owner must examine the use to which the property was put during that twelve months. "Use"in this context means the taxable or exempt use of the property. This percentage of taxable use will usually be readily identifiable by the owner as it is based directly on the use of the property. However, in some cases a property may be used as a headquarters of a business that is engaged in various taxable and exempt activities. In these cases, the percentage of taxable use will depend on the overall mix of taxable and exempt activities carried on by the business.

Where the percentage of taxable use during the first year differs from the percentage of the VAT deducted by the owner on the acquisition or development of the property, then an adjustment is required. If the percentage of taxable use for the initial interval is less than the percentage of the VAT deducted on the acquisition or development of the property, VAT is payable by the owner. If the percentage of taxable use for the initial interval is greater than the percentage of the VAT deducted on the acquisition or development of the property, then the owner is entitled to additional deductible VAT. Clearly, if the owner deducts all of the VAT and uses the property for fully taxable purposes, there is no adjustment required. Examples 27 and 28 below illustrate how these rules work in practice.

Note – There is an exception to the normal rules at the end of the initial interval. If a property developer rents out residential properties (exempt – option not allowed), then there is no obligation to carry out the adjustment at the end of the initial interval.

Example 27 – Adjustment at the end of the Initial Interval (tax payable)

ABC Ltd purchases a property on 13 September 2010. The cost of the property is €10,000,000 + VAT €1,350,000. This is the *'total tax incurred'*. ABC deducts all of this VAT on the basis that the company intends to put the property to a fully taxable use.

At the end of the initial interval (12 Sept 2011) ABC calculates that the use to which the property is put during the Initial Interval was 80% taxable. As ABC deducted 100% of the VAT charged it is obliged to make an adjustment (because there is a difference between these two figures) and repay the excess amount deducted.

For the purposes of the adjustment ABC must calculate the *'total reviewed deductible amount'* which is calculated by multiplying the *'total tax incurred'* by the *'initial interval proportion of deductible use'* (80%) –

'total reviewed deductible amount' = €1,350,000 × 80% = €1,080,000.

This figure represents the tax deducible in relation to the property on the basis of the taxable use during the initial interval and is the benchmark VAT deductibility figure for the remaining 19 intervals.

The adjustment required at the end of the initial interval is calculated as the difference between the amount of the VAT deducted and the *'total reviewed deductible amount'* using the formula -

A – B (A = amount of total tax deducted, B = *'total reviewed deductible amount'*)

A – B = €1,350,000 – €1,080,000 = €270,000.

As A is greater than B, this amount is payable as VAT due for the taxable period immediately after the end of initial interval which will be Nov/Dec 2011. The effect of the calculation is that there is a claw-back of €270,000 from ABC (20% of the VAT initially deducted.)

Example 28 – Adjustment at the end of the initial interval (tax deductible)

> XYZ Ltd purchases a property on 7 April 2010. The cost of the property is €1,000,000 + VAT €135,000. This is the 'total tax incurred'. XYZ deducts 10% (€13,500) of the VAT on the basis that it intends to use the property for 10% taxable activities (90% exempt activities).
>
> At the end of the initial interval (6 April 2011) XYZ calculate that the use to which the property is put during the year was 20% taxable. As it deducted 10% of the VAT charged it is obliged to make an adjustment because there is a difference between these two figures. For the purposes of the adjustment XYZ must calculate the 'total reviewed deductible amount' which is simply the 'total tax incurred' multiplied by the percentage of taxable use for the initial interval (20%) –
>
> $$€135,000 \times 20\% = €27,000.$$
>
> The adjustment is calculated as the difference between the amount of the VAT deducted and the total reviewed deductible amount –
>
> $$A - B$$
>
> (A = amount of total tax incurred deducted, B = 'total reviewed deductible amt')
>
> €13,500 – €27,000
>
> = –€13,500
>
> As B is greater than A, this amount is given as a VAT credit to XYZ for the taxable period immediately after the end of initial interval which will be May/June 2011. The effect of the calculation is that XYZ is entitled to an additional input credit of €13,500 (10% of the VAT charged to them).

6.8 Second and subsequent intervals (Section 12E(5))

At the end of the second and each subsequent interval the owner should examine the use to which the property is put during that interval and compare that use with the use to which the property was put during the initial interval. *Where the percentage of taxable use during the interval in questions differs from the percentage of taxable use for the initial interval, then an adjustment is required.*

If the percentage of taxable use for the interval is less than the percentage of taxable use for the initial interval then an additional amount of VAT is payable by the owner. If the percentage of taxable use for the interval is greater than the percentage of taxable use for the initial interval, then the owner is entitled to an additional VAT deduction. Of course, if the percentage of taxable use for the interval is the same as the percentage of taxable use for the initial interval, no adjustment is required.

The adjustments at the end of the second and each subsequent interval are calculated using certain defined terms.

- The 'base tax amount' is calculated by dividing the 'total tax incurred' by the number of intervals in the adjustment period.

- The *'reference deduction amount'* is calculated by dividing the *'total reviewed deductible amount'* by the number of intervals in the adjustment period. This amount is treated as if it were the amount that was deducted by the owner at the beginning of the second and each subsequent interval.

- The *'interval deductible amount'* is the amount of the *'base tax amount'* that is deductible on the basis of the use in the interval in question (i. e. the second or subsequent interval). For example if the *"proportion of deductible use"* for the second interval is 70%, then the *"interval deductible amount"* is calculated by multiplying the "base tax amount" by 70%.

Example 29 below illustrates all of these concepts.

Example 29 – Adjustments at the end of second and subsequent intervals

Using the same figures as Example 27 above with company ABC Ltd and property acquired 13 September 2010. Accounting year ends 31/12.
'total tax incurred' = €1,350,000
'base tax amount' = €67,500 (€1,350,000/20). This is the 'total tax incurred' divided by the number of intervals in the adjustment period.

As illustrated in Example 27 the 'initial interval proportion of deductible use' was 80%. 'total reviewed deductible amount' = €1,080,000
'reference deduction amount' = €54,000. (€1,080,000/20). This is calculated by dividing 'total reviewed deductible amount'by the number of intervals in the adjustment period and is used for any calculations required at the end of the second or subsequent intervals. The reference deduction amount is the same for the second and each subsequent interval. Where the deductible amount for the second or any subsequent interval (known as the *'interval deductible amount'*) differs from this amount an adjustment will be required.

2nd Interval – no adjustment
For the second interval (which ends on 31/12/2011) ABC's taxable use was 80%. (This is known as the *'proportion of deductible use'* for the interval.) As this is the same as the use for the initial interval, no adjustment is required.

3rd, 4th & 5th interval – no adjustment
For the 3rd (ending 31/12/2012), 4th (ending 31/12/2013) and 5th (ending 31/12/2014) intervals the *'proportion of deductible'* use was still 80% so adjustments are not required for those intervals.

6th & 7th interval – change in taxable use – VAT payable on adjustment
For the 6th interval (ending 31/12/2015) the *'proportion of deductible use'*is 70%. As this differs from 80% (use during initial interval) an adjustment is required. In order to carry out the calculation ABC is obliged to calculate the *'interval deductible amount'* which is the *"proportion of deductible use"* for that interval multiplied by the *'base tax amount'* €67,500 × 70% = €47,250.

The adjustment is the difference between the *'reference deduction amount'* and the *'interval deductible amount'* -

C − D

(C = reference deduction amount, D = interval deductible amount)

€54,000 − € 47,250 = €6,750

As C is greater than D €6,750 is payable as tax due for the taxable period following the end of the interval, which is Jan/Feb 2016.

For the 7th interval (ending 31/12/2016) the *'proportion of deductible use'* was 70%. Again, an adjustment is required –

C − D

€54,000 − €47,250 = €6,750

As C is greater than D €6,750 is payable as tax due for the taxable period following the end of the interval, which is Jan/Feb 2017.

8th & 9th interval – no adjustment required

For the 8th (ending 31/12/2017) and 9th intervals (ending 31/12/2018) the *'proportion of deductible use'* for the interval was 80%, so no adjustment required.

10th interval – change in taxable use – VAT deductible on adjustment

For the 10th interval (ending 31/12/2019) the 'proportion of deductible use' was 95%. As this differs from 80% (used during initial interval) an adjustment is required. Similar to above, the 'interval deductible amount' is

€67,500 × 95% = €64,125

Adjustment for the interval –

C − D

€54,000 − €64,125 = − €10,125

As D is greater than C €10,125 is given as a VAT credit for the taxable period following end of the interval, which is Jan/Feb 2020.

For the remainder of the intervals the *'proportion of deductible use'* is 80% which means there are no adjustments made at the end of all the intervals. The 20th interval ends on 31/12/2029. After this date there are no further obligations under the scheme.

As can be seen from Example 29, the scheme ensures that the total deductibility allowable in respect of the property reflects the use to which the property is put over the adjustment period. Table 2 below illustrates how the figures from Example 29 lead to adjustments at the end of the initial interval (based on the full amount of VAT incurred) as well as the 6th, 7th, and 10th interval based on 1/20th of the VAT incurred.

Table 2 – Adjustments for intervals

Interval	Amt Deducted €	Total Rev Ded Amt €	Adjustment €	VAT
1	1,350,000	1,080,000	270,000	Payable
		Base tax amount = €67,500 for all intervals		

Interval	Ref Deduction Amt €	Interval Deduction Amt €	Adjustment €	VAT
2	54,000	54,000	-	-
3	54,000	54,000	-	-
4	54,000	54,000	-	-
5	54,000	54,000	-	-
6	54,000	47,250	6,750	Payable
7	54,000	47,250	6,750	Payable
8	54,000	54,000	-	-
9	54,000	54,000	-	-
10	54,000	64,125	-10,125	Deductible
11	54,000	54,000	-	-
12	54,000	54,000	-	-
13	54,000	54,000	-	-
14	54,000	54,000	-	-
15	54,000	54,000	-	-
16	54,000	54,000	-	-
17	54,000	54,000	-	-
18	54,000	54,000	-	-
19	54,000	54,000	-	-
20	54,000	54,000	-	-

6.9 Adjustment where property use is linked to overheads

Where the taxable use of a property is determined by reference to the overheads of the taxpayer (i. e. a HQ building) Revenue will allow the adjustment (either tax payable or deductible) to be made in any of the three taxable periods following the end of any interval. This follows Revenue's position that allows taxpayers who engage in both taxable and exempt supplies up to three taxable periods to calculate their proportion of taxable use. It should be noted that if a taxpayer attempts to abuse these rules for avoidance/deferral of tax purposes the treatment may be withdrawn for that taxpayer at the discretion of Revenue.

This procedure will not apply in the majority of cases as the taxable use of a property will be determined by direct attribution i.e. the use to which the property itself is put. In the majority of cases the adjustment must be made at the end of the interval and any tax payable or deductible must be accounted for in the VAT return for the taxable period following the end of that interval.

6.10 **Big-Swing in taxable use (Section 12E(6))**

So far, this Chapter has outlined the rules for the adjustments at the end of an interval where there is a change in the taxable use of a property when compared with the taxable use during the initial interval. Such adjustments are based on 1/20th (1/10th in the case of refurbishment) of the VAT incurred on the capital good.

There are special rules that apply where the taxable use for an interval differs by more than fifty percentage points from the taxable use for the initial interval. These rules recognise the fact that there has been a significant change in the taxable activities of the business and require a full adjustment. This adjustment is not based on 1/20th of the VAT incurred but is based on the full VAT incurred reduced by the number of intervals that have already expired in the adjustment period.

The big-swing rule operates by providing for an adjustment at the end of an interval where there has been a change of more than fifty percentage points when compared to the initial interval. This adjustment is based on the full amount of VAT deducted for the initial interval (as opposed to 1/20 under the normal rules). Where such an adjustment is required there is a "re-balancing" of the benchmark figures and the re-balanced benchmark figures are then used for all remaining intervals after the interval in which the big-swing occurs.

Example 30 – Changes of more than fifty percentage points in taxable use

C Ltd is an IT company. It provides both software services and training services. The breakdown of the business over the last number of years is 30% software (taxable), 70% training (exempt). Its accounting year ends on 31/3 each year. C Ltd purchases a property on 21/8/2011 for €3m 1 VAT €405,000 ('total tax incurred').

'base tax amount' = €20,250 (€405,000/20)

The initial interval begins on the date of purchase (21/8/2011). C Ltd deducts 30% of the VAT charged.
At the end of the initial interval (20/8/2012) the 'initial interval proportion of deductible use' = 30% so no adjustment is required.

'total reviewed deductible amount' = €121,500 (€405,000 × 30%)

'reference deduction amount' = €6,075 (€121,500/20)

For the 2nd (ending 31/3/2013)[8], 3rd (ending 31/3/2014), 4th (ending 31/3/2015) intervals the 'proportion of deductible use' is 30% so no adjustment is required.

During 2015 C Ltd wins a high value contract to develop software for a large multinational. As a result for the 5th interval (ending 31/3/2016) the 'proportion of deductible use' is 90%. As this differs from the 'initial interval' proportion of deductible use' by more than 50 percentage points (90% less 30%) a big-swing adjustment is triggered[9].

---

[8] The 2nd interval ends on the date of the end of the next accounting year which in this example is 31/3/2013 as the accounting year of C Ltd ends on 31/3 each year.
[9] When such an adjustment occurs, there is no "normal" adjustment as described in Chapter 6 based on 1/20 of the deductibility.

The 'interval deductible amount' = €18,225 (base tax amount × 90%)

Adjustment is calculated as follows –

(C − D) × N

(C = reference deduction amount, D = interval deductible amount, N = number of full intervals remaining +1)

(€6,075 − €18,225) × 16 = −€194,400

As D is greater than C, €194,400 is given as an additional VAT credit to C Ltd in the taxable period following the end of the interval (May/June 2016).

As part of the big swing adjustment the benchmark figures for the capital good are also changed.

The 'initial interval' proportion of deductible use' is changed to 90%, from 30%. This is necessary, as essentially C Ltd has been given a VAT credit of 90% for 16 intervals.

'total reviewed deductible amount' = €364,500 (€405,000 × 90%)
'reference deduction amount' = €18,225 (€364,500/20)

The 'total tax incurred' and the 'base tax amount' stay the same as they are based on the VAT charged at acquisition.

For the 6th interval (ending 31/3/2017) the 'proportion of deductible use' = 90% so no adjustment is required as this is the same as the new 'initial interval proportion of deductible use'.

For the 7th interval (31/3/2018) the 'proportion of deductible use' = 75% so an adjustment is required.
The 'interval deductible amount' = €15,188 (base tax amount × 75%)
C − D
€18,225 − €15,188
= €3,037

As C is greater than D, €3,037 is payable as tax due by C Ltd for the taxable period following the end of interval (May/Jun 2018).

For all the remaining intervals 8th – 20th the 'proportion of taxable use' is 90% so no further adjustments are required.

Example 30 illustrates how adjustments are calculated when there is a change of more than fifty percentage points in the proportion of taxable use of the property when compared with the use during the initial interval. In that particular example, the use increased by more than fifty percentage points so there was a VAT credit given. The rule also applies where there is a decrease in the taxable use by more than fifty percentage points. The decrease results in a claw-back of VAT. The benchmark figures are re-balanced.

6.11 **Development by the tenant (Section 12E(8))**

Where a tenant has a leasehold interest in a completed property and carries out development work on that property then the tenant "creates" a capital good. The tenant is regarded as the owner of this capital good. This development is a refurbishment and the adjustment period is ten years. All of the obligations in relation to the initial, second and subsequent intervals above arise for the tenant in relation to the development work carried out. Any change in use must be adjusted for over the adjustment period, which is ten intervals.

6.12 **Obligations – the "capital good record" (Section 12E(12))**

Every owner is obliged to create and maintain a "capital good record"for each property[10] they own. The record must contain the following information about the property –

- The amount of VAT charged in relation to the owner's acquisition or development of the property. (This is known as the *"total tax incurred"*. See examples above).

- The amount of the VAT charged that was deducted initially.

- The date on which the adjustment period begins (date of acquisition, where the property was acquired or date of completion of development where property constructed or refurbished).

- The number of intervals in the adjustment period. This may be 10 or 20 depending on the situation.

- The Initial Interval proportion of deductible use, i. e. the percentage of taxable use for the first 12 months. (See examples above).

- The total reviewed deductible amount, i.e. total tax incurred multiplied by the percentage of taxable use for the initial interval. (See examples above).

- The proportion of deductible use for each interval, i.e. the percentage of taxable use for each interval (second, third, fourth, etc).

- Details of any adjustments under the scheme. (See examples above).

- Details of any sale of the property.

---

[10] In the case of a property that has been refurbished there may be two or more capital goods attributable to that property. A "capital good record" must be created and maintained for all capital goods that a taxpayer has.

Chapter 7

Capital Goods Scheme: Other adjustments

This Chapter deals with the CGS rules relating to sales, assignments/surrenders of leases and the landlord's option to tax.

7.1 Sales of capital goods

There are a number of rules within the scheme for dealing with sales of capital goods (properties) during the adjustment period. The basic rule is that if the sale is taxable (subject to VAT), then for the remaining intervals in the adjustment period, the property is treated as being used for taxable purposes by the taxable person who sells it. If the sale is exempt, then for the remaining intervals in the adjustment period, the property is treated as being used for fully exempt purposes by the seller. The adjustments required are made for the VAT period in which the sale takes place. The rules for whether or not the sale of a property is taxable or exempt are contained in Chapter 2.

7.2 Taxable sale during the adjustment period (Section 12E(7))

If the sale is taxable there are two possible scenarios –

- if the owner was not entitled to deduct some or all of the VAT on the acquisition or development of the property, then a VAT credit is given to the owner at the time of the sale based on the non-deductible VAT and the number of intervals remaining in the adjustment period; or

- if the owner was entitled to deduct all of the VAT on the acquisition or development of the property,[11] then there is no adjustment required.

---

[11] The owner must also have used the property for 100% taxable activities for the initial interval. This condition obviously does not have to be met if the property is sold before the end of the initial interval.

7.3 Exempt sale during the adjustment period (Section 12E(7))

If the sale is exempt there are two possible scenarios –

- where the owner was entitled to deduct some or all of the VAT, then there is a claw-back based on of the amount of VAT deductible by the owner and the number of intervals remaining in the adjustment period, or

- where the owner was not entitled to deduct any of the VAT,[12] then there is no adjustment required.

Example 31 below illustrates whether or not an adjustment is required when the sale of a property occurs during the adjustment period.

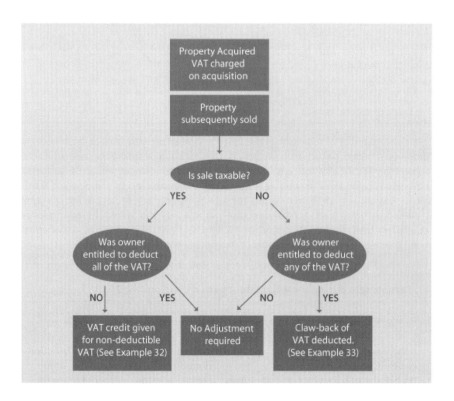

When a property is sold there are no further obligations for the owner under the CGS scheme. In all cases the sale brings the adjustment period for a property to an end for the seller.

---

[12] The owner must also have used the property for 100% exempt activities for the initial interval. This condition obviously does not have to be met if the property is sold before the end of the initial interval.

7.4 Obligations for the purchaser

Whether or not the purchaser has any obligations under the scheme is determined by the normal rules as described in Chapter 6. If the purchaser acquires a property (capital good) on which VAT is chargeable and the purchaser is engaged in an economic activity, then the purchaser has acquired a capital good and is subject to the rules of the scheme and must make adjustments as required over a twenty interval adjustment period. The following examples illustrate the various scenarios that can arise on a sale during the adjustment period and outline the obligations for the seller and the purchaser in each case.

7.5 Taxable Sale

The following example outlines the CGS rules when a taxable sale occurs.

Example 32 – Taxable sale, credit for non-deductible VAT

BL owns a green field site. It engages a builder to construct a new office. The builder charges €5m + VAT €675,000 ('*total tax incurred*'). BL deducts 15% of this VAT on the basis that it intends to use the property for 15% taxable activities. The building is completed on 3/2/2010. The initial interval begins on this date. At the end of the initial interval (2/2/2011) the '*initial interval proportion of deductible use*' = 15% so no adjustment required.
'*total reviewed deductible amount*' = €101,250
'*non-deductible amount*' = €573,750 (€675,000 – €101,250).

For the 2nd, 3rd, 4th, 5th and 6th interval the "*proportion of deductible use*" = 15% so no adjustment required at the end of those intervals.

On the 6/5/2016 (during the 7th interval) BL sells the property to JB Ltd. The sale is exempt as it is over 5 years since the completion of the building. However, BL and JB exercise the joint option to tax the sale. The sale price is €7million. An adjustment is required by BL which gives it a credit for part of the non-deductible VAT – The adjustment is calculated using the formula:

$$\frac{E \times N}{T}$$

(E = non-deductible amount, N = number of full intervals remaining + 1, T = Total number intervals in the adjustment period)

$$\frac{€573,750 \times 14}{20}$$
$$= €401,625$$

BL claims €401,625 VAT credit for the taxable period in which the sale occurs (May/June 2016). BL has no further obligations under the scheme. As the sale is subject to the joint option to tax, it is reverse charged[13] and JB must account for VAT on the sale - €7m x 13.5% = €945,000.

Obligations for JB
JB has acquired a developed property on which VAT is chargeable. JB is an owner for the purpose of the scheme. The initial interval for JB begins on 6/5/2016. There will be 20 intervals and the '*total tax incurred*' = €945,000.

---

[13] See Chapter 2.

It should be noted that Example 32 deals with a situation where the sale is exempt but a joint option to tax is exercised. The VAT credit given to BL also applies to situations where the sale takes place while the property is "new"[14] (for example if the property was sold by BL within 5 years of its completion[15]).

Example 32 illustrates how the credit given to BL ensures that when VAT is charged on the sale that any non-deductible VAT for the remainder of the VAT-life (twenty years reduced by the number of intervals that have expired) is given as a VAT credit. Obviously, if the seller had been entitled to deduct the full VAT charged (the total reviewed deductible amount was the full VAT charged) no further input credit arises.

7.6 Exempt Sale

The following example outlines the CGS rules when an exempt sale occurs.

Example 33 – Claw-back of VAT on exempt sale

M Ltd purchases a new property[16] from B Ltd on 6/10/2012 for €3m + VAT €405,000 ('total tax incurred'). The initial interval for the property begins on that day. M deducts all of the VAT on the basis it intends to use the property for a fully taxable activity. M 'occupies' the property on 25/10/2012[17]. At end of the initial interval (5/10/2013) –
'initial interval proportion of deductible use' = 100%
'total reviewed deductible amount' = €405,000.

The property is used for 100% taxable purposes until sold on 4/5/2015 to RS Ltd. As it is the second or subsequent sale following completion and the property has been occupied for a period of more than 2 years[18] the sale is exempt. The exempt sale triggers an adjustment. The formula is:

$$\frac{B \times N}{T}$$

(B = total reviewed deductible amount, N and M – see Example 32 above)

$$\frac{€405,000 \times 17}{20}$$
$$= €344,250$$

€344,250 is payable as tax due by M in the taxable period in which the sale occurs (May/June 2015). There are no further obligations under the scheme for M.

Obligations for RS Ltd
RS acquires a developed property but no VAT is chargeable on the acquisition. Therefore, the property is not subject to the CGS in the hands of RS.

---

[14] See Chapter 2
[15] Note – In cases where the sale is taxable while "new", the tax payable on the sale is not "reverse charged" as described in Example 32. BL will charge VAT to JB in the normal way. BL will remit the VAT to Revenue and JB will deduct whatever proportion of the VAT to which it is entitled.
[16] The property was completed on 1/9/2012 and never occupied by B Ltd.
[17] See Chapter 2.
[18] Occupied 25/10/2012, sold 4/5/2015, more than 24 months occupation – sale is exempt. See Chapter 2.

7.7 Development by a tenant (Section 12E(8))

As discussed in Chapter 6.11, where a tenant has a leasehold interest in a property and carries out development work in that property, then the tenant "creates" a capital good. Where such a development occurs the adjustment period is ten years as, for the purposes of the scheme, the development is considered a "refurbishment" (development work on a previously completed building). There are certain other obligations in such circumstances aside from the change of use provisions. Where a tenant assigns or surrenders the lease there are special rules as described below.

7.8 Assignment or surrender of lease where development carried out by tenant

If, during the ten-interval adjustment period, a tenant assigns or surrenders a lease of a property in which they have "created" a capital good, an adjustment arises. Essentially a claw-back of the VAT deducted (reduced by the number of years that have elapsed in the adjustment period) arises in the hands of the tenant.

Example 34 – Development by tenant, subsequent assignment

PH Ltd takes a lease in a property from 1 June 2010. PH carries out development work on the property installing air-conditioning units, a lift and other fixtures to prepare the unit for trading. The total cost of this work is €500,000 + VAT €60,750. PH deducts 90% of this VAT on the basis that the property is to be used to the extent of 90% for taxable activities.

'total tax incurred' = €67,500
'base tax amount' = €6,750 (€67,500/10)
The development work is completed on 23 July 2010. The initial interval for the capital good begins on that day. At the end of the initial interval (22/7/2011) PH's exempt activity is greater than forecast; the 'initial proportion of deductible use' is 65%. As this differs from 90% an adjustment is required.

The 'total reviewed deductible amount' = €43,875 (€67,500 × 65%)
'reference deduction amount' = €4,388 (€43,875/10).
Adjustment calculated as follows –
A − B
€60,750 − €43,875 = €16,875

As A is greater than B €16, 875 is payable as tax due in the taxable period following the end of initial interval (Sept/Oct 2011). For the 2nd (31/12/2011), 3rd (31/12/2012) and 4th (31/12/2013) intervals 'proportion of deductible use' = 65% so no adjustments are required.

During 2014 (fifth interval) PH decide to upscale and move to a new property. It surrenders the lease to the landlord on 1 April 2014. This triggers an adjustment under the scheme calculated as follows –

$$\frac{B \times N}{T} \qquad \text{(See Example 33 for B, N and T)}$$

$$\frac{€43,875 \times 6}{10}$$

= €26,325 payable as tax due in taxable period when surrender occurs (Mar/Apr 2014).

7.9 Passing on scheme liabilities in certain circumstances (Section 12E(8))

There are two exceptions to the rule described above, whereby there is a claw-back of VAT deducted, where the tenant assigns or surrenders a lease on a property in which the tenant has carried out a development.

The first exception is where the tenant used the property for 100% taxable use during the initial interval. In such cases where the lease is assigned or surrendered and where the tenant enters into a written agreement with the person to whom the lease is being assigned or surrendered, then the tenant's obligations under the CGS can be "passed on" to that person. The tenant is obliged to issue a copy of the *capital good record* to the other party and that person uses the information in the record for the purposes of operating the scheme.

Example 35 – Assignment/surrender – passing on obligations

GR Ltd takes a lease in a property from 1 April 2010. The property is a shell and GR Ltd intends to open a restaurant. GR Ltd carries out development work on the property installing a bar, kitchen and air-conditioning units, etc. The total cost of this work is €1,500,000 + VAT €202,500. GR Ltd deducts all this VAT on the basis it intends to make fully taxable supplies. The development work is completed on 6 Aug 2010. *'total tax incurred'* = €202,500

At the end of initial interval *'initial interval proportion of deductible use'* = 100%. Therefore, no adjustment required.

'total reviewed deductible amount' = €202,500 (€202,500 × 100%)

During the 3rd interval GR Ltd ceases trading. GR's landlord is willing to accept the surrender of the lease from 1 Sept 2012. The landlord is willing to leave the tenant's fixtures in place as another tenant might wish to run a restaurant from the premises. The landlord agrees in writing with GR to "take over" the responsibilities under the CGS scheme from the date of the assignment. GR issues a copy of the capital good record and the landlord will have to make adjustments at the end of each of the remaining intervals for any changes of use, etc. until the end of the adjustment period (31/12/2019).

The second exception to the claw-back from the tenant is where there is an assignment or surrender of a lease where the development work is essentially "ripped out". For example, if a kitchen and bar has been installed and the kitchen and bar are taken out of the property prior to the assignment or surrender of the lease, then there is no claw-back from the tenant under the scheme.

7.10 Exercising and terminating a landlord's option to tax a letting (Section 12E(6))

Chapter 4 outlines the rules regarding the VAT treatment of the letting of property. The basic rule is that the letting of a property is exempt from VAT. However, a landlord may opt to tax the letting. The effect of so opting is that the property is then put to a fully taxable use and the landlord is entitled to deduct the acquisition and development VAT costs.

As the option can be exercised or cancelled at anytime, there are clear implications for the Capital Goods Scheme as a property can move from taxable to exempt use (or vice-versa). The basic rule is that if a landlord terminates an option to tax a letting or exercises an option to tax a previously exempt letting, the landlord is deemed for the purposes of the CGS to have supplied the property and immediately re-acquired it. Where the landlord terminates the option to tax, the 'supply' is deemed to be exempt, which gives rise to a withdrawal of deductibility already allowed. Where the landlord exercises an option to tax a letting where the letting was previously exempt, the 'supply' is deemed to be taxable, thus giving input credit for previously non-deductible VAT. Examples 36 and 37 illustrate how this operates in practice. The adjustment period for the capital good commences at the deemed acquisition date and comprises the number of full intervals remaining in the original adjustment period plus one.

Example 36 – Terminating the landlord's option to tax

L acquired a property on 12/7/2010. His accounting year ends on 31/12 each year. The property cost €15m + VAT €2,025,000 ('total tax incurred'). L deducted all of the VAT on the basis that he intends to rent the property and exercise the landlord's option to tax and charge VAT on the rents. L enters into a 21-year lease with an un-connected tenant beginning on 1/9/2010 and charges VAT on the rents.

'total reviewed deductible amount' = €2,025,000

The initial interval begins on 12/7/2010. After ten years the tenant exercises the break clause in the lease. L secures a new tenant. The new tenant K has no entitlement to deduct VAT and therefore does not want to be charged VAT on the rents.

L creates a new 15-year lease to K beginning on 1/10/2020. He does not charge VAT on the rents and so "terminates" the landlord's option to tax. This is deemed to be an exempt sale of the property by L. This triggers an adjustment on 1/10/2020. The formula is the same above in Example 33 (exempt sale) –

$$\frac{B \times N}{T}$$

$$\frac{€2,025,000 \times 10}{20}$$

$$= €1,012,500$$

€1,012,500 is payable by L for the taxable period during which the option to tax is terminated (Sept/Oct 2020).

L is deemed to immediately reacquire the property and the property is deemed to be a capital good for the purposes of the scheme.

'total tax incurred' is deemed to be €1,012,500

'non-deductible amount' = €1,012,500

'total reviewed deductible amount' = Nil (since the property will be subject to an exempt letting). The adjustment period will have 10 intervals beginning with the initial interval that commences on 1/10/2020 and ends on 30/9/2021. (The second interval begins on 1/10/2021 and ends on 31/12/2021, etc).

There is no variation in the lease and the adjustment period ends (with no further adjustments during the remaining 10 intervals) on 31/12/2029.

Example 37 – Exercising the landlord's option to tax with previously exempt letting

OCS purchases a property on 17/2/2010 for €6m + VAT €810,000. (*'total tax incurred'*) It did not deduct any of the VAT on the basis that it intended to make an exempt letting of the property. OCS's accounting year ends on 31/12. OCS secures a tenant and creates a 25 year lease which begins on 1/4/2010.

'non-deductible amount' = €810,000

'total reviewed deductible amount' = Nil

The letting continues for 8 years until the tenant exercises a break clause and exits from the lease. OCS secures a new tenant who is fully taxable and so is indifferent as to whether VAT is charged or not as it will be fully deductible.

On 1/5/2018 OCS creates a new lease for 20 years to T Ltd and exercises the "landlord's option to tax". This is deemed to be a taxable sale of the property by OCS. This triggers an adjustment under the scheme. The formula is the same as above in Example 32 (taxable sale) –

$$\frac{E \times N}{T}$$

$$\frac{€810,000 \times 12}{20}$$

= €486,000 which is given as VAT credit for the taxable period when the option is exercised (May/June 2018).

OCS is deemed to immediately re-acquire the property on 1/5/2018. It is a capital good as it was acquired for a business purpose and VAT was deemed to have been charged. For the purposes of the scheme –

'total tax incurred' is deemed to be €486,000

OCS is deemed to have fully deducted this amount.

'total reviewed deductible amount' = €486,000

The adjustment period will have 12 intervals beginning with the initial interval that commences on 1/5/2018 and ends on 30/4/2019. (The second interval begins on 1/5/2019 and ends on 31/12/2019).

There is no variation in the lease and the adjustment period ends (with no further adjustments during the remaining 12 intervals) on 31/12/2029.

7.11 **Property Developer/ Builder lets residential property prior to supply**

Paragraph 2.10 sets out an exception to the two and five-year rules whereby the supply of a residential property by the property developer/builder who developed the property is always treated as taxable regardless of when it takes place. Where the property developer/builder lets the property this letting is exempt, as an option to tax residential property is not allowed. Under the normal CGS rules the exempt letting of a property leads to a full adjustment of the tax deducted as set out in paragraph 7.10 above. However, in the case of the property developer/builder the adjustment set out in paragraph 7.10 does not apply and the CGS adjustment is treated under the 'normal' CGS rules for change of use and the adjustment is as set out in Chapter 6. (See note on page 45.)

Chapter 8

Capital Goods Scheme – Transfer of Business as a Going Concern

8.1 **Background**

Where a transfer of ownership of goods takes place in the course of the transfer of a business or part of a business that transfer is deemed not to be a supply for VAT purposes. This means that no VAT is chargeable on such a transfer.

8.2 **CGS and transfer of a business**

As no VAT is chargeable on the transfer of a property in the course of a transfer of a business, there are special rules within the CGS to deal with such transactions. There are basically two main rules dealing with the transferee to enable him or her to operate the scheme. One applies where the transfer occurs during the period when the sale of the property would have been taxable but for the transfer of business relief (i.e. while the property was considered "new").[19] The second rule applies when the transfer of the property occurs outside this period i.e. when if it were supplied other than as part of a transfer of a business, the sale would have been exempt. There are also rules dealing with the transferor.

8.3 **Transfer of property during the period when property considered "new" (Section 12E(3) and (7))**

Where a transfer of a property occurs in the course of a transfer of a business no VAT is charged on the sale of the property to the transferee. If this occurs during the period when a property is considered "new" (i.e. if the property was supplied at the time the transfer takes place it would be inherently taxable) then for CGS purposes:

---

[19] See Chapter 2.

- the transferor is treated as having made a taxed supply of the property; and

- the transferee is deemed to have been charged the VAT that would have been charged but for the fact that relief for the transfer of business applied. The amount of tax that would have been charged is treated as the *'total tax incurred'*. The transferee must pay to Revenue the difference between this amount and the amount that would have been deductible if this amount of VAT had been charged on the supply of the property.

Example 38 below illustrates how this operates in practice.

Example 38 – Transfer of business while property is "new"– taxable transferor/ transferee

B Ltd constructs a property that is completed on 6 Oct 2009 for a cost of €1,000, 000 + VAT €135,000 (*'total tax incurred'*). It deducts all of the VAT on the basis it intends to run a fully taxable bookshop business. B Ltd operates a fully taxable business for three years so there are no adjustments required under the CGS scheme. During their 3rd year of occupation of the property, C Ltd makes B Ltd an offer to buy their business for €2,000,000. Of this, the property is valued at €1,500,000, the stock at €100,000 and the goodwill of €400,000. As this is a transfer of a business no VAT applies. The business is sold to C Ltd on 14/11/2012.

CGS Implications for B Ltd (transferor) –
B Ltd is treated as having made a taxable supply of the property. There are no CGS implications on the transfer as B Ltd has already deducted all of the VAT and used the property for fully taxable purposes. The CGS rules for properties acquired through the transfer of business rules mirror those for taxable supplies from the perspective of the transferor.

CGS Implications for C Ltd (transferee) –
C Ltd is treated as having incurred VAT on the acquisition of the property. As C Ltd is using the property for fully taxable purposes there is no difference between the amount of VAT deemed to have been charged and the amount of that VAT that would have been deductible.

Using the formula to calculate the amount payable:

$F - G$

(F= amount of VAT that would have been chargeable if the transfer of business relief had not applied, G= amount of that VAT that would have been deductible)
€202,500 − €202,500 = €0 (i.e. amount payable by C Ltd is nil)

A new CGS adjustment period begins for C Ltd
'total tax incurred' = €202,500 (Amount that would have been chargeable €1, 500,000 × 13.5%)
C Ltd is deemed to have fully deducted this amount.
'base tax amount' = €10,125 (€202,500/20)
The initial interval begins on 14/11/2012 and ends on 13/11/2013.
At the end of the initial interval the 'initial interval proportion of deductible use' = 100% so no adjustment required.

'total reviewed deductible amount' = €202,500
'reference deduction amount' = €10,125

C Ltd must then operate the CGS scheme for the property for the remaining 19 intervals in the normal way and account for any change of use or any possible adjustments required when the property is sold, etc.

Example 39 – Transfer while property "new" – exempt transferor/transferee

Training Ltd (TL) purchases a new property on 7 Nov 2010 for €4m + VAT €540, 000 ('total tax incurred'). TL are engaged in the fully exempt activity of vocational training and do not deduct any of the VAT. At the end of the initial interval (6/11/2011) there is no adjustment as the 'initial interval proportion of deductible use' is 0%.
'total reviewed deductible amount' = 0
'non-deductible amount' = €540,000 (€540,000 − 0)

During 2011 an international consortium (IC) make an offer to buy the business for c6m. The valuation of the property as part of the offer is €4.5m. TL agrees to sell the business to IC on 1/12/2011. As there is a transfer of a business as a going concern, no VAT applies.

CGS implications for TL (transferor) –
The transfer however triggers a CGS adjustment for TL. The adjustment mirrors the credit that would be given if the property were subject to a taxable supply –

$$\frac{E \times N}{T}$$

(E= non-deductible amount, N= number of full intervals remaining +1, T= total number of intervals in adjustment period)

$$\frac{€540,000 \times 19}{20}$$
$$= €513,000$$

This is given as a VAT credit to TL for the taxable period when the transfer occurs (Nov/Dec 2011).

CGS obligations for IC (transferee) –
IC is treated as having been charged VAT that would have been charged on the supply of the property if the transfer of business relief had not applied.

'total tax incurred' = €607,500 (Amount that would have been chargeable if the transfer of business relief had not applied €4,500,000 × 13.5%).
As IC would not have been entitled to deduct all of the VAT that would have been chargeable, there is an adjustment triggered in the taxable period when the transfer occurs (Nov/Dec 2011) –

F − G

(F = amount of VAT that would have been chargeable had property been supplied,
G = amount of that VAT that would have been deductible)
€607,500 − 0
€607,500 payable as tax due by IC.
IC is deemed to have deducted none of the "total tax incurred".

The initial interval begins on 1/12/2011 and ends on 30/11/2012.
"initial interval proportion of deductible use" = 0%.
"total reviewed deductible amount"= 0
"non-deductible amount"= €607,500.

IC must operate the scheme for the remaining 19 intervals in the normal way and will be entitled to a VAT input credit at the end of any interval during which the property is used for taxable/partly taxable purposes. It will also be entitled to a credit if the property is sold during the adjustment period and the sale is taxable.

It should be noted that the obligations on the exempt transferor and exempt transferee as illustrated in Example 39 applies only to transfers that occur during the period while the property is "new" .

8.4 Transfer of property during the period when property outside "new"period (Section 12E(10))

If a transfer occurs outside the period where a property is considered "new" (i.e. if the property was sold at the time the transfer takes place it would be exempt from VAT) then the transferee essentially "steps into the shoes" of the transferor. The transferee takes over from the transferor and "inherits" the adjustment period of the property, i.e. if six intervals have elapsed then there will be fourteen intervals remaining in the adjustment period for the transferee. Example 40 below illustrates how this operates in practice.

Example 40 – Transfer outside period where property is "new"

Mr S is a sole trader who runs a fully taxable business. He purchased his current office space for his business on 13/4/2010 for €3m + VAT €405,000. He has no adjustment at the end of the initial interval as his 'initial proportion of deductible use' = 100%. 'total reviewed deductible amount' = €405,000

Mr S continues to trade for 6 years engaging in fully taxable activities. (No adjustment at end of any intervals to that point). During 2016 (7th interval) Mr S begins to plan his retirement. A big firm (BF) becomes aware of this and makes Mr S an offer for the business of €5m. The property is valued at €4m. Mr S accepts the offer and sells the business on 1/7/2016. As there is a transfer of a business as a going concern, no VAT applies. If the transfer of business relief had not applied, the supply of the property would have been exempt from VAT. Because of this the treatment of the transfer for the purposes of the CGS is different to that as outlined in Examples 38 and 39.

Essentially BF becomes the successor to Mr S and "steps into the shoes" of Mr S for the purposes of the CGS scheme. Mr S is obliged to provide a copy of the "capital good record" to BF and BF continues to operate the CGS as if it had owned the property from the date it was acquired by Mr S (13/4/2010).

BF must comply with the scheme for the remaining 14 intervals in the normal way and account for any change of use or any possible adjustments required when the property is sold, etc.

8.5 Interaction with Section 13A VAT Act 1972 (as amended)

Section 13A VAT Act 1972 (as amended) provides for the zero-rating of most supplies to exporters who qualify for authorisation under that provision. These supplies would include the sale of property to the exporter and construction services and other services and goods used by an exporter for the purpose of developing property. Where, as a result of Section 13A, an exporter has had costs relating to the acquisition or redevelopment of a property zero rated – including refurbishment by the exporter as a tenant – then, for the purposes of the CGS, those inputs are treated as if Section 13A had not applied to them and as if the VAT had been charged at the rates appropriate to the goods or services concerned and fully deducted by the exporter. The exporter therefore has the same responsibility within the CGS in respect of capital goods acquired or developed and zero rated under a Section 13A authorisation as he would if the authorisation had not applied.

Appendix A

Section 7A(3) of the VAT Act, 1972 (as amended), which outlines the circumstances under which a person shall be determined to be connected with another person, is reproduced below:

"(3)   (a)   For the purposes of this section any question of whether a person is connected with another person shall be determined in accordance with the following:

        (i)   a person is connected with an individual if that person is the individual's spouse, or is a relative, or the spouse of a relative, of the individual or of the individual's spouse,

        (ii)   a person is connected with any person with whom he or she is in partnership, and with the spouse or a relative of any individual with whom he or she is in partnership,

        (iii)   subject to clauses (IV) and (V) of subparagraph (v), a person is connected with another person if he or she has control over that other person, or if the other person has control over the first-mentioned person, or if both persons are controlled by another person or persons,

        (iv)   a body of persons is connected with another person if that person, or persons connected with him or her, have control of that body of persons, or the person and persons connected with him or her together have control of it,

        (v)   a body of persons is connected with another body of persons –

            (I)   if the same person has control of both or a person has control of one and persons connected with that person or that person and persons connected with that person have control of the other,

            (II)   if a group of 2 or more persons has control of each body of persons and the groups either consist of the same persons or could be regarded as consisting of the same persons by treating (in one or more cases) a member of either group as replaced by a person with whom he or she is connected,

            (III)   if both bodies of persons act in pursuit of a common purpose,

            (IV)   if any person or any group of persons or groups of persons having a reasonable commonality of identity have or had the means or power, either directly or indirectly, to determine the activities carried on or to be carried on by both bodies of persons, or

            (V)   if both bodies of persons are under the control of any person or group of persons or groups of persons having a reasonable commonality of identity,

        (vi)   a person in the capacity as trustee of a settlement is connected with –

            (I)   any person who in relation to the settlement is a settlor, or

            (II)   any person who is a beneficiary under the settlement.

    (b)   In this subsection –

        'control', in the case of a body corporate or in the case of a partnership, has the meaning assigned to it by section 8(3B);

        'relative' means a brother, sister, ancestor or lineal descendant."

Appendix 2

E-Brief 37/2008: FAQs 2008 VAT on Property

This collection of replies to frequently asked questions in relation to the new VAT on property provisions has been prepared by Revenue in response to questions that were submitted by the representative bodies on the TALC Indirect Taxed Sub-Committee. It is expected that the number of questions and answers will be added to over time as further issues arise.

1. **At the end of April 2008 the Revenue posted the New VAT on Property Guide. On 6 May 2008 the Revenue posted a slightly different version of the New VAT on Property Guide. Can the Revenue explain the difference between the new version and the old version?**

There were two changes:

- page 20, para 3.5 - addition of sentence 'However....required'

- page 31, para 4.11 - addition of ...'or a legacy lease (see Chapter 3.7)'

2. **Under Section 7A(1)(d)(iii) it is provided that a landlord's option to tax is terminated where the landlord and the tenant become connected persons after the lease has been granted. Upon a strict reading of the legislation this applies whether or not the tenant has the ability to recover at least 90% of VAT on input costs.**

Where a landlord and tenant become connected the landlord's option to tax is terminated. However, if the tenant is entitled to at least 90% deductibility in relation to the VAT on rents, the option to tax may remain in place. Similarly if the tenant sub-lets the property to a person who is connected to the landlord, the landlord's option is terminated. However, if the person connected to the landlord is entitled to at least 90% deductibility in relation to the VAT on rents, the option to tax may remain in place. Accordingly, in Example 17 VAT on Property Guide, the termination of the option would not arise if 'C' has at least 90% VAT recovery entitlement.

3. **Section 5(3B) provides for a blanket period of twenty years following the acquisition or development of the goods by the accountable person. This does not take account of the fact that the adjustment period will be twenty intervals and not twenty years, the adjustment period for a refurbished property is ten intervals and the adjustment period for a legacy lease or a property acquired under transfer of business rules could be any period but will inevitably be less than twenty years.**

The provisions in Section 5(3B) deal with diversion to non-business or private use. These rules are independent of the CGS. The rules for adjusting deductibility in Section 12E relate to diversions to exempt use. Twenty years is the period over which the taxpayer must account for the VAT where a deduction has been taken and the property is subsequently diverted to a non-business use in accordance with Section 5(3B). The amount on which VAT is chargeable as a result of this supply is based on this same twenty-year period in accordance with Section 10(4D). See also Regulation 21B of S.I. No. 548 of 2006 - VAT Regulations 2006 (inserted by S.I. No. 238 of 2008 - VAT (Amendment) Regulations 2008).

4. **The final paragraph of Chapter 3.18 VAT on Property Guide confirms that the existing practice as regards 'shared services' (i.e. where a landlord passes on VAT on such services to tenant) is continued for legacy lease after 1 July 2008. Is this practice also extended to new leases created after 1 July 2008?**

Yes this practice extends to such leases.

5. **Where a tenant carries out a refurbishment in say year fifteen of a twenty-year lease and the lease expires at the end of the twenty years without being renewed, is the tenant responsible for a capital goods adjustment in respect of the refurbishment when the lease expires?**

In the case described above there is no obligation on the tenant to make an adjustment since the lease simply expires. It is not assigned or surrendered. It should be noted that Revenue will examine cases where a tenant carries out a significant refurbishment approaching the end of the lease to see if in fact the refurbishment is for the benefit of the landlord and the issue of entitlement to input credit of the landlord, etc., would need to be considered.

6. **What is the VAT treatment of a premium/reverse premium payable by the tenant to his landlord on the surrender/assignment of a legacy lease on/after 1 July?**

The payment of a reverse premium to the landlord by the tenant on the surrender of a 'legacy' lease is not taxable: it is considered outside the scope of VAT. The consideration for the assignment/surrender of a legacy lease is based on the CGS amount as per Section 4C(7). The position of premiums generally is set out in paragraph 4.11 of the VAT on Property Guide.

7. **Where after 30 June a landlord makes a letting by way of an occupational lease to a tenant and exercises the landlord's option to tax, what is the VAT treatment if the tenant then makes a sub-letting of part only of the original property to a person connected with the landlord where the sub tenant does not have at least 90% VAT recoverability? Is the landlord's option to tax terminated for the entire of the property let by the landlord or only in respect of part of it, namely the part occupied by the connected sub tenant?**

Only the part occupied is effected by the termination of the option to tax. Section 12E(6)(c) has the effect of clawing-back the proportion of the landlord's deduction that relates to the part occupied by the connected tenant.

7a. **What is the position as regards charging VAT on such an occupational lease if, for example, 25% of the property was sub-let to a connected person with less than 90% recovery. The claw-back would be based on 25% of the VAT recovered by the landlord. Would the landlord only charge VAT on 75% of the rent paid under the occupational lease?**

Yes, the landlord would only charge VAT based on 75% of the rent charge to the main (unconnected) tenant. Please note that the apportionment of the rent between the taxable and exempt use would have to be made on a fair and reasonable basis. For example, if the ground floor represented 25% of the floor space but was more valuable in terms of the amount of rent receivable this would affect the amount of the claw-back under section 12E(6)(c) and the corresponding amount of the rent subject to VAT.

8.   **Section 4C(11) provides that the adjustment period for an assigned or surrendered legacy leasehold interest in the hands of the assignee or person who makes the surrender is 20 years. The capital goods scheme operates by intervals. Can the Revenue explain how the capital goods scheme will work in relation to an assigned or surrendered legacy lease?**

Where a legacy lease is assigned/surrendered from 1 July onwards, the person who is assigning or surrendering the lease calculates the number of intervals remaining in the adjustment. This is calculated from Section 4C(11)(c).

The adjustment period for the new owner (assignee/landlord) is advised by the assignor/surrendering tenant per section 4C(8)(b)(i), which will be the number of intervals remaining (being the number of intervals remaining in the latter's adjustment period, including that in which the assignment/surrender takes place).

Section 4C(8)(b) provides that the assignee/landlord is a capital goods owner for the purposes of Section 12E. The initial interval runs for a full twelve months from the date on which the assignment and surrender occurs. The second interval (as per Section 12E) will end on the date of the end of the accounting year of the capital goods owner. (Example 1 in Appendix A illustrates how this operates in practice.)

9.   **In Section 12E(3)(a) the adjustment periods for various classes of capital goods are set out. This sub section does not refer to shorter adjustment periods which will apply in the case of capital goods to which the transfer of business applies and legacy leases. The words 'in all other cases 20 years' give cause for concern. Can the Revenue confirm that different periods than those set out in Section 12E(3) can apply in the case of properties transferred under transfer of business rules and legacy leases?**

The adjustment period for legacy leases for the person who holds the interest on 1 July is provided for in Section 4C(11). For a person to whom a lease is assigned or surrendered post 1 July the adjustment period is provided for in Section 4C(8)(b)(i).

In relation to a transfer of business there are two separate scenarios. If a transfer of business occurs during the period where the property is considered 'new' then the adjustment period is 20 intervals as per

Section 12E(3)(a)(iii) for the transferee and the 'total tax incurred' is the amount of tax that would have been chargeable on the transfer but for the application of Section 3(5)(b)(iii) as per section 12E(3)(b)(ii).

If the transfer occurs outside the period where the property is considered 'new' then Section 12E(10) provides that the transferee will effectively 'step into the shoes' of the transferor and must make adjustments for the remainder of the adjustment period as provided for in Section 12E(10) (c). Where the transferee's accounting year ends on a different date to the transferor's, the transferee may align the end of the CGS intervals with his or her end of accounting year. See Regulation 21A of S.I. No. 548 of 2006 - VAT Regulations 2006 (inserted by S.I. No. 238 of 2008 - VAT (Amendment) Regulations 2008).

10. **Can a body that is considered outside the scope of VAT, such as a local authority avail of the option to tax the sale of a transitional property under Section 4C(2)?**

A local authority, or any other person or entity to the extent that their activities are outside the scope of VAT, cannot avail of the option to tax since they are not a 'taxable person' and therefore do not come within the provisions of Section 4C which only applies to immovable goods acquired or developed by a taxable person. Similarly the CGS will not apply to such a person since it only applies to taxable persons.

11. **When a person leaves a VAT Group and is either the landlord or the tenant of a person who remains a member, can the landlord avoid a deductibility adjustment by opting to tax the letting?**

Yes, subject to the connected persons rule in Section 7A.

12. **Does a CGS positive adjustment apply where a landlord has a short term letting pre 1 July 2008 without a waiver and opts to tax the letting on or after 1 July 2008?**

A CGS positive adjustment is not provided for in these circumstances as transitional properties are not subject to the change of use provisions in Section 12E.

13. **More clarification is needed regarding the meaning of 'freehold equivalent' - What is the position of a lease for 50 years, for 70 years, for 80 years that do not fall foul of the '50% rule'?**

The length of the lease is not of great importance. The amount of the payment and the nature of the payment(s) is the most significant issue.

However, as a very general rule of thumb, leases of 75 years duration or longer are likely to be considered as 'freehold equivalent'.

14. **What is the position for a waived letting between connected persons (where the connected tenant is not entitled to at least 90% deducibility) where the VAT on the rents prior to 1 July satisfies the minimum test in the 12-year rule?**

In such cases the landlord simply continues to charge VAT on the rents. The landlord must however ensure that the VAT on the rents continues to satisfy the minimum amount provided for in the 12-year rule.

15. **What is the position for a waived letting between connected persons (where the connected tenant is not entitled to at least 90% deducibility) where the VAT on the rents prior to 1 July is less than the minimum amount provided for in the 12-year rule?**

In such cases the waiver is cancelled with effect from 1 July. However, the landlord may increase the rents so that the VAT on the rents is at least equal to the minimum amount provided for in the 12-year rule on 1 July. Rents will not have to apply on a monthly or bimonthly basis in order to satisfy the 12-year rule. However, rent payable from 1 July 2008 should, irrespective of the period for which it is payable, be at such a level that when 'annualised' the 12-year rule will be satisfied. The VAT on the rents, which meets the minimum amount1, must be accounted for in the July/Aug VAT return.

It is important to note that the 12-year rule is subject to the landlord paying the resulting VAT liabilities on time. It is not a requirement that the tenant must have paid the VAT to the landlord. Note – bad debt relief does not apply in such a case. See Regulation 16A of S.I. No. 548 of 2006 - VAT Regulations 2006 (inserted by S.I. No. 272 of 2007 - VAT (Amendment) Regulations 2007 as amended by S.I. No. 238 of 2008 - VAT (Amendment) Regulations 2008).

16. **Will there be flexibility with the practical application of the CGS in regard to the first and second interval? For some businesses, the partial exemption calculation is a major task performed once a year - the application of the CGS would require partial exemption calculations throughout the year. Would it be acceptable to allow some flexibility in the timing of calculating the initial interval adjustment?**

In practice this major task of calculating the partial exemption calculation is likely to be dealt with in Large Cases Division (LCD) and should be taken up by each business with LCD. In the majority of cases the proportion of taxable use should be readily identifiable by direct attribution. See paragraph 6.9 of the VAT on Property Guide. Revenue appreciate the practical application of the CGS may give rise in certain circumstances to some issues and some flexibility will be considered as these issues come to light.

For example, if the minimum VAT as calculated by the formula is €12,000 per year, the minimum amount for each taxable period is €2,000. Therefore €2,000 must be accounted for in the July/Aug VAT return.

17. **Example 3 in the VAT on Property Guide would appear to relate to repairs not development. Can Revenue clarify the example?**

Expenditure on repairs and renewals does not fall to be taken into account when calculating development expenditure. Example 3 in future editions of the Guide will be amended to enhance clarity.

18. **Has the exclusion for supplies of immovable goods in the grouping provisions been removed?**

The exclusion has not been removed. The grouping provisions do not apply to the supply of immovable goods.

19. **Can a person who carries on an exempt business avail of the joint option for taxation and is such a person subject to the CGS?**

Any person who carries on a business in the State (even an exempt business) is a 'taxable person'. The joint option for taxation is allowed when the sale is between taxable persons. The CGS applies to properties where VAT was chargeable on the acquisition or development of that property to a **taxable person.** This should not be confused with a person or body who is involved in activities that are outside the scope of VAT. (See Q10).

20. **In relation to Section 12E(8) – are paragraphs (b)(i) and (b)(ii) separate exclusions?**

The conditions for the non-application of Section 12E(8)(a) set out in (i), (ii) and (iii) of Section 12E(8)(b) are not separate - they are cumulative. The taxpayer must satisfy the three conditions in order to avoid the CGS adjustment.

21. **Does Section 12E(8) apply to 'legacy leases'?**

Yes. It is separate to the tax charge that arises on the assignment or surrender of a legacy lease under Section 4C.

22. **Can Revenue confirm that, where a long lease that is subject to VAT is granted before 1 July 2008 (passing EVT, etc.) and the landlord then disposes of the reversionary interest in that lease after 1 July 2008 in circumstances where S.4(9) applies, the landlord will not suffer any CGS adjustment on that disposal of the reversion?**

A CGS adjustment will not apply in these circumstances.

23. **Is VAT chargeable on the sale of commercial or residential 'transitional' property post cancellation of waiver after payment of cancellation sum?**

Generally no VAT due on sale but see Tax Briefing 64 in respect of sales by a developer/builder - otherwise no change in treatment intended under new rules.

24. **When does development constitute 'refurbishment'? Is it subject to the 25% rule?**

Refurbishment is a concept within the CGS. Whenever a person carries out a development on a previously completed building, this constitutes a refurbishment and essentially 'creates' a capital good. The adjustment period for a refurbishment is ten intervals, the first of which begins when that refurbishment is completed.

If a property is sold, the 25% test and the materially altered test apply to determine whether or not a property is 'new'. For example, suppose a property was acquired in 1985 without VAT and developed at a cost of €1,000,000 + VAT €135,000 in Apr 2007 (the development was completed 5 July 2007). A further development was carried out in Jan 2008 (completed 18 Mar 2008) at a cost of €200,000 + VAT €27,000. Both developments constitute refurbishment and 'create' two separate capital goods with ten intervals for each capital good. The adjustment period for the first capital good (development completed 5 July 2007) begins on 5 July 2007. The adjustment period for the second capital good (development completed 18 Mar 2008) begins on 18 Mar 2008.

If the property is subsequently sold, it is necessary to determine whether or not the sale is taxable or exempt. This means looking at all development carried out in the five years before the sale occurs. The property is sold in Feb 2009 for €4,000,000. The total cost of the development (neither of which materially altered the property) in the previous five years is €1,200,000. Since this is more than 25% of the consideration for sale the sale is taxable.

If the property had been sold for €6,000,000 the cost of the development would not breach the 25% rule and so the sale would be exempt. In order to avoid a CGS claw-back (separate claw-back for each capital good), the joint option for taxation would have to be exercised.

Note — if the property is not sold there are simply two capital goods - each with an adjustment period of ten intervals. Neither of these capital goods is subject to the annual adjustment provisions under the CGS since the development which 'created' them was completed prior to 1 July 2008.

25. **If a developer disposes of a holiday cottage after 1 July 2008, what are the VAT implications for the developer and the investor? Is the investor entitled to recover VAT on the purchase price and let the property to the management company as the letting of a holiday cottage is a taxable activity?**

The position for such arrangements post 1 July 2008 is as follows. The developer charges VAT to the investor on the sale of the holiday home. As there is no distinction between long and short leases under the new system for VAT on property the granting of the lease from the investor to the management company is an exempt supply of a service. There is no entitlement to deductibility for the purchaser. However, the investor can choose to register for VAT and exercise the landlord's option to tax in accordance with Section 7A and opt to tax the letting to the management company (assuming that the investor and the management company are not connected, or if connected the tenant is entitled to at least 90% deductibility). The investor must then charge VAT on the periodic rents to the management company at 21.5% over the term of the lease. The management company who are engaged in the provision of holiday accommodation are obliged to charge VAT at 13.5% (para (xiii)(b) Sixth Schedule) on the moneys received for providing the holiday homes to its customers.

26. **Can a waiver of exemption be backdated to a letting that commences prior to 1 July 2008?**

Yes, providing all the normal criteria as provided for in Regulation 4(4) VAT Regulations 2006 are applicable, e.g. tenant must be entitled to full deductibility, a waiver may be backdated in respect of an **individual letting.** The backdated waiver will not extend to any of the landlord's other lettings.

27. **Where a property, in which there is a short-term letting that is subject to a waiver, is sold and the sale is subject to VAT Revenue have traditionally allowed the amount of VAT charged on the sale be included in the 'tax paid' for the purposes of the cancellation adjustment. Will this practice continue for waivers that are cancelled after 1 July?**

Yes, this practice will continue where VAT is chargeable on the sale of a property and the waiver is subsequently cancelled.

28. **A landlord creates a 25-year letting in a property on or after 1 July and the landlord's option to tax is exercised. Two years later the landlord sells the property. Can the transfer of business relief in Section 3(5)(b)(iii) apply to such a situation where the purchaser will continue to apply the landlord's option to tax?**

Yes the transfer of business relief can apply where a landlord sells a property in which there is a sitting tenant and where the purchaser (landlord 2) will continue with the landlord's option to tax and charge VAT on the rents to the sitting tenant.

29. **A landlord has two properties that are let short-term and are subject to a waiver of exemption on 1 July 2008. In December 2008 the landlord wises to cancel his or her waiver of exemption. Can he or she cancel in respect of just one of the properties?**

No, the normal waiver cancellation rules as contained in Regulation 4 of S.I. No. 548 of 2006 - VAT Regulations 2006 apply and the cancellation amount must be calculated in respect of both properties.

30. **What is the VAT treatment of a premium/reverse premium payable by a landlord to a tenant or a tenant to a landlord on or after 1 July in respect of leases created prior to 1 July?**

There are essentially four possible scenarios –

1. Long lease created prior to 1 July on which VAT was chargeable when created.

2. Long lease created prior to 1 July on which VAT was **not** chargeable when created.

3. Short lease created prior to 1 July where waiver of exemption did not apply (i.e. exempt lease).

4. Short lease created prior to 1 July where waiver of exemption did apply (i.e. landlord charges VAT at 21.5% on the rents).

In respect of (1) the VAT chargeable on the assignment or surrender of the lease is restricted to the amount specified in Section 4C(7). (See question 6 above.)

In respect of (2) and (3) no VAT is chargeable on the assignment or surrender of the lease in such cases.

In respect of (4) VAT is chargeable at 21.5% the payment on the assignment or surrender of the lease is linked to the taxable waived letting.

Note – the treatment of premiums and reverse premiums on leases created on or after 1 July is explained in paragraph 4.11 VAT on Property Guide.

Appendix A

Example 1 – CGS intervals for legacy leases

Mr X grants Ms Y a 35-year lease on 1 July 2000. VAT is charged on the capitalised value of the lease of €1million. Ms Y is still the tenant (and so has the 'interest' in the property on 1 July 2008.) The adjustment period for the legacy lease for the person who holds the legacy on 1 July 2008, i.e. Mr Y, is 20 years from 1 July 2000. (This is determined from Section 4C(11)(c).

On the 15 April 2012 Ms Y assigns the lease to Mr J. The assignment is taxable, on the reverse charge basis, as it occurs within the 20-year adjustment period.

VAT charged on the assignment is calculated as follows –

$$\frac{T \times N}{Y}$$

$$\frac{€1,000,000 \times 9}{20}$$

$$= €450,000$$

The assignment is reverse charged which means that Mr J is liable to account for VAT of €450,000 on the supply in his Mar/Apr 2012 VAT return. Mr Y must issue a document to Mr J which contains–

- The amount of tax due on the assignment (€450,000)

- The number of intervals remaining in the adjustment period at the time of the assignment2, which is in this case is 9 intervals.

Section 4C(8)(b) deems Mr J to be a capital goods owner for the purposes of Section 12E. Therefore, the interest that he owns is subject to the annual adjustments and all the other rules in the CGS. The number of intervals in the adjustment period for the person to whom a legacy lease is assigned or surrendered after 1 July 2008, is determined by Section 4C(8)(b)(i). For Mr J it is 9 intervals. The initial interval for Mr J begins on 15/14/2012 and end on 14/4/2013. Mr J's accounting year ends on 31/12. The second interval for the interest will begin on 15/4/2013 end on 31/12/2013. Mr J must make any adjustments required under the CGS until the end of the adjustment period (9 intervals) the last of which will end on 31/12/2020.

Appendix 3

Revenue: Tax Briefing, Issue 69, September 2008

VAT treatment of property developers renting out residential properties

Introduction

New rules for VAT on property transactions came into effect on 1 July 2008. This article deals with situations where a property developer (or a person connected with a property developer) who was entitled to deduct the VAT incurred on the acquisition or development of residential property subsequently rents out that residential property on or after that date. There are two separate VAT rules for such scenarios depending on when the property was completed.

When is a property considered 'completed'?

'Completed' is defined in legislation [1]. Generally speaking, a property is completed when it is ready to be used for the purposes for which it was designed. There are certain criteria that must be met before a property can be considered completed. For example, the utility services required for the purposes for which it was designed must be connected. However, the fact that the utility services are connected does not in itself necessarily mean that a property is completed. Revenue is prepared to accept, in cases to which this article applies, that a property may be regarded as not having been completed until it has been rented.

Properties completed before 1 July 2008 and rented on or after that date

Where a property developer develops a residential property, that property is completed before 1 July 2008, and that property is rented on or after 1 July 2008, then there is a full claw-back of the VAT deducted by the developer. This claw-back is triggered by *Section 4C(3) VAT Act 1972* (as amended) and is effected at the time the letting of the residential property is created. Example 1 below illustrates how this operates.

Example 1

Developer D constructs a house for sale. The cost of constructing this house is €1,000,000 + VAT €135,000. D deducts all of this VAT. The development of the house is completed on 1 Feb 2008. D is unable to sell the house and instead rents it out. The letting is for two years and is created on 4 Aug 2008. This triggers an immediate claw-back under *Section 4C(3)* VAT Act 1972 (as amended) using the formula in *Section 4(3)(ab)* —

$$\frac{T \times (Y - N)}{Y}$$

T = amount of tax deducted
Y = 20
N = 0 (number of full years since development occurred)

$$\frac{135,000 \times (20 - 0)}{20}$$

= €135,000 VAT payable by D in taxable period in which the letting is created (Jul/Aug 2008).

D must account for this amount in the VAT return for Jul/Aug.

It should be noted that the adjustment that Developer D makes in the above example as a result of letting the house from 4 August is the same that would have been required if the letting had commenced prior to 1 July 2008. The only difference is that, under the new rules, the formula in *Section 4(3)(ab)* is applied through the operation of the new *Section 4C(3)*; prior to 1 July, *Section 4(3)(ab)* applied directly to such a transaction.

[1] See *Section 4B(1) VAT Act 1972* (as amended).

Properties completed on or after 1 July 2008 and rented on or after that date

Where a property developer develops a residential property, that property is completed on or after 1 July 2008, and that property is rented on or after 1 July 2008, no immediate claw-back occurs. Instead, the developer will be required to adjust the VAT deductibility at the end of the second capital goods scheme (CGS) interval [2] - and each subsequent interval - until the property is sold. Example 2 below illustrates how this operates.

Example 2

Developer E constructs a house for sale. The cost of constructing this house is €1,000,000 + VAT €135,000. E deducts all of this VAT. The development of the house is completed on 15 Jul 2008. E is unable to sell the house and instead rents it out. The letting is for two years and is created on 4 August 2008. There is no immediate claw-back of the VAT deducted. E's accounting year ends on 31 December each year.

The CGS initial interval for E in respect of the property begins on 15 Jul 2008. It ends on 14 Jul 2009. The second interval ends on 31 December 2009 (end of accounting year). An adjustment arises at this point in accordance with *Section 12E(5) VAT Act 1972* (as amended) as follows –

$$C - D$$

C = reference deduction amount
D = interval deductible amount (see VAT on Property Guide for details [see Appendix 1])

$$6,750 - 0$$

= €6,750 payable as tax due by E for the taxable period following end of second interval: that is, the tax is due for the Jan/Feb 2009 VAT period.

This payment essentially amounts to E paying back 1/20th of the VAT deducted in respect of the development of the property. At the end of each subsequent interval (in the taxable period following the end of each 31/12 financial year) the same amount (€6,750) will be payable by E for as long as the property is not used for a taxable purpose.

[2] See VAT on Property Guide Chapter 6 for full details. Available from www.revenue.ie

What is the position when a residential property - such as the properties in Examples 1 and 2 above - is subsequently sold after being rented?

In both cases, the sale is subject to VAT on the full consideration received regardless of how long a period of time the properties have been let. However, there are two different treatments in relation to the deductibility that has been clawed back depending on the scenario. This is illustrated by the example below.

Example 1 Continued

At the end of the lease (3 Aug 2010) D sells the property for €1,200,000. The sale is subject to VAT @ 13.5% = €162,000.

There is a VAT credit given to D for the VAT that was clawed back on the letting of the property, but this credit is reduced by the number of years that have elapsed since the property was completed —

$$\frac{E \times N}{T}$$

E = non-deductible amount [3]
N = 18 (no of full intervals remaining in adjustment period + 1)
T = 20 (total number of intervals in adjustment period)

$$\frac{135,000 \times 18}{20}$$

= €121,500 given as VAT credit for the taxable period in which sale occurs (Jul/Aug 2010). D must, however, also account for VAT of €162,000 for that period, being the VAT due on the sale of the property, for a net liability of €40,500.

---

[3] Where there has been an adjustment using the formula in *Section 4(3)(ab)* - whether by the operation of that section or via *Section 4C(3)* - the 'non-deductible amount' is the total amount of tax that the person had an entitlement to deduct in respect of the acquisition or development of the property, as employed originally in the formula in *Section 4(3)(ab)* for the purpose of calculating the deductibility adjustment. In some cases this non-deductible amount may be greater

than the deductibility adjustment made as a result of applying the formula in *Section 4(3)(ab)*; but in the majority of cases - as in this example - the figures will be the same.

Example 2 Continued

At the end of the lease (3 Aug 2010) E sells the property for €1,200,000. The sale is subject to VAT @ 13.5% = €162,000.

There is no VAT credit given as the claw-back of €6,750 that occurred in the Jan/Feb 2010 taxable period was in respect of the use to which the property was put during the second interval - i.e. an exempt use. No further claw-back of inputs arises as the taxable supply of the property in August 2010 constitutes a taxable use for the third and all subsequent intervals.

E must account for VAT of €162,000 for the Jul/Aug 2010 taxable period, being the VAT due on the sale of the property.

While the net amounts that Developers D and E will return in respect of their sales of the two houses differ greatly, this reflects the fact that Developer D, in making the deductibility adjustment in 2008 had already accounted for the potential exempt use of the property for the full remaining portion of its CGS adjustment period, and will therefore benefit from its diversion to taxable use via its taxable sale in 2010. Developer E, on the other hand, would have made adjustments for exempt use only on an interval by interval basis. In consequence, both developers have consistent entitlements to deductibility for the remaining intervals in the adjustment periods.

Treatment for Stamp Duty

Where an intended purchaser occupies a new house under 'a rent with an option to buy scheme' and the house is subsequently purchased by that person as part of the scheme, the property will be regarded as new for the purposes of reliefs that apply on the purchase of a new house.

INDEX

compiled by Julitta Clancy

Note: references are to **paragraph numbers.**